THE ADOLESCENT YEARS

THE ADOLESCENT YEARS

A Guide for Parents

PAT PETRIE

MICHAEL JOSEPH
London

Acknowledgements

I am grateful to many individuals and organisations who have made a contribution to this book, whether by discussion, by putting resources and information at my disposal or in other ways – while making it quite clear that I alone am responsible for the content.

I would like to thank: Isobel Allen; Len Almond; Neil Armstrong; Eileen Barker; Anne Charlton; John Coleman; Malcolm Grey; Jim Horne; Doris Kelly; Tim Lang; Petra Longstaff; Anne Matton; Ann Phoenix; Janet Pidcock; Sandra Perry; Delwyn Tattum; John Tiernan; Barbara Thompson; The Advisory Centre for Education; Action on Smoking and Health; Alcohol Concern; Anorexic Family Concern; Belfast Law Centre; British Dental Health Association; Children's Legal Centre; Coronary Prevention Group; Eating Disorders Association; Eye Care Information Bureau; Gamblers Anonymous; Health Education Authority; Family Planning Association Information Service; London Food Commission; National Association for the Welfare of Children in Hospital; National Confederation of Parent-Teacher Associations; National Eczema Society; National Society for the Prevention of Cruelty to Children; Sports Council; Vegetarian Society; Vegan Society and Scottish Child Law Centre. I would also like to thank Louise Haines, Vivien James and Susan Watt at Michael Joseph for their encouragement and expert support and, as always, Vivien Green of Richard Scott Simon Ltd.

MICHAEL JOSEPH LTD

Published by the Penguin Group
27 Wrights Lane, London W8 5TZ, England
Viking Penguin Inc., 40 West 23rd Street, New York, New York 10010, USA
Penguin Books Australia Ltd, Ringwood, Victoria, Australia
Penguin Books Canada Ltd, 2801 John Street, Markham, Ontario, Canada L3R 1B4
Penguin Books (NZ) Ltd, 182–190 Wairau Road, Auckland 10, New Zealand

Penguin Books Ltd, Registered Offices: Harmondsworth, Middlesex, England

First published in 1990

Typeset in Lasercomp 11/12½pt Palatino,
printed and bound in Great Britain by
Butler & Tanner Ltd,
Frome, Somerset

A CIP catalogue record for this book is available from the British Library

ISBN 0 7181 3150 9

CONTENTS

Introduction

THIS BOOK IS addressed to mothers and fathers equally. Although looking after children has traditionally been the work of mothers, we are, at the end of the twentieth century, moving away from the uneven divisions of earlier times. The business of bringing up children is now more frequently a matter of co-operation between parents, and both mothers and fathers need the sort of information this book contains. And because many parents are bringing up children alone it is for single parents as well as those with partners. It aims to be of use from the time when children are still approaching adolescence and throughout the teenage years.

We all have a fairly clear idea of what an adolescent is: a teenager, someone who goes to secondary school, who is growing quickly, falling in and out of love, troubled by spots, who has particular tastes in fashion and is following the current craze in music and dancing. We have all been there and can remember the feelings, excitements and disappointments of growing up.

However, the experience of becoming an adult varies from society to society and from age to age. In many ways, it is not the same process for our children as it was for us, still less for our grandparents and great-grandparents. We are used to thinking of adolescence as one stage in development, the period of transition that comes between childhood and adult life. This concept is a relatively new one, dating only from the last century and the time when adults and children started to lead separate lives.[1] Before, children and adults had spent much of their time together. Most children neither went to school nor enjoyed the company of large groups of other youngsters. There were always, it is true, some grammar schools attended by the sons of relatively well-to-do townspeople, but these were in the minority. For the sons and daughters of land-owners, the more usual pattern was to be educated at home by tutors and governesses. The expansion of boys' public schools occurred throughout the nineteenth century, followed by the development of girls' boarding schools. At the same time there was a growth in the number of elementary schools for the children of the working-classes, who had previously worked alongside their parents at home, in the fields, or in factories and mines where their contribution was necessary for the family economy. For these youngsters there was no 'youth culture' as we know it today, nor distinguishable points marking the passage from childhood to adult life, such as leaving school, starting work, or obtaining the vote. By the time they married or had children of their own, they may well have been recognised as adults for some years.

In some traditional societies, likewise, there is no special adolescent status. At a certain stage of development, linked to becoming physically and sexually mature, a young person ceases to be regarded as a child and, perhaps after an initiation ceremony, becomes an adult.

In our society, however, we need the 'in-between stage' of adolescence, with all its ambiguities, because modern life enforces a prolonged period of dependency on young people during their early and mid-teens; even though they may be physically mature, they are not yet equipped to survive in the modern world. This is because the complexities of high technology demand a long apprenticeship of education and training, with the result that young people need financial and other support even though, in the physical sense, they may have reached adult life. They are kept in a suspended state, physically adult but still dependent, segregated by school and college from adults at work and, except at home, from adults at leisure.

The transition from childhood to adult life can span many years. It has a clear physical beginning, the onset of puberty, but its end is less clearly defined. A young woman may be physically adult, that is, fully grown, sexually mature and fertile, at the age of fourteen or even younger; some boys are also physically adult at around the same age, in that they are capable of reproduction. To be an adult has legal and economic meanings, however; it is not measured merely in terms of physical maturity. There is an array of laws which mark the ages at which young people are, on the one hand, allowed the same rights as adults and, on the other, are expected to be responsible in the same way as adults: at the age of eighteen they may exercise the rights of citizenship, politically, by voting for Members of Parliament and local councillors, but from the age of ten they are held to be legally responsible for criminal offences and may have to face legal proceedings. (At many points in *The Adolescent Years: A Guide for Parents*, there is information about the law and young people.) For those who enter higher education, or for those who are unemployed, adult independence, in terms of financial independence, may not arrive for some years after physical and legal maturity.

During the 'in-between' stage, it is not always clear how young people should be treated. In many areas of life there are no clear rules about how they should behave, what freedoms they should be allowed, and what levels of responsibility are appropriate. This is especially so at a time when society is changing and developing in such a manner that children are being brought up in a very different way from their parents.

- Many adolescents now live in reconstituted families with step-parents and new brothers and sisters; others live in lone-parent households.
- The world of employment is very different now from twenty or thirty years ago; technology evolves rapidly and there is a greater risk of unemployment for people without technological skills, and for people in towns which developed around traditional industries.
- Ethnic minority communities are not now composed of recent immigrants; the parents of adolescents were often brought up in this country and their children are born here. Their ways of bringing up children may differ from the ways of their parents.
- More mothers go out to work.
- The development of feminism has brought about a new awareness of the position of girls and women in society and the need for positive steps to redress the balance towards equality between the sexes.
- Many fathers, especially those with younger children, now play some part in child-care.
- There is greater openness about sexual behaviour and what is considered acceptable.
- Schools and education are changing, with new examinations and new legislation; legislation includes moves to integrate youngsters with disabilities into mainstream schools.

During the last, important stage of child-rearing parents have to observe a careful balance between protecting their sons and daughters and, at the same time, enabling them to function independently. Parents retain certain responsibilities for their adolescents' health, safety, education and welfare, and can offer information and help as appropriate for different ages throughout the teens. On the other hand, there are some areas in which adolescents should take responsibility for themselves: deciding with their parents about what is appropriate behaviour; organising and carrying out their own studies; looking after their own basic health needs depending on their age.

It is also important for parents to realise that some responsibility for their adolescent offspring lies outside the family. The policy of successive governments and local authorities is very influential. For example, legislation about education, about benefit payments to and on behalf of young people, about employment and training, and about the provision of recreational facilities can make the task of bringing up adolescents either easier or more difficult. Other outside bodies, most notably the school, also have an important part to play in bringing up children to become competent adults, and can make either a positive or a negative contribution to their development. And the influence of groups such as the food industry, the brewers and distillers, the tobacco trade and other leisure industries and their advertising agencies is also significant. So it should be remembered that responsibilities for the health, education and well-being of young people in our society is a collaborative effort.

It is hoped that this book will provide information and suggestions that will be helpful to parents. Few parents will want to read it through from beginning to end; it is meant, rather, to be a source of information to be turned to when needed. It does not set out to promote a spirit of perfectionism in parents, or to achieve the 'perfect parent' or the 'perfect teenager'. Child psychologist Bruno Bettelheim makes a point of reminding parents that all that is required of them is to be 'good enough'.[2] Parents should not take all the blame on themselves if things go wrong at times; there are other forces active in society as well. Similarly, it is only fair to adolescents that parents should be prepared to settle for a 'good enough adolescent'. Adolescents may not always live up to their parents' expectations of them, and dreams of a perfect, talented, studious teenager will place an unnecessary burden on both parents and children alike. People have their own temperaments, their own talents, and their own disabilities, and parents and adolescents are equally liable to make mistakes. However, the crises and problems that may crop up can be learning-points, and not disasters, if communications are kept open and teenagers feel assured of their parents' love, support and respect.

CHAPTER ONE

THE DEVELOPING ADOLESCENT

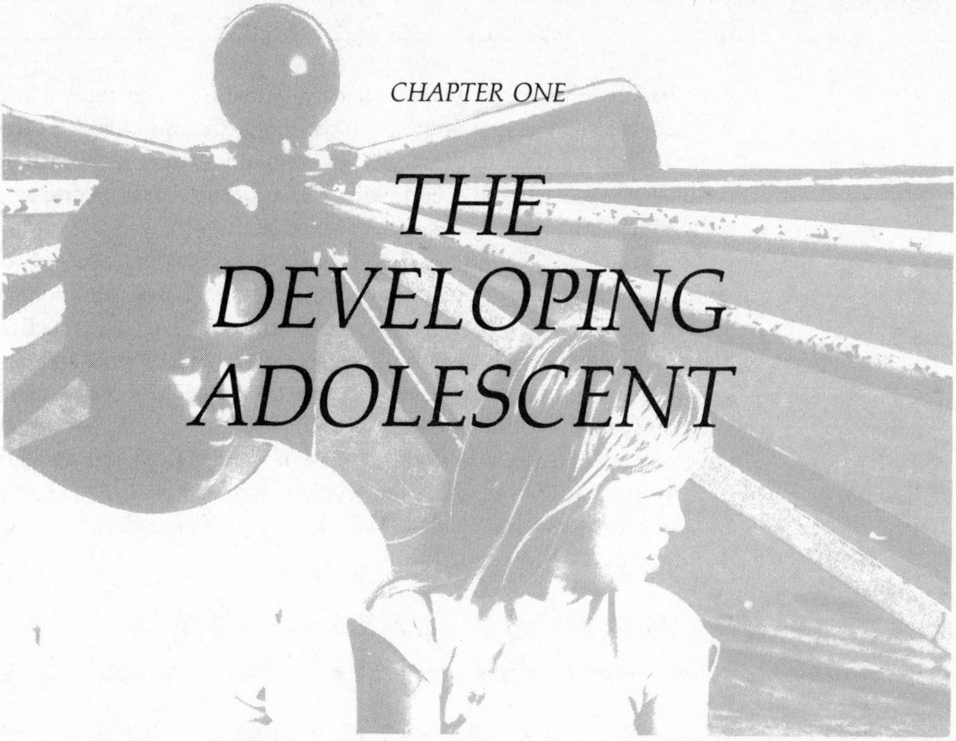

IN ADOLESCENCE YOUR child undergoes major physical and sexual developments that are normally accomplished within a period of four years. There are also changes in intellectual functioning. The experience of new developments and emerging competence can be rewarding for both of you, but the thought of change and the unknown can also be unsettling. It is hoped that what follows will give you helpful information about the kind of changes to expect.

This is not the first time you have lived through rapid developments in your child. Remember your first year together. That also involved the excitement of living with an individual who was growing and developing at high speed. During the first year of life, your child's physical growth and intellectual development were fast. Birth weight doubled and then trebled; muscles developed and grew strong; a new tooth, or a new word, could appear overnight. The tiny, powerless baby quickly became the robust toddler – adventurous, curious and increasingly competent. And then, after the first eventful year, developments slowed down: clothes were out-grown, but over the course of a year rather than within a few months as in babyhood. Progress – physical, intellectual and social – continued throughout the years of childhood but in a gradual, leisurely way so that you both had time to adapt, perhaps hardly noticing the changes. Now, with adolescence, comes another phase of speedy and radical change as your child becomes biologically and sexually mature, approaching full stature and strength and with the capacity for thinking and reasoning which approaches that of an adult.

This chapter looks at the growth and developments which adolescents undergo during this important life-stage and at some of the consequences of this development: the feelings, problems and practical matters which arise. There are three sections: the first is about biological growth and developments, the second is about developments in adolescents' mental abilities, and the third is about how they develop their own standards and ideals: moral development. In all of these areas, we shall see how the feelings and ideas that adolescents have about themselves – their self-identity – also undergo change and development.

How does it all start?

Biological Growth and Development

Hormonal changes

Adolescent biological development depends, to a large extent, on the action of hormones. Hormones are chemical substances which are formed in glands in various parts of the body; they are released into the bloodstream and their job is to stimulate and regulate growth and development.

From birth, children's lives are affected by hormones. Growth hormones, for example, stimulate a baby's rapid growth and sex hormones affect development as male or female (see pages 50–1). In adolescence the production of both sex and growth hormones increases; it is this, together with the complex interactions between different hormones, which accounts for many of the changes that come about in the teenage years.

An important part in hormonal activity is played by the hypothalamus – a nerve centre in the brain which controls the activities of the different glands. Throughout childhood the hypothalamus is sensitive to the amounts of sex hormone in the bloodstream and when the level is too high it sends out signals which slow down hormonal output. It does this by its action on the pituitary gland, located just beneath the brain, which in turn regulates the hormonal output of other glands.

As adolescence approaches, the following events take place. First the hypothalamus loses its sensitivity to the sex hormones circulating in the blood and, as a result, produces substances which stimulate the pituitary gland. The pituitary gland now secretes the hormones which had previously been inhibited. These hormones activate other glands – the ovaries, testes, adrenal and thyroid glands – which then produce more sex and growth hormones and send them out into the bloodstream to promote growth and sexual development. The hypothalamus becomes increasingly accustomed, as it were, to the higher levels of sex hormones and continues to stimulate the pituitary gland, which, in turn, continues to produce the hormones that trigger the activities of other glands ... It is these complex chain reactions which produce all the physical changes of adolescence. Of special importance are:

- *Human growth hormone*, produced by the pituitary which, as its name suggests, accelerates bone and muscle development.
- *Androgens* – 'masculinising' hormones – which promote male characteristics and include:

  testosterone which is produced by the testes and helps the development of the main male characteristics, including the growth of the penis and scrotum, the development of facial and body hair and changes in muscle strength and physique. It also promotes the growth spurt in boys;
  adrenal androgen which stimulates growth, and the development of pubic hair, in girls.

(It is the 'masculine' hormones which are associated, for both boys and girls, with acne [see page 130].)

- *Oestrogens* – 'feminising' hormones – which promote female characteristics. These stimulate breast development, the growth of pubic hair, and a 'feminine' distribution of fat in the body. They are involved in the process of menstruation.
- *Progesterone* – the pregnancy hormone which also plays a part in regulating the menstrual cycle.

All of these hormones are produced by boys and girls alike; indeed girls need androgen to promote adolescent growth, and its secretion is increased at this time. But the proportion of female to male hormones increases for girls whereas the opposite happens for boys. The differences become more and more marked as adolescence progresses and adult hormone levels are reached.[1]

Physical changes

It may be a couple of years after the onset of the hormonal activity which paves the way for adolescence before you notice any physical changes in your child. Then, one day, you will suddenly realise that he or she seems to have grown very quickly recently, and that adolescence has already begun. On average, girls grow and mature two years earlier than boys, a difference that is clearly visible in any class of eleven-year-olds where adolescent girls are inches taller than boys.

Growing pains

Just as teething troubles are associated with babies and toddlers, so growing pains are seen as being especially connected with adolescence. Growing pains do not figure in paediatric textbooks because there is, in fact, no pain connected with growing. But the term is nevertheless used by some doctors to describe the experience of a few children and adolescents whose limbs ache and feel heavy when they lie down at night. Doctors use the expression to reassure parents and children that the pains, although uncomfortable, are harmless. If an adolescent experiences frequent aches and pains, however, the family doctor should be consulted.[2]

Individual differences

There are considerable differences in the ages at which individual boys and girls begin the process of adolescence and reach its various milestones. For example, a few girls begin menstruating as early as nine years of age, while others do not start for another six or seven years. Similarly, boys may experience their first emission of semen as early as the age of eleven, or as late as sixteen.[3] The age at which such developments occur depends, to a large extent, on the characteristics which boys and girls inherit from their parents. It is the genetic factors present at the moment when sperm and ovum fuse at conception that make it likely that girls will start menstruating, and boys will start growing, around the same age as their mothers and fathers did.[4] Another example of genetic influence comes from research by J.M. Tanner, which found that identical twins have their first period nearer together than non-identical twins.[5] But other influences are also important and malnutrition, illness and stress can all hold children back.

The growth and development of girls

Growth spurt

The beginning of adolescence, the time when hormonal activity increases (see page 6), is known as prepubescence, the stage which precedes puberty and the outward signs of emerging sexual maturity. It is during this period that the growth spurt begins, on average at nine years of age. It continues for about four years, and for many girls it reaches its peak at around the age of eleven. How tall a girl grows, what weight she gains, and her own particular shape depend to a large extent on inherited characteristics – although eating habits can also play a part. Sometimes parents are worried that a girl who has started the growth spurt sooner than her classmates may end up exceptionally tall. In fact, an early start means that she will slow down before the others and things will even themselves out. For most girls, the period of rapid growth has tapered off by the age of thirteen, although it continues at a slower pace for several more years.

During this time, a girl not only grows taller and heavier but also stronger: her muscles increase and her heart and lungs grow stronger. The strength of girls does not, on average, equal that of boys but this is not a general rule. Some girls are as strong as some boys and some are even more so. Growth does not happen at an even rate over the entire body. The head, hands and feet show the first signs of growth, followed by arms and legs and, lastly, the trunk.

Sexual maturation in girls

At the age of about ten or eleven, for most girls, the first downy pubic hairs make their appearance, their breasts begin to bud and hips to grow round. This is followed by the growth of soft, unpigmented hair under the arms.

Within a year or so the sexual organs increase in size, both internally – the vagina and the womb – and externally – the labia and the clitoris – and these become more pleasurably sensitive. The pubic hair becomes more profuse, curly and pigmented. The breasts and nipples develop further – they may feel tender – including the pink area surrounding the nipple, called the areola. One breast may appear larger or a slightly different shape from the other – human beings are not totally symmetrical! Later, under-arm hair becomes darker in colour and sweat glands develop in the armpits and in the genital area (see page 129). Sometimes there is also a little white discharge from the vagina.

A girl has her first period on average at the age of twelve or thirteen, eighteen months or so after reaching her growth peak.[6] For a few girls this happens two or three years earlier, or two or three years later, than average. It may take a little time for the periods to settle down into a regular pattern. The girl is probably not fertile yet and may not become capable of pregnancy for another year or more. However, no young woman who is sexually active should rely on this – some girls are fertile from the time of their first period and, therefore, capable of conceiving and having a baby.

By this time the girl's face is changing, losing its childishness, becoming adult, and her figure is more rounded. The weight she gained while she was growing rapidly was largely a result of increasing muscle tissue, but later she plumps out more. When she was still prepubescent her shape was straight up and straight down, her shoulders wider than her hips (the opposite is true of boys at the same stage). Over the course of adolescence these proportions gradually change so that the girl's hips become wider than her shoulders. She may find that hair grows more strongly on her arms and legs than it did in childhood and there may be a few hairs on her abdomen or around her nipples; this is quite normal. In late adolescence, the breasts, pubic hair and under-arm hair all reach their adult form: the biological process of growing up is complete. Most young women reach maturity between sixteen and eighteen years of age, depending on when the process of growing up started.

Early maturation

For girls there are some disadvantages in maturing early. A girl who develops early is not always adequately, if at all, prepared for her first period. She needs extra support because her friends are not at the same stage and there is no one in her age-group with whom to share her experiences; if she has an older sister to talk to and compare notes with, she will find things easier. If your daughter is growing rapidly, shooting ahead of her classmates with early breast development and light pubic hair, she is entering adolescence. Even if she is only nine years old she needs to be told what is happening to her and prepared for her first period, which will happen about eighteen months after the peak of the growth spurt (see page 9). It is important that her first period should not be the frightening event it could be for a girl who does not expect and understand it.

A further problem for the early maturer is that the current fashion favours slimness and as she develops she may feel self-consciously, and unacceptably, fat in comparison with other girls of her age. Some girls even become round-shouldered and slouch in order to disguise breast development. She may also be embarrassed by her periods which make her different from other children in the class. If she is one of the older pupils in a junior school, then her different level of maturity will be emphasised. Things are likely to improve for her when she goes on to secondary school and is among other girls at the same stage of development. If she talks to you about these worries, listen to them carefully and do not try to brush them under the carpet: they are real enough for her (see pages 38–43). Talk about her development in a positive way; tell her that even though she is more grown up, more advanced than other girls now, they will catch up with her in a year or so's time.

Meanwhile, think of ways to encourage her interests and talents so that she is not too preoccupied with herself and her appearance. Perhaps, if she is so inclined, arrange coaching or informal lessons in a new sport – tennis or riding, for example (see pages 125–8); or maybe there is a music, art or dance group which she could join, with girls and boys of different ages, so that she does not feel conspicuous, as she may do at school. Be positive about her appearance and, if your budget allows, encourage her to choose clothes she enjoys wearing.

Because she is biologically more mature than other girls, and looks it, it is possible that she will become interested in boys at an earlier age than her friends and that boys will also start taking notice of her. She may want to have a boyfriend and start dating earlier than other girls. If so, she needs your understanding and support; although she is biologically maturing she is not at all experienced and you can help her by talking to her and finding her helpful books (see pages 299–300). She especially needs encouragement to take her schoolwork seriously in the face of what may be more interesting competition.

Late maturation

In many ways girls who are late developers are at an advantage compared with early developers. In the years preceding adolescence, of course, they will not realise that they are late developers and, being untroubled by preoccupations about themselves and their changing bodies, will have extra energy to expend on their schoolwork. When, by the age of thirteen or fourteen, it becomes obvious that they are falling behind their contemporaries, this may cause them some anxiety. They may feel immature and childlike and wonder when their periods will start. If your daughter is a late developer she needs you to listen sympathetically to her worries and answer her questions. Explain that there is a wide variation in the ages at which girls mature and that she will catch up with her friends eventually.

If, at the age of thirteen, your daughter still has a childlike appearance, shows no signs of fast growth, breast development or pubic hair, then it is wise to take her to see your family doctor. Should she be one of the few girls who have some underlying condition which is delaying puberty, then it is better – both psychologically and physically – for this to be diagnosed and treated early rather than late.

Preparing your daughter for menstruation

A girl's attitude towards menstruation is tied up with feelings about herself, her body and her developing sexuality. It is important that such a significant event as her first period should be as positive an experience as possible. Many girls feel that menstruation is just a nuisance, others that it is rather shameful, and still others – the lucky ones – that it is an exciting sign of growing up.[7]

Before discussing menstruation with your daughter, it is helpful to sort out your own feelings about it. How enlightened were your parents (or others) in explaining it to you? And how do you feel about it now? Would you find it useful to discuss menstruation, and your attitudes towards it, with a friend? If you are aware of your feelings about menstruation you will be less likely to pass on negative attitudes to your daughter. Here are some points to bear in mind:

1 Prepare your daughter well in advance

- If your daughter is maturing at the same rate as her contemporaries, it is likely that they will discuss menstruation together, but if she has started her periods early – at the age of ten or younger – she will have no support from age-mates. Whatever your daughter's age or rate of development, she needs to be authoritatively informed about the events taking place in her body and you are the ideal person to do this. Unless she understands what is happening, the first bleeding can be a great shock. Blood is usually associated with injury or she may think that she is suffering from some life-threatening illness.
- Talk to your daughter about periods around the time when her breasts are beginning to develop and she is showing signs of starting to grow quickly. It could be that she raises the subject herself because a girl at school has already started her periods, in which case she will need information, and perhaps reassurance.
- Tell your daughter that if her first period should occur while she is at school, her teacher can provide sanitary towels. Also give her a stock of disposable sanitary towels to keep in her own room so that she feels in charge of the situation. She will need a small bag – a pretty cosmetic bag, for example – for carrying them to school.
- Tell her that she will not need to change every time she goes to the toilet, only every few hours or if she does not feel fresh. Also point out the instructions for disposing of used towels, printed on the packet.
- Tell her that, if she wishes, she can use tampons. The hymen does

not cover the opening of the vagina completely (otherwise the flow could not escape) and it is possible, in most cases, for a small tampon to be inserted. These should be changed at least three times a day and she should be sure to wash her hands before inserting a tampon. Remind her to remove the last tampon at the end of her period.

The final choice of sanitary protection is probably best left to your daughter, but you may prefer not to suggest tampons for the first few months. If your daughter is at all anxious about using them, she may find it difficult to position a tampon at first, particularly as – until ovulation takes place, which may be some months after the first period – her vagina may be rather dry and not receive a tampon easily.

■ Preparing your daughter for her first period is important but do not give her all the information at once, since this could be confusing.

Be ready to repeat what you have told her and to answer questions (see pages 32–33). If she is an early maturer (a nine- or ten-year-old) then it may be wise to let her teacher know that she is having her first period and to ask what facilities there are for coping with periods at school (see page 215).

2 Periods should not be a cause of embarrassment. There is no need to be secretive or mysterious about them

■ Tell your daughter that periods are a normal part of growing up. The lining of the womb is built up each month in order to receive and nourish a fertilised ovum if conception should take place. If there is no conception, then this lining is shed and flows out through the vagina. This happens about every four weeks, although to start with periods may be irregular and for some women they continue to be so.

■ Explain that the blood which comes out of the opening of the vagina may be darker or browner than blood which comes from a cut, and that the actual amount of blood lost is small, only a few ounces each month, but it can look more when it mixes with water in the lavatory, as happens when she urinates or gets rid of a disposable sanitary towel. Periods last for about four days.

■ Don't be secretive about your own periods; leave packets of sanitary towels and tampons openly in the bathroom and buy them, without any concealment, when your daughter is with you.

■ Call periods by their proper name rather than using words that suggest they are something to be ashamed of. Refer to your own periods in a matter-of-fact way in the family.

■ Share your own experience with her. For example, tell her how old you were when you started and how your periods stopped while you were expecting her.

3 A period is not an illness

■ Be especially careful not to refer to periods as 'feeling unwell' or 'the curse'; periods are a normal part of life and all healthy young women have them.

■ There is no need, usually, for a girl to let her period interfere with any of her usual activities and so she can go to school, wash her hair, take a bath and join in sports (including swimming if she wears a tampon) as usual.

■ However, once their periods have settled down into a regular pattern, quite a large proportion of girls suffer from stomach cramps, which last for a few hours.[8] Some girls, a minority, find that the pain is severe. If your daughter should be one of these unfortunate few she can take aspirin to relieve the pain or, if you prefer, consult the family doctor.

4 Starting her periods is a sure sign that she will soon be a woman. Congratulate her and make a special fuss of her. This is an important occasion

Note: If you are a father bringing up your daughter alone, it may be helpful to ask a woman friend, or relative – someone your daughter trusts – to talk to her from her own experience, as well as offering information and support yourself.

The growth and development of boys

Growth spurt

Like girls, boys grow slowly and steadily throughout childhood. A couple of years later than girls, on average at about the age of eleven, a boy starts to grow more rapidly and this growth spurt reaches its peak after two years. At this time boys are producing bone and muscle rather than fat, and tend to thin out, losing the characteristic roundness of childhood. Rapid growth lasts for four years in all before tapering off; it then continues slowly for several more years. How tall a boy becomes is largely a matter of genetics (the characteristics he inherits from his parents), but inadequate diet, severe stress and illness can hold him back, just as over-eating can make him fat (see pages 115–16).

Growth does not follow an even pattern. In most, but not all, boys, the hands and feet grow rather more rapidly than the rest of the body; you will notice particularly how quickly your son grows out of his shoes and how large his hands are becoming. Next his arms and legs lengthen so that his sleeves and trouser-legs seem to have shrunk, exposing his wrists and ankles. Later his spine lengthens and his shoulders become broader. He is taking on the appearance of a young man. You will see this also in his face as his nose and chin lengthen and his lips fill out.

At the same time, but out of sight, his lungs and heart also grow rapidly and these, together with his bone and muscle growth, make for an increase in strength and endurance which continue to develop in young adult life.

Sexual maturation in boys

In response to hormonal activity (see page 6), on average between the ages of eleven and twelve, the first signs of sexual development appear as the testes start to enlarge and the skin of the scrotum (the bag which encloses the testes) begins to redden and coarsen. At the same time, a little downy pubic hair may appear. Boys' breasts, as well as girls', change during adolescence, with the areola growing and the nipple standing out. In about a quarter of all boys there is also an enlargement of the breasts at this time, and these may be tender. This tenderness is perfectly normal and in many cases disappears after a year or so.

At the age when the growth spurt is most rapid, the penis starts to grow in length and diameter and boys are easily sexually aroused. Strong pubic hair begins to appear, straight at the base of the penis and curly above it. The voice begins to deepen as the vocal cords lengthen. Some boys experience their voice cracking or breaking from time to time, but others are only aware of a gradual lowering of pitch. In order to house the lengthening vocal cords the Adam's apple, or voice box, also enlarges and can be seen clearly moving when the boy swallows. (In girls the vocal cords are shorter, the voice box is less enlarged and it is hidden by a greater layer of fat under the skin.)

Hair begins to appear, downy at first, on the arms, legs and face, and in the armpits. New sweat glands become active under the arms and near the genitals (see page 129). The first emissions of semen occur at about this time (on average, at the age of fourteen although it is quite normal for this to happen a year or two earlier or later). This can occur spontaneously during sleep or as a result of masturbation (see page 18). At the time of the first emissions the semen contains only few sperm but a boy becomes increasingly fertile with time. It is important to understand that there is no way in which a boy can know to what extent he is fertile. Intercourse has resulted in boys in their early to mid-teens becoming fathers (see page 82).

Over the next few years facial hair grows more vigorously; pubic, armpit and body hair become more profuse. The boy's voice continues to deepen and breaking ceases. The penis and testes continue to grow.

By the time he is eighteen to twenty years of age he is entering manhood. Sexually he is mature and fertile. He has reached, or is within a few centimetres of, his full adult height. As an adult he may become more hairy and there may be further muscle development but the main work of growing up is completed.

Early maturation

While girls who develop early are at something of a disadvantage, the opposite is true for boys. The characteristics which society admires in males are those which an early-developing boy acquires ahead of his age-mates. He becomes taller and, with developing muscles, stronger. He can use his superior physique to advantage in sports; girls of his own age may find him more attractive than his fellows; he may be generally more popular and treated as a leader. As a result, his own self-esteem can be higher than that of late developers.

There are some disadvantages for the early developer though. He has to experience the changes he undergoes and adjust to them at a younger age than most boys. Also, because of his apparent manliness, adults may expect greater personal maturity and responsibility from him than is at his command – he is expected to act his size, rather than his age. So if your son is an early developer, remember that he is not necessarily more responsible and wiser than others of his age. He, too, needs your support and understanding as he undergoes the changes of adolescence. He also needs advice about personal relationships and sexuality earlier than his friends.

Late maturation

The late maturer, with his extended childhood, has more time to gather experience and to understand himself before starting to come to terms with sexuality. He may therefore arrive at adulthood with more self-insight than the early maturer. However, there are difficulties in being physically childlike when your peers are developing into young men. It may lead him to over-compensate among his friends, to be something of a rebel, an attention-seeker. If you are aware of what lies behind this sort of behaviour in a late developer, it is easier to make allowances for it. It is important to treat him in a way that is appropriate for a young person of his age rather than according to his rather childlike appearance. He needs to be assured that he will grow and develop like his friends and, if this is important to him, that his strength and athletic prowess will accordingly increase. Listen to his worries and take them seriously (see page 38).

If, in his early teens, you think he is showing no signs of rapid growth and looks too young for his years, consult your doctor so that, if he is one of the very few boys who needs treatment, this can begin early, rather than late.

Nocturnal emissions

About a year after the beginning of the growth spurt, the testes become mature and, just as girls need to know about periods, so boys need to be prepared for the emission of semen. As maturing young men, they are becoming fertile, capable of fatherhood, and the sign of this is the production of semen and its emission from the penis. For a boy who does not understand what is happening, this can be disturbing because he may interpret it as a symptom of illness rather than as a natural and welcome sign of growing up.

The first emission may take place during masturbation (see page 18) or it may happen at night, during sleep. In this case it is often (not always) accompanied by erotic dreams – 'wet dreams'. According to research into sexual behaviour, most men experience nocturnal emissions at some time during their lives, especially if they are taking part in no other form of sexual activity leading to orgasm.[9]

Starting to shave

Small boys (and small girls) watch their fathers shave with great fascination and, for a boy, starting to shave is a sure sign of approaching manhood. The following notes are for mothers who are bringing up a son without an adult male in the household and cannot draw on their own experience in this matter!

Your son himself is probably the best person to decide when he ought to start shaving – remember that shaving is only a social convention and there is no health hazard in growing a beard or moustache, however sparse and wispy! If he matures at the same age as most of his friends, then no doubt they will be a source of advice to one another. Should he mature early and feel that he wants to tidy up whiskery growth on his upper lip or round his jaw, then he will need you to advise him about the necessary equipment – indeed, you may find that the first you know of it is that he has borrowed, and blunted, your own razor. Nuisance apart, this is not a good idea.

- One of the first rules about shaving is not to use other people's razors. This can be a source of cross-infection.
- It is equally important, for the sake of hygiene, to rinse the razor after each use.

Perhaps the most convenient razors are the disposable ones sold in packets of five or ten. With these, there is no need to dismantle the razor and wash and dry the blade separately after each use. The razor is simply held under running water until soap and debris are washed out. How often the razor needs changing (or the blade, if the non-disposable type of razor is used) depends on the heaviness of the hair growth. Using a blunt razor can irritate the skin.

- A foaming shaving soap can be used – which is the most convenient kind – or ordinary shaving soap, either with a brush to work up lather, or without. The use of soap softens the hair and without it shaving can set up irritations.

If your son has sensitive skin, and develops a shaving rash, then it is a good idea for him to use a non-perfumed shaving soap. Should he suffer badly from spots or acne, then shaving may be a problem and you should consult your doctor (see pages 130–31).

Masturbation

Masturbation is people stimulating their own sex organs because of the pleasurable feelings this produces, including the pleasure of orgasm. From babyhood, children explore and discover their own bodies – think of the fascination three-month-old babies have with their own hands! In the course of these explorations they discover that feeling their genitals produces a pleasant sensation. For boys this may be accompanied from infancy with erection of the penis, when the blood vessels in the penis become engorged and it grows hard and stands up.

Adolescence, with its hormonal activity and sexual development, is a period of increased sexual arousal and this frequently leads to masturbation. In time young people learn to value their sexuality as a powerful means of communicating with another person, of giving and receiving pleasure. During adolescence, masturbation should be seen as a normal part of growing up, a way in which many boys and girls find out about themselves and explore newly available experiences. It is essentially private, only the business of the young person concerned; it will not lead to any disease or dysfunction, and there is no need for any anxiety about it.

Feelings about Adolescence

At a biological level adolescence is very eventful and it would be strange if all the changes, which take place over a relatively short time, should pass by without any emotional effects on young people and their parents. The results of growing up can be clearly seen in adolescents' demands for independence, which can cause turbulence between parents and children. Later chapters cover many of the ways in which the lives and activities of adolescents shift from what seem, in retrospect, to have been the much safer ways of childhood. Both being an adolescent and being the parent of an adolescent are challenging as well as rewarding stages in life.

Young people's feelings

You may be able to remember some of the emotions which you yourself experienced as you came to realise that you were leaving childhood behind; what was exciting and enjoyable and in which areas you felt uncertain, or even miserable. Your child's experience may, in its particular details, be quite different from your own, but there are also deep similarities.

The onset of adolescence marks a transition in the child's life; he or she is leaving childhood behind and entering a new phase, a phase which, admittedly, points to the future and to future responsibilities but which also has its own realities, its special experiences, delights and anxieties. And because it is a time of transition and change it is also a time when young people are especially concerned with the crucial question: 'Who am I?' – they may not voice this in so many words, but finding themselves and recognising themselves can occupy much of their energy. Also at this time, adolescents develop new intellectual powers (page 21), which means that they can arrive at different, and competing, hypotheses to answer the problems which perplex them.

In the early years of adolescence the search for identity is connected with very apparent physical changes: rapid growth, changing proportions and sexual maturation. Boys and girls start to look different and feel different. Clothes are quickly out-grown; their very bodies take up a different space; hands and feet, which used to be taken for granted, may seem large and clumsy. Visiting grandparents and relatives who have not seen a youngster for a few months often comment on these changes. 'She's nearly as tall as her mother' ... 'He's going to be a big man like his father' ... 'Isn't she filling out?' are the sort of statements which adolescents overhear and which reinforce their own self-consciousness about their appearance. Other remarks which make adolescents cringe include comments about spots, moustaches and croaky voices. These may be totally acceptable from trusted parents but not from other people. If you know that your child is feeling vulnerable, ask visitors not to make personal remarks and explain that he or she feels shy at present.

Pressures about physical appearance and identity also come from outside the family. We live in a society which emphasises the importance of personal appearance and attractiveness, possibly even more than in the past. Television, videos, popular music and magazines all present young people with ideal pictures against which to measure their own, rather unstable self-image. There is nothing new in this: in the 1950s and early 1960s it was acceptable – indeed desirable – for women to have large breasts. In imitation of film stars like Jane Russell and Marilyn Monroe, some girls used to pad their bras with 'falsies'. But a decade or so later fashion changed and a slim, childlike figure became the 'ideal' feminine shape. Girls cannot help but be aware of such standards imposed by the media and may see themselves as failures if they do not match up to them.

Friends and classmates also have an influence. They seem to be very sure of what constitutes attractiveness and of what is unacceptable. This, too, adds to a young person's anxiety and preoccupation with changing looks. As we have seen (page 10), girls who develop early can be self-conscious about their shape because it is more womanly than that of other children of the same age and may seem unacceptable on that account. Girls, compared with boys, place more importance on being attractive[10] and value themselves accordingly. This difference between the sexes relates to current stereotypes about women and their status in society: women are often judged, and think they are judged, according to whether they are attractive or not by the standards of the day. The changes a girl notices in her figure, and the way her face and features are altering, can be a source of preoccupation and anxiety because of her desire to be 'attractive'. As our thinking develops about the position of women in society, and we move towards equal opportunities between the sexes, it is hoped that women and girls will come to value themselves more realistically: for their competence, skills and personal worth rather than how they look to other people. Boys, on the other hand, may be anxious about being sufficiently strong and muscular. For both boys and girls the question of gender identity can present problems, and they may be concerned if they are – or ever will be – 'masculine enough' or 'feminine enough' by popular standards. In addition, they experience the sensations of awakening sexuality which also alter the way they think about themselves and their identity, and this in turn can produce its own anxieties (see page 49).

As adolescence progresses these insecurities and uncertainties, based on physical changes, diminish as young people 'grow into' their bodies, become more sure about their physical identity and more self-accepting.[11] In late adolescence, young people are more likely to be concerned about preparations for the future, about preparing for examinations and getting a job rather than about how they look.

Being supportive about adolescents' feelings

As a parent, you are aware of some of your adolescent's feelings and preoccupations about themselves. But as they start to grow, to approach your own height even, this in itself puts your relationship on a slightly different footing. Perhaps you are no longer able, physically, to take your son or daughter on your knee for a reassuring cuddle and while your support is still essential, the events of your child's life are no longer so closely under your control. For example, he or she may have certain areas of life which are validly private, which they do not wish to share with you, and these wishes should be respected. Sometimes they may not wish you to express your affection physically but at other times they want, as much as ever, hugs and kisses and physical contact.

They need you to be sensitive and supportive towards their feelings and the mood swings connected with the physical changes they are experiencing or observing: an adolescent will spend hours looking in the mirror, either in self-satisfaction – 'Being her own Barbie doll' as one disgruntled father put it – or in near despair. Make-up, skin lotions, body-building equipment seem to offer some control over a changing and not always satisfactory appearance. All this may seem to you to be egocentric, distasteful, or even narcissistic, but it is important to remember that to adolescents such anxieties can be very real and that they need, in this phase of change and biological upheaval, the reassurance that your love and acceptance are constant. Sometimes you can offer them practical help: acne can be treated (see page 130), a healthy diet adopted (see page 100), something can be done about irregular teeth (see page 141). It is the worries which seem to you to be unrealistic which are more difficult to cope with and yet they need just as much patience and understanding as 'real' problems. It is important to listen, not to be dismissive, and to see things from your adolescent's point of view. Listening attentively does not always come easily. The next chapter (see pages 38–43) will offer some suggestions about how to listen in a supportive way so that adolescents know that they are not alone with feelings which may at times be tumultuous.

Intellectual Development

As well as growing taller and achieving sexual maturity, adolescents make progress intellectually. It is during this time that they acquire ways of thinking needed for adult life in a technological and democratic society. They also find new ways of thinking about moral issues, whether these involve themselves or other people.

For the adolescent these developments open up a new world, different from the world of childhood. They are a necessary part of the growing independence which equips young people, in time, to stand on their own feet and to make their own judgements and decisions as responsible adults.

New ways of thinking

Children do not think – cannot think – in the more sophisticated ways of which adults are generally capable. It is not just that we know more facts than our children – as big buckets hold more water than little buckets. It is rather that adults, as well as having greater experience and knowledge, can actually think in ways that are more advanced than those available to children. This realisation is not new. 'When I was a child I thought like a child' was self-evident for St Paul and his followers two thousand years ago!

In the last forty years researchers have started to tease out the differences between the way adults think and the way children think. They have also studied how children's ability to think develops throughout childhood. For many youngsters, there are distinct changes in the way they think which take place during adolescence and start around the age of twelve. When you listen to your child you may notice that he or she is much more grown up in what they say and in how they reason things out than they used to be, although you might not be able to put your finger on what the difference is.

Intellectual changes in adolescence

Younger children think about the world that can be seen, felt and touched: when they want to solve a problem they draw on actual physical things and their observable qualities. (They can use their imagination, but they rely on their experience of the concrete world to furnish their imagination.)

When adolescents want to tackle a problem, they rely less on thinking about concrete examples and become capable of thinking scientifically. They start to develop ideas about the world and about their own experiences – and go on to think about these ideas, to evaluate them and to compare their ideas with those of other people. They are using what is known as *reflective* thinking.

Here are some of the thought processes that open up to adolescents, with important effects for themselves and their families:

Using hypotheses

Adolescents become interested in possibilities as well as realities – they can develop hypotheses. That is, they begin to ask the question 'What if . . .';

for example, 'What if nuclear arms aren't a deterrent?'

When they are dealing with practical problems they can test their hypothesis and be ready to abandon it for a new one if necessary. This is important for problem-solving. When younger children are faced with an intellectual problem they tackle it by a process of trial and error. Adolescents, on the other hand, can adopt a logical approach and reach a satisfactory solution more quickly.

> In a well-known experiment[12] children and adolescents were asked to discover what controlled the speed of a swinging pendulum. There were various possibilities: the weight of the object on the end of the pendulum, the length of the string, the force with which it was swung and the height from which it was swung could all have an effect, either separately or in combination.
>
> The experiment showed that adolescents are more likely than younger children to go about solving such a problem in a logical way. They realise that they need to test each factor separately and to follow a systematic order, so they develop some sort of strategy. For example, they might ask themselves, 'What if the weight of the object is most important?' and test their hypothesis by keeping all the other factors the same but trying objects of different weights, in a series of trials. They also realise that it is possible that not one, but two or more factors in combination, may be responsible for speed and they build this into their systematic search. Eventually, by working through all possible combinations, it becomes clear that the factor which makes the difference is the length of the string.

Younger children do not solve problems in this way. They tackle them in a hit-or-miss fashion, trying everything out as it occurs to them and repeating tests which they have already carried out and which have been unproductive.

The development of this more systematic, hypothesis-testing approach has implications for what young people are capable of at school and at work. When they are able to think in this way they are potential scientists and problem-solvers and can study school subjects at a sophisticated level.

Abstract thinking

Adolescents can think in an abstract way; they do not need concrete examples.

In the problem about the pendulum, above, someone thinking scientifically can take all the relevant factors into account and produce a rational strategy for solving the problem without seeing a pendulum or even producing a mental image of one. Abstract concepts like weight, length, force and height now have meaning *in themselves*. It is no longer necessary for them to be linked to actual objects. This is very liberating for adolescents who are now entering the realm of ideas – heady territory, in more senses than one! Concepts like beauty, truth, justice, poverty, oppression are discovered and thought about. School subjects open up: not only the sciences but literature, history and social studies.

These new abilities allow youngsters to develop their own theories about life or politics and some become very idealistic. In fact they may become so engrossed with their own interpretations of how things are and how they ought to be that they refuse to contemplate any other point of view. Sometimes the difference between how things are and how they *should* be can lead an idealistic teenager to become sad or depressed. Teenagers suffering physical disability can be similarly affected; they are able to think about their condition in a more objective way and may become more strongly aware of how life could have worked out differently.

At home, arguments about the practicalities of everyday life, and how teenage sons and daughters want to spend their time, can take on a much more theoretical dimension. 'Because parents belong to a different generation . . .' a young person begins in an effort to persuade you that an unsupervised trip abroad, with other youngsters, is desirable. Arguments of this sort can be tiring but it is difficult not to feel admiration for the sophisticated thinking involved.

Realism about the future

Adolescents come to think about the future in a realistic way.

A very young child can hardly wait for tomorrow – and Christmas is an unrealistic eternity away. Over the years, however, future possibilities come to have greater reality and importance. When young people think about the future they can see the advantages and disadvantages of different courses of action. As they progress through their teens they are more likely to take future as well as immediate consequences into account. This is evident from a study carried out with a group of adolescents, aged from twelve to eighteen. They were asked to listen to recordings of other teenagers talking about decisions they had to make, and then to suggest factors which should influence those decisions. One such decision concerned the wisdom of having an operation to remove an unsightly lump on the face. The older group saw reasons both for and against the operation, the risks as well as the advantages, but the younger ones did not take such a balanced view. The older group was also more likely to take the future as well as the present into consideration, while the younger adolescents were more concerned with immediate problems such as being teased at school.

It can be hard to convince young teenagers that the future, some years ahead, is real or important. They may not want to listen to your advice about doing homework or wearing sensible shoes. The long-term benefits do not have the same relevance as having more leisure and being fashionable in the here-and-now. It is probably not worth while for parents to dwell too much on the more distant future when adolescents will respond more readily to arguments like 'You will get behind at school if you don't do your homework'.

Nevertheless, as the teenage years progress, adult life and decisions about the future become more important, something they can think about, hypothesise about, now. 'If I want to study physics at a more advanced level, then I ought to try to get good grades in maths now. On the other hand, if I go for languages, maths is not quite so important.' Similarly they can make plans about work and exercise some forethought about personal relationships; for example, 'I don't think I shall get married until I've settled down in a steady job.'

Improvements in memory

There are marked improvements in how much adolescents can remember, compared with children.

In adolescence the brain is more physically mature, as is the nervous system, and at the same time adolescents are finding ways to make remembering easier. If they are called on to remember details, in history or science, they can use mnemonics or associations as a memory aid (see page 225).

They can also organise information in a logical way, remembering first the main headings under which facts or ideas can be grouped, and then the sub-headings which come under each main heading (see page 225).

Age of intellectual development

It is not really possible to say at what age these different powers of thought emerge; as with physical maturity there are individual differences in intellectual development. Some very bright children may show signs of advanced ways of thinking before adolescence which, for others, do not appear until the mid-teens. Some youngsters and adults do not acquire advanced ways of thinking at all. It is possible that people who are under-functioning in this way (unless they are suffering from a disabling condition) have not been exposed to experiences which challenge them to extend their powers of thinking. Parents can help youngsters to try different strategies for solving problems, can suggest a number of hypotheses to explore when adolescents are confronted by a puzzle and suggest different ways of organising material which they are trying to commit to memory.

Not all adolescents, and not all adults, who are capable of advanced ways of thinking use them consistently. In many areas of life people do not need to think in a sophisticated way at all; the most intellectual adult can get dressed without too much thought. On other occasions, all too easily, adults can slip into 'childish' ways of thinking. For example, when someone is having problems with a word processor he or she may try the same unsuccessful strategies several times, knowing that they have failed in the past. Adolescents can be equally inconsistent in their approach to solving problems.

Moral Development

The intellectual development of adolescents has important bearings on their plans for future education and work. Parents are obviously concerned about these and all too aware of the significance of wise choices as adult life approaches. They hope that their sons and daughters will find work that suits them, satisfactory housing and so on. But parents also value less tangible assets. They want adolescents to grow up with a sense of morality: to know the difference between right and wrong, to be honest, not to let people down, to care for others, to understand their responsibility towards the community as well as to other people – and to act accordingly.

Adolescence is a time of rapidly developing independence. The world of young people is enlarging and they need to be able to function as responsible individuals without constant help and supervision. They move away from their junior schools and perhaps travel out of the immediate district to go to secondary school where they are likely to come into contact with a more varied group of friends whose values may not be shared by their parents; they develop an interest in members of the opposite sex; they will shortly have to enter the world of work or of higher education and will need to make complex choices; within the foreseeable future they will have the vote, be members of trade unions, sit on a jury, choose a life partner and perhaps in a surprisingly few years will have children of their own.

In all of these new enterprises, parents hope that their children will bring mature moral values to the decisions they make and it is natural to want to give them the maximum help. As it happens, alongside the intellectual developments of the teenage years – and ma… by them – young people also develop a more mature moral judge… than they had at an earlier age. Let us consider what stage you… adolescent has reached in his or her ability to reason about moral issues and look at the stages through which he or she has already passed. The main work in defining the stages of morality has been carried out by Lawrence Kohlberg[13] and Jean Piaget.[14]

Researchers have tested the reactions of children, young people and adults to various moral dilemmas. For example, should a man steal expensive drugs, which he cannot afford to buy, when these are needed by his desperately ill wife? The responses they have collected have led them to conclude that there are distinct stages of moral thinking through which individuals pass.

Stage 1 For young children – around the age of three to six years – being good is mainly a case of avoiding parental displeasure. They do what they are told, or avoid doing things which they know they should not do, so as not to be told off or punished. It is quite likely that they cannot yet tell the difference between cause and effect: are they told off because they have been naughty or is what they do naughty because they have been scolded? At this stage 'might is right' prevails.

Stage 2 Children move on from wanting to avoid punishment to being 'good' in order to win approval. They like their parents to think highly of them. Until they reach the age of about nine, they judge actions to some extent by their consequences, rather than by any intention on the part of the person who carries them out. Children who were asked who was naughtier – a boy who, while helping his mother, accidentally broke fifteen glasses or another boy who, while stealing a biscuit, broke one glass – more often than not replied that it was the first boy, on the grounds that he broke many more glasses! Around this age, also, children tend to think that rules are rules, with a life of their own, hence parents should never be disobeyed (although they frequently are!) and the rules of games are immutable. With their friends they operate on the basis of reciprocal obligations: 'He didn't lend me his ball so I'm not going to give him any of my cake.'

Stage 3 By the time they reach the age of eleven, some youngsters want to do the 'right thing' for the sake of their own self-esteem as well as to please others. They want to be able to approve of themselves, to be a good person in their own eyes and in other people's. At this stage they become able to put themselves in another person's shoes and work out how they would want to be treated if they were that person. They begin to see that such qualities as trust and loyalty should feature in relationships – not just the sort of tit-for-tat standards that they recognised earlier. And they know that other people's interests can come before their own.

Stage 4 Still later, the function of society and its laws, together with the duties of the individual, begin to assume importance. The guiding principle seems to be that the laws of society are there to be obeyed and if people do not obey them, then the system will break down. Similarly all members of the community should play their part in that community. It is an understanding which sees morality as contained within society, but which does not permit the individual to make any judgements about society. Someone who reasons in this way does not acknowledge that laws may sometimes be unjust, and therefore ought not to be obeyed.

Stage 5 At this stage it is recognised that while laws about what is allowed and what is forbidden differ from society to society, people should usually, as members of a society, obey them for the common good. At the same time they feel that fundamental values, like liberty or life, should be upheld in any society, whether doing so goes against the law or not.

For some young people, the realisation that different societies have different standards can be unsettling; they may come to think, for a time, that morality is all relative. The certainties of earlier stages have gone, without being replaced by the confident moral judgement of the final stage. One teenager described his feelings thus: '... it seems that the views of society don't really have any basis as being right and in that case, most people, I think, would tend to say forget it and I'll do what I want.'

Stage 6 By the time the final stage is reached, an individual has chosen his or her own moral principles. These are abstract rather than concrete: for example, the equality of human rights is considered more important than a set of rules or laws. The individual believes that just laws depend on these principles, which are universal, and that unjust laws should be disobeyed.

A greater capacity for moral reasoning does not necessarily lead to moral behaviour; experiments have shown, for example, that some people who are capable of a high level of moral judgement may none the less cheat in tests, but they are in a minority.[15]

Some adolescents – and adults – do not progress beyond a morality centred on fixed rules and the maintenance of law and order (Stage 4, above), but circumstances can lend a helping hand. Various real-life dilemmas can force people to think afresh about what is right and what is wrong, whether in the area of personal relationships, social justice, or international affairs. There is also some evidence from studies of families in America and India that the parents of morally advanced children are themselves more advanced in their moral judgements.[16] It is likely that such children have greater opportunity for discussing problems concerning their own behaviour, and that their relations with their parents are based on mutual respect rather than on complying with a rigid set of rules (see page 189). There are also suggestions that such parents take opportunities as they present themselves, whether on television programmes or in real life, to put their own point of view and to discuss moral issues with their adolescents. In schools it has been found that teachers who draw youngsters into discussions about moral dilemmas are successful in raising the level at which adolescents are able to form their own judgements. Preaching to young people about honesty and service, on the other hand, seems to have little effect.

Independent thinking in adolescence

In the course of adolescence most youngsters move forward in their thinking about morality. But the higher levels of judgement can only be exercised by people who have a strong sense of their own individuality and have become less dependent on the opinions of others, their friends, their parents and their teachers. Some may move away from their parents' religious or political beliefs (see pages 286–7) or come to have different standards about sexual behaviour based on their own sense of morality. These differences can sometimes lead to conflict between parents and children, but they can also be a sign that young people are preparing to stand on their own feet. People who hold different views can still respect one another and conflict of this kind does not necessarily have to have a negative outcome.

CHAPTER TWO

SEX EDUCATION AND THE ADOLESCENT

BRINGING UP CHILDREN and young people to be competent and responsible members of society includes educating them about sex. This, together with the rest of their education, is a process which takes many years and involves facts, understanding and feelings.

Sex education can take many forms. It can be systematic and planned, as in a school syllabus, or it can be less structured, as, for example, when discussions about personal relationships are encouraged in a youth club where there is an emphasis on social education. It can also happen spontaneously at home when an adolescent's questions are answered by the parent as they arise. Some of the ways children learn about sex take place in situations which are largely outside your control or that of any other educator, whether teacher or youth leader. Youngsters come across sexual material on television and in magazines, which can add both to their knowledge and to their perplexities. In trying to make sense of what they see they may draw conclusions that are not accurate. Often they turn to their friends and to older brothers and sisters to compare notes and to ask questions, even though they know that parents and teachers are more reliable sources of information.[1]

Leaving adolescents to learn about sex in a haphazard way can result in misinformation and ignorance, a poor preparation and one which holds real hazards for young people and for their future partners. There are other dangers involved in leaving adolescents to find out about sex for themselves from the mass media. The messages about sex and personal relationships which young people pick up from videos and magazines are in some cases misleading and harmful, for example presenting an over-romantic, unrealistic picture of the relationships between the sexes; others can be brutal and pornographic. At a time when adolescents are working towards discovering their own identity as young men and women they meet stereotypes of feminine and masculine behaviour, which portray women as dependent, and as sex objects, and men as supremely macho. These role models can provoke anxiety and feelings of inadequacy in young people of both sexes. They are also poor patterns for everyday life in which both men and women are called upon to be competent, tender and caring. The example of parents is likely to be most powerful in forming an adolescent's view of how men and women should behave towards each other; but it is still essential for adolescents to have a chance to air their opinions and feelings about these important matters, including the approach taken by the media. Being able to discuss things openly in this way is a vital part of sex education.

Sex education cannot be left to chance. It is necessary for adults, both at home and at school, to take responsibility for giving adolescents the resources they need for such an important dimension of life. Not all parents are happy about this. Some are afraid that sex education can itself be dangerous for young people. They think that the more adolescents know, the more likely they are to experiment and therefore to run into trouble. But research carried out in the UK and in the USA has shown that such fears are groundless.[2] It is youngsters who are not provided with information about sex, at home or at school, and who rely on what they can pick up from friends and the media, who are more at risk. Uninformed adolescents engage in sexual intercourse at a younger age than better informed youngsters and are less likely to take contraceptive precautions when they do so. There is an obvious explanation for this: in the absence of trustworthy advice, one way for teenagers to find out about sex is by experimenting for themselves. Because they do so without any reliable knowledge or understanding of what they are doing, they are unequipped to act in a responsible way towards their partners and themselves.

As children enter adolescence it is particularly vital that they should be given clear information about sex and about themselves as developing sexual beings. If they are to cope with the changes of puberty in a responsible way they must understand what is happening to them and be prepared for developments before they arise (see pages 6–18). Knowledge can help to free young people from guilt and anxiety: for example, it is good for them to know that masturbation is normal and not harmful, that menstruation is healthy, and that most males at some time experience embarrassing erections. Knowledge can also increase their social competence and independence. Informed youngsters are less at the mercy of false information and myths, and are more able to behave in a responsible manner towards themselves and other people.

Good sex education can give adolescents the dignity which comes with being able to understand and respect both themselves and their friends as sexual beings. It can help them to realise that affectionate relationships do not necessarily involve sexual intercourse. There are many other ways of communicating, spoken and unspoken, which convey messages of friendship, attraction and affection. Sexual intercourse is not obligatory for young people and good sex education can help to relieve pressure on them, whether from friends in general, a particular boyfriend or girlfriend, or from the media, to have full sexual relationships before they themselves feel ready. Sex education allows them to understand that it is acceptable to say 'no' if they do not want to have sex.

Subjects that should be covered in sex education

Lack of information and education about sexual matters can be disastrous; the consequences can include unwanted pregnancy, interrupted education and VD as well as unhappy relationships and anxiety. (Chapter 4 looks in detail at some possible consequences when teenagers do not have, or do not act upon, information about sex.)

Good sex education aims to give adolescents accurate information and a helpful understanding of themselves and other people as sexual beings. It covers the physical aspects of sex but it is not just a matter of biology. Sexuality and sexual relationships involve more than the clinical facts covered by a medical textbook. To regard sex as merely a means of reproduction or a source of physical pleasure is not to do it justice. Other important issues in sex education include:

Sexual identity

Sex education should aim at fostering a positive attitude towards sexuality in young people and an acceptance of their identity as sexual human beings. Becoming sexually mature marks the boundary between childhood and adult life and opens up options and uncertainties which need consideration. The changing shape and features, not to mention the skin problems, that come with puberty make it difficult for adolescents to accept themselves as they are. They can be anxious about whether they are attractive to members of the opposite sex and whether they will find a boyfriend or girlfriend. For some teenagers there is the question 'Am I or am I not a homosexual?'

Personal relationships

Sexual acts are a powerful means of communication between people, conveying messages of love, tenderness, trust and playfulness. (They can, unfortunately, convey messages of power and abuse as well.) Because sexual maturity introduces the possibility of relating to other people in a different, more intimate way, the role played by sex in personal relationships, and the questions of morality that can arise, are an essential part of sex education. At a practical level teenagers need to know about subjects related to sexual relationships, such as birth control, pregnancy, abortion and sexually transmitted diseases; at a more fundamental level, they should be encouraged to consider their responsibilities in personal relationships, whether these are sexual or not.

Life partners

Young people should also, over the teenage years, be developing a more mature understanding of stable, long-lasting relationships and of marriage. They need time to consider and discuss what qualities they would look for in a partner, what their expectations would be for themselves and their partner in such a relationship. In addition they should have an opportunity to learn something about the realities of childcare and the attention and love which children need.

To sum up, sex education comprises many subjects, some of which are biological or technical and others which are about the closest of relationships and what they involve. In attempting to explain these, it is only too easy for adults to take a negative line about sexuality in order to impress young people with some of the risks involved, and to overlook another important message: that sex is a normal part of life and one which can give great joy. This too needs to be communicated in the course of helping adolescents to understand about:

- the physical and sexual development of both boys and girls (see pages 6–18);
- menstruation (see pages 12–14);
- erections and wet dreams (see pages 15 and 17);
- masturbation (see page 18);

- sexual intercourse (see pages 62–4);
- fertility, pregnancy, birth and the needs of children (see pages 81–7);
- contraception (see pages 72–80);
- abortion (see pages 87–90);
- sexually transmitted diseases (see pages 92–7);
- homosexuality (see pages 66–9);
- personal relationships;
- marriage and life partners.

Different adolescents will need to know about these various subjects at different ages, according to their own physical development, and in more detail and greater depth as they grow older. Boys and girls alike need to be told about all of them so that they understand something of the experience of members of the opposite sex. For example, boys should know about menstruation and girls about erections. Secrecy can cause embarrassment and a lack of mutual understanding, while being well informed allows young people to see things from the other person's point of view, to be supportive and to make allowances. It is a prerequisite for sensitive relationships between the sexes.

The Role of Parents in Sex Education

Parents can find sex education very daunting but by the time a child reaches adolescence it is a task they have already, consciously or otherwise, been involved in for a long time. From the earliest years, children acquire from their parents information and understanding which relate, perhaps indirectly, to sex, to reproduction and to sexual relationships and behaviour. You have taught them names for the different parts of their bodies; you have given them an understanding of privacy and modesty by letting them know when and where nudity is acceptable; your own loving care will have conveyed important lessons about close personal relationships and trust between people; and its physical expression – the cuddles and kisses which say more than words – will have introduced them to communicating love and playfulness through touch.

This process continues when your child enters adolescence and you do what you can to support them and promote their self-confidence. You listen to teenagers' worries about their appearance, about friendships and about school and show that you understand how they are feeling; you welcome their boyfriends and girlfriends and you encourage, but at the same time establish boundaries for, their growing independence. None of this may sound like sex education, but all of it provides the security which eases their acceptance and understanding of the 'facts of life' when these are presented to them.

When it comes to talking about sex and reproduction with their adolescent children, some parents have difficulties. If you are one of these you may find it reassuring to know that research in Britain[3] and in the United States[4] shows that many others feel as you do and would like at least some aspects of sex education to be taught in school. These difficulties are quite understandable. Some parents believe that their own sex education was inadequate and that they do not have enough information to be able to cover subjects in detail. Others feel that they do not know the correct words to use and are afraid that the use of slang words demeans sex and turns it into something dirty, an attitude they do not wish to pass on to their children.

Yet others have sufficient knowledge but they feel embarrassed to talk about sex with their children and, again, this reluctance is understandable. Often, in explaining things to adolescents, parents turn to familiar examples drawn from their own experiences: an approach which, in matters of sex and reproduction, may not feel comfortable. Even in the open climate of the present day many adults are diffident when it comes to talking about this area of life, and especially with their own children. This is perhaps because of the strong conventions in our society which seek to exclude children from sexual life and which may have their roots in protecting them from incest. Another reason may be that in teaching their children about sex, parents are forced to acknowledge that their child's sexual potential is becoming a reality, and they can have mixed feelings about this. On the one hand they may feel pride but on the other they may feel envy or anxiety when they realise that their child is approaching what can be an exciting, tumultuous and even dangerous stage of life.

Parents may sometimes find it difficult to talk to their adolescents about sex because the young people themselves are reluctant to listen. This may be due to an unwillingness to admit that they do not know all there is to know about it. Such an admission could threaten their own insecure sense of becoming adult and independent of their parents.

Questions of identity also come to the fore in discussions about sex. Sexuality is intensely personal, and in learning about it there is the implicit assumption that the adolescent is a sexual being who has, or will have, sexual experiences. Some adolescents may not yet feel easy with this new aspect of their identity; they may make a quick getaway if you bring the subject up. The problem facing parents is that they feel a real obligation to see that their son or daughter is well informed but they do not want to draw them into a conversation that they may not be ready for. In such cases it would be unwise to force the issue. If a boy or girl is experiencing feelings of embarrassment or anxiety, he or she will be unlikely to pay much attention to what you are saying anyway (see pages 39–41).

If you are reluctant to talk to your adolescent about certain sexual matters, whether the reason comes from you or from them, it is nevertheless important that they are adequately informed. School can be a great help here. Both American and British research shows that some teenagers feel more comfortable learning about sex at school in the company of people of their own age.[5]

Mothers or fathers?

In general it is mothers rather than fathers who play the major role in sex education, perhaps because women carry out the largest part of childcare and of home-based education. This is especially true where a marriage or partnership has broken down; in such circumstances it is usually the mother who has custody of the children and brings them up. It is also possible that many men feel less easy talking about intimate, personal matters than women, owing to the different ways boys and girls are brought up and the different expectations we have of them (see page 55). How things are managed in your family will depend on your own personal circumstances – for example, if yours is a single-parent household, or if you are bringing up your child with the help of a step-parent. There is the question, too, of how often a youngster sees an absent parent and how well they get on together.

Where there are two adults involved in bringing up an adolescent they may find it helpful to decide jointly who is going to be responsible and, if it is agreed that both will take some share, the areas which each is best-equipped to deal with.

Boys and girls

Research indicates that boys are less likely to have spoken to their parents about sex and reproduction than are girls.[6] Perhaps this is because mothers tend to leave boys to their fathers – and then fathers dodge the issue! Also, parents are more strongly motivated to provide sex education where girls are concerned, both because girls need to be prepared for menstruation and also because of the risk of unwanted pregnancy for those who are left in ignorance.

It also seems likely that fewer boys than girls get sex education at school and this is a real deprivation for them. They need just as much information as girls; males as well as females are involved in any unwanted pregnancy and for both there are risks of sexually transmitted diseases, which can be avoided. These are the most important reasons for ensuring that both boys and girls receive education about sex and personal relationships at the start of adolescence.

Sex Education at Home

Sex education at home is very different from that given at school where there may be a systematic curriculum and specialist staff. At home, much of the instruction you give your child occurs spontaneously as opportunities arise. Incidents on television provoke questions and discussion; having a pet in the family provides the opportunity to explain about pregnancy and birth. Sometimes you need to seize these opportunities – they are too good to miss. On other occasions your adolescent will ask you direct questions or a chance remark will lead you to clear up a misunderstanding.

But even at home there is a case for passing on information directly and making opportunities to discuss sex and personal relationships, especially when you think there is a real gap in what an adolescent knows and understands. Here are some ideas that might be helpful:

- Choose a time when you are not likely to be interrupted and also when you both feel calm and unharassed. Some people might find a walk together a good opportunity, or a chance to chat over a late night drink when the television is switched off. Sharing a household chore, like washing up, could also be an opportune moment.
- Be aware of your own feelings when talking about sex. If, for example, you feel at all anxious, acknowledging this to yourself puts you more in command of the situation and makes you less likely to pass on your anxiety to your son or daughter.
- Think about where you stand on various moral issues, like abortion and sexual intercourse outside marriage, before talking about them. It could be that your values have changed over the years. Discussing difficulties with a friend or partner can help you to be clearer about your own position. If you remain undecided, admit this to your

teenager. You can say something like 'I used to think that is was wrong, now I'm not quite so sure ... I think it depends on the circumstances.' Your honesty can help your adolescent to understand that life is not always simple.

■ Be positive about sex. It is a normal, healthy part of life which can be very pleasurable and it is good to convey this to young people. Although you need to give information about subjects like venereal disease and unwanted pregnancy, these are not the whole picture.

■ Give the information as simply as you can and use at least some of the scientific words, perhaps alongside more familiar ones. In this way young people will be more at home when they meet them, or want to use them, outside the family. They will feel more confident, for example, in talking to the doctor.

■ Do not try to cover everything there is to say on a subject in one conversation. Remember that sex education is an ongoing process. Be prepared for your son or daughter to ask questions or to make their own contribution to the conversation; always ask if there is anything they would like to know more about.

Passing on information once is not enough. Young people tend to forget, partially or completely, what parents have told them, possibly because they are embarrassed or because it has not been fully understood. Be ready to raise subjects that have already been talked about, to give them an opportunity to clear up misunderstandings; you could also do this by recommending a book which covers the same ground. Remember, too, that what you have said to your child at one age may need to be enlarged upon later; obviously a conversation with a nine-year-old about pregnancy and birth would not include the details required by a teenager.

Listening

Listening has an important part to play in communicating with young people about sex and about other matters, so what follows also has relevance for other parts of this book.

So far we have been concerned with giving your son or daughter knowledge and information. But sex education is not just a matter of talking; it is a two-way process and includes listening to your son or daughter and giving them your support, interest and understanding. There are many times when adolescents need people who are responsive and sensitive to them. They may be worried about how things are going at school, about friendships and about their own development. If you encourage them to talk – and the best way is by showing that you are listening – you will help them to come to terms with their experience and perhaps to solve problems for themselves. Most importantly, when they see that you are listening carefully they will realise you are taking them seriously, that you are treating what they have to say with respect, that they are being accepted.

For your part, in listening attentively you come to understand your teenager better and begin to see things from their vantage point, no longer from the point of view of a child but of an adolescent and, eventually, of a young adult.

Listening is not always easy

While listening is essential it is not always easy; people who have perfectly good hearing can, in some circumstances, be poor listeners: listening and hearing are not the same thing. Imagine concentrating on reading a book, for example; you are so involved in reading that you are scarcely aware of household or street sounds. But when the book is laid aside the various noises around you come more into focus; and if you actually choose to listen, a variety of sounds can be distinguished: a car passing in the street, a radio playing, rain beating against the window. These noises were present while you were reading but they were not claiming your attention.

Something similar can happen in conversation. In certain circumstances, although an adolescent is perfectly capable of *hearing* what a parent says, he or she may not be listening. It is as though the information is sabotaged in some way; either it is completely blocked, or whatever gets through is distorted and muddled. Here are two examples:

A father decides that it is time to talk with his son John about the physical and sexual developments of adolescence. The main thing on John's mind is to ask his father if he can go to a football match with his friends. His father says he will not discuss this at the moment but it is time they had a quiet talk together about boys growing up. As his father talks, John mentally rehearses the good reasons he can give his father about why he should go to the match. Perhaps he should have asked his mother instead. John feels so resentful that his father will not give him an answer that he pays no attention to what is being said.

Jenny wants to tell her mother that she has been asked to a

party by a boy in her class. This is her first date. She does not know whether to go or not. She approaches her mother, who is preoccupied with a phone call she has just had. Because she is concerned about it she only hears that Jenny wants to go to a party with a boy and thinks she is being asked permission. She does not really listen to what Jenny is saying, neither to her words nor to her tone of voice. So she does not pick up the fact that Jenny is worried. 'That sounds really nice,' she says and hurries back to the telephone.

When communications do not get through there is often some distraction blocking the way. These can include:

- *Discomfort or physical pain.* It is difficult to listen if you have a headache or feel cold.
- *Interruptions.* Parents and adolescents find it difficult to give serious attention to each other if there are frequent interruptions from a younger brother or sister, wanting attention at the same time.
- *Emotions such as anger, anxiety or sadness.* An angry teenager may not listen to what a parent has to say; anxious parents find it difficult to listen to sons and daughters.
- *Thinking about other matters.* It is unlikely that someone trying to work out how many tiles are needed for the bathroom has much attention to spare for anyone else.
- *Noise.* Some people have difficulty concentrating against a background of other people's music.

Avoiding distractions

It is plainly not sensible to expect your teenager to be able to listen to you if he or she is distracted.

It may be that you want to talk about some aspect of life over which you do not see eye-to-eye with your adolescent (see page 183). Or you may want to tell them a piece of news which will have serious effects on the family, such as that there is going to be a major change, like the introduction of a step-parent (see pages 187–9). Or you may want to make sure that they have a good understanding of menstruation and other changes of adolescence (see page 12). If there is something important to be said, it is a good idea to decide whether this is the right time and place for your adolescent to listen attentively and to postpone the discussion if necessary.

If, on the other hand, your teenager wants to talk to you and you are distracted, you have a choice to make. Either you can explain that at the moment things are a bit hectic and you would like to be able to concentrate on what they want to tell you. Ask if you can talk later on, when things have quietened down. Or, if you can see that what they have to say needs saying now, you may decide that it is better not to put them off. In this case, it is wise to reduce whatever distractions there may be.

If you are aware of possible sources of distraction in yourself, such as a headache, or feelings of anxiety, or preoccupation with other matters, then you need to remind yourself to listen as carefully as you can and make a conscious effort to do so.

Do not interrupt

Attentive listening means giving your full attention to what is being said, letting the other person have their complete say and not interrupting, although this may not be easy. You may find that you desperately want to break in with a question, or that you would like to put your point of view or offer some advice. However necessary this may seem, bide your time. When youngsters really need to talk, interruptions can shut them up or make them change the subject.

Here is an example of how attentive, encouraging listening can help whatever is worrying a person come to the surface, while offering advice or asking too many questions could be frustrating.

An adolescent, David, is worried that he is not getting on with his biology teacher. At the back of his mind is an anxiety that he will not do well in his exam and that his parents will be disappointed or angry. He thinks the teacher has misunderstood him and treated him unjustly in class today. David mentions it first to his father. His father hardly gives him a chance to explain what is on his mind. After the opening words he rushes in with reassurances that you cannot get on well with everyone and that his son should cheer up. How long has the teacher been at the school? How old is she? She might not have settled down to teaching yet. David, put off by the information and questions, answers to the best of his ability and goes away still burdened with an anxiety he needed to share.

When David's mother comes home and he tells her what is on his mind, she quietly hears him out. He is very relieved that she is really listening and taking him seriously. He feels able to go on and confide his worries about the exam. His mother accepts what he has to say before offering some suggestions. David feels better for having shared his anxieties and is able to listen to his mother's advice.

Let them know you are listening

It is not enough just to listen to adolescents; you have to let them know you are listening by showing that you are. Sometimes this comes naturally but it is more difficult when what is being said provokes strong feelings in the listener. When adolescents have something important to say, they need space and time to say it and the assurance that they are being listened to. This is especially necessary if they are excited or upset. On such occasions it is reassuring if the listener looks at the young person while they are speaking. If a listener's gaze wanders, it gives the impression that he or she is thinking of other things. Encouraging words like 'yes', 'I see' or even 'mm' can reassure an adolescent that a parent is following what is being said and that it is all right to go on talking.

On many occasions careful, attentive listening can be more valuable than having a discussion about the problem in question. You show by your encouragement that you are interested, that your teenager is not boring you, and that you are putting their needs first.

Responding

You can also let them know that you understand by repeating back the essential things they have said, being a sort of mirror for them, in fact. So you might say to a young person who has just told you about a quarrel: 'You feel that Jane has let you down and you're really angry about it.' Notice that the reflecting back lets them know that you have heard what they said and recognise how they are feeling. It also gives your son or daughter a chance to put you right if you have misunderstood. Having feelings and experience accepted in this way, instead of being weighed down by advice or distracted by questions, can be a positive experience for an adolescent and a way in which parents can learn more about how life looks from the teenage point of view.

When you do not want to listen

There will be occasions when you do not feel like being a patient listener, when your own concerns are uppermost and when you do not give your adolescent your complete attention or offer to do so later. However, parents and adolescents have travelled a long way together by this stage and young people are coming to realise that their parents are not always perfect! If you are not always completely available to them, they may be disappointed, but they will nevertheless survive and remain confident of your love.

If listening to your adolescent's problems is very painful for you, perhaps because your own feelings are also involved due to a family breakdown or bereavement, then try to find someone else in whom he or she can confide. You could arrange for a trusted friend to visit or make it possible for your adolescent to go and see other relatives. At times of family crisis, young people also turn increasingly to friends of their own age for help and support (see page 281).

Sex Education at School

There are few countries where, by law, schools have to include sex education in their curriculum – Sweden and Denmark are among the exceptions. At the other end of the spectrum are those countries where sex education is frowned upon and not at all common, while in Britain whether or not a school provides sex education is the responsibility of the school governors (see page 201).

Most parents and most children, according to research carried out both in Britain and in the USA, welcome the idea of school-based sex education.[7] Schools are a major resource in the upbringing of children and offer a variety of educational experiences, intellectual, artistic, physical and social, so why not education about sex and personal relationships? What help can you expect to get from schools in this important area?

Not all the schools which provide sex education cover the ground necessary for adolescents. You really need to know what happens in the school your son or daughter attends because there may be gaps which need to be covered in your discussions at home. In Britain schools must, by law (Education Act 1981), inform parents about any sex education they provide. The Department of Education and Science (DES) encourages schools to go further than this and says that sex education should be carried out 'in consultation' with parents. Your opinions are important and should be heard. So if your adolescent goes to a school which takes sex education seriously, you may find yourself invited to parents' evenings where you can discuss your concerns and ask questions.

Despite the law, some schools are not very forthcoming about sex education and you may hear little about it from the school your child attends. This may be because the governors, the head teacher and staff have not yet developed any policy about sex education so that it 'crops up' rather than having a place of its own; or there is no sex education; or that the school does not publicise it in case some parents object. If this is true of the school your child attends, you will need to talk to teachers in order to get a fuller picture. The teachers to approach are those who have pastoral responsibilities towards your child, a year tutor, for example (see page 203), or another senior member of staff who understands the school's policy.

Sex education in primary schools

In primary schools sex education is fairly informal. Teachers take opportunities to explain subjects like birth and pregnancy as they come up, perhaps when a child has a new brother or sister or if the classroom pet gives birth. Sometimes teachers will pass on information in answer to questions and at other times they will correct children's obvious misunderstandings, gauging what children understand and explaining things at their level. In some primary schools there are lessons for older children about menstruation and the physical changes of adolescence, but boys may not be included in such classes and they may also come too late for girls who have matured early.

Sex education in secondary schools

In the secondary school sex education comes in many guises, which you may or may not recognise. It may be included under any of the following subjects: Education for Adult Life, Biology, Personal Relationships, Preparation for Parenthood, Child Development, Hygiene, or Health Education.

There are also opportunities for young people to explore their own ideas about life and sex in the general school curriculum. Literature is full of stories about the joys and pains of love, not to mention the dilemmas inherent in personal relationships, and these can be the focus of discussion in an English class. Similarly, history lessons may look at royal marriages, the problems of heirs, succession, and infidelity; geography, history and social studies may deal with population growth and control; religious studies have a moral component and can deal with questions of sexual ethics and responsibility in personal relationships.

Teaching methods

Sex education can be carried out in a variety of ways as well as in formal lessons. Schools find video and film very helpful both to inform youngsters and to spark off discussion. Young people welcome the opportunity to talk about sex with their friends, both informally – although they know that any information they receive may be less than accurate – and in discussion groups led by adults.[8] Listening to others of the same age can help them to sort things out and seeing things from other people's points of view helps them to understand more about the ethical dimension. They also like to hear questions asked which they might feel shy about asking themselves, for fear of appearing ignorant. Sometimes experts are brought in from outside to provide input which can also provoke discussion.

What should you look for in sex education at school?

There may be times when you will be able to influence the sort of sex education your adolescent son or daughter receives at school. Perhaps your choice of school will partly depend on how the school deals with sex education and what you want for your child. It is possible that an occasion could arise when you are consulted and your opinion asked at a parents' meeting. And, if you wish, you can raise the subject with other parents at a meeting of the Parent-Teacher Association (PTA – see page 201), with a school governor or at the annual meeting when governors report to parents (see page 201).

What should schools be doing about sex education?

- They should tackle the subject head on, having worked out a curriculum of sex education for the whole school. The coincidental opportunities that arise, in subjects like English, for discussing material related to sex make a useful contribution, but they are too haphazard to be relied on to cover the subject.
- Sex education should be systematic and meet the needs of youngsters of different ages. The syllabus should see that information is given in good time, not 'too little, too late'.
- The emphasis should not be on the physical aspects of sex and reproduction only. The syllabus should integrate the emotional, physical, social and ethical dimensions of sex education.
- The same material needs to be covered for boys and girls, even though teachers may occasionally separate the sexes.[9]
- Sex education should be available for all students. In some schools it is dealt with in an option like Child Development, which not everyone takes.

It is also a good idea to find out what help the school offers students in matters relating to sex and personal relationships.

- Are there counsellors or teachers with special responsibility for pastoral care who can be approached for advice and help? Young people can find it very useful to talk about things in confidence to a sensitive person outside the family.
- Does the school seem sensitive to the special needs of adolescents at this stage in their lives?
- What provision is there to help young girls cope with their periods? Are there dispensers for sanitary towels and tampons in the toilets? Are there good means for disposing of them?
- Is consideration given to young people's needs for privacy at a time when they may feel awkward about their development and physical appearance? Do the lavatory doors lock? Is there some privacy in the showers after sports lessons? Youngsters can become very anxious about such things.

The attitude of the school towards its adolescents at this important practical level is just as important as its formal sex education syllabus.

Taking a child out of sex education

In Britain parents may apply to take their child out of sex education, but this is not to be recommended. Adolescents do not like to appear different from others, especially when the subject matter is already sensitive. They may feel that other students think they are being treated as children in not being allowed to receive adult information, and they may be teased about it. In addition they can feel left out and curious about what the others are learning.

Books

If you think that the school your child attends does not provide an adequate programme of sex education (see page 44), there are several books aimed at teenagers which could prove useful. While young people usually welcome the opportunity to talk about adult subjects with their parents, books have a useful part to play in sex education. Some are written in a chatty, familiar style, using current jargon and humorous illustrations as well as informative diagrams; textbooks about human biology can also be helpful if they are at the right level for your teenager. Young people can return to books to check up on anything you have told them and books are always there to be consulted. Your local library may have suitable books but these will not necessarily be displayed on an open shelf in the children's department. It is the policy of some libraries to make books on sex education available only on request so parents and adolescents may need to ask what books the library holds or request the librarian to obtain those required. A list of useful books is given on pages 299–300.

Sex education for adolescents with physical disabilities

Adolescents with physical disabilities develop towards sexual maturity just like other young people and youngsters with certain conditions, for example spina bifida, reach puberty at an earlier age than other children. Just like other adolescents, those with physical disabilities need information about the changes that are happening to their bodies and support in coming to terms with their sexuality.

They need to know if their disability will have any effect on how they are able to function sexually; will they be able to have sexual intercourse, for instance? They need to be able to ask questions and to get practical advice. Both boys and girls will want to know if they will be able to have children and to what extent there is a risk of their disability being passed on. But sexuality is not only about the physical side of life; it also has to do with feelings, relationships, self-identity and self-esteem. Young people with physical disabilities need the chance to bring into the open their anxieties about sexuality, about having boyfriends and girlfriends, how they feel about themselves and their bodies, whether with a trusted adult or in discussion with other youngsters.

Sex education should be part of the curriculum for adolescents with physical disabilities whether they are at special or mainstream schools (see page 241) and they will also need individual advice about their own condition. The school nurse should be able to give advice about the practicalities concerning menstruation, and various support organisations for specific conditions can give practical advice on other matters.

Sex education for adolescents with mental handicaps

Most young people with mental handicaps develop sexually and have normal sexual feelings. This can be hard for parents, and society at large, to accept because it is sometimes more comfortable, if mistaken, to regard people with mental handicaps as perpetual children and, therefore, asexual.

Confusingly, there also exists another belief which is in contradiction to this. This belief has its roots in the past and holds that men and women with mental handicaps experience very strong sexual feelings which they are unable to control. Both of these myths may still colour our attitudes towards adolescents with mental handicaps but they are, nevertheless, myths. The United Nations' Declaration of Rights of the Mentally Handicapped (1971) states that the mentally retarded person has the same rights as other citizens of the same country and of the same age. Equally, adolescents with mental handicaps, however slight or severe, need information about sexual development, if only as a protection against people who might take advantage of them. Young women with mental handicaps need help in coping with menstruation and the reassurance of their parents, through their attitudes towards it, that periods are normal and healthy.

Some adolescents with mental handicaps will eventually be able to lead independent lives, others will only manage to achieve semi-dependence. For all, however, information about reproduction is both feasible and necessary. They do not need to understand all the underlying biology but they do need to know that babies start through an act of sexual intercourse.[10] They also need to know how to deal with their developing sexuality: what is, and what is not, socially acceptable behaviour; that it is inappropriate to hug strangers; that they have the right to say 'no' to any touch or kiss.

The school may have a health and personal relationships programme which covers these things. For parents it is especially important to know what the programme contains and what approach is followed, so that they are prepared for questions or remarks at home. There is also the possibility of setting up a parents' support group, where parents can exchange experiences about their adolescents and about their concern regarding independence and sex education.[11]

CHAPTER THREE

GENDER AND SEXUALITY IN ADOLESCENCE

In adolescence there is an increase in hormonal activity triggering the physical changes which turn a child into a young man or woman (see pages 6–18). Young people start to become aware of aspects of their sexual identity that have not been relevant before. More clearly and obviously than in childhood, they are sexual beings. This emerging identity presents them with the choices that belong to their new stage of development.

Because young people reach puberty earlier than ever before, there are now more young, sexually mature people who are still in full-time education and living with their parents. This uncomfortable mixture of biological maturity and economic and social dependency can present parents and adolescents with dilemmas not met in the past. For an increasing number of young people, sexual feelings culminate in sexual intercourse. Some youngsters, spurred on by their own development, both intellectual and physical, take a fresh look at what is expected of males and females in our society, and compare this with their own developing sexual identity and with what they want from life as young men and women. Do they want a boyfriend or girlfriend? How would they like to spend their leisure-time? What sort of career choices do they wish to make? Some find that they are attracted to members of the same sex and wonder if they are homosexual.

Sexual identity, whether it is concerned with sexual behaviour in the erotic sense or simply with behaviour thought to be appropriate for one sex or the other, is not just a matter of biology. Much depends on the standards set by the rest of society, whether by parents, teachers, friends or by the images conveyed in the mass media.

The first part of this chapter is about how sex roles develop; it goes on to deal with the subject of sexuality in adolescence, and concludes with heterosexuality and homosexuality.

Sexual Identity: Males or Females?

When we start to think about the development of sexual identity, it is necessary to go right back to the beginning, to babyhood or before. You may remember that the first question asked as people peeped into the pram to look at your newborn child was: 'Is it a little boy or a little girl?' This is an enormously important question in our society, where we so often think about people according to whether they are male or female. Differences between the sexes seem to be so immediately obvious and important that they are often used as a way of organising people. In school, teachers frequently say 'Boys stand over there, girls over there', when they want to divide their classes – even when there is no intrinsic reason for sorting children out into groups of the same sex.

In recent years psychologists have given a lot of attention to how children acquire their sexual identity and how this affects their lives. Girls and boys become aware of gender differences very quickly and these have a profound influence on their development. Whether a child is male or female influences how they think about themselves and how other people think about them and treat them. It can open up some possibilities and close down others.

Becoming male and female

From the moment of conception different forces have been at work in determining your child's sexual identity; your teenager behaves as a male or as a female for complex reasons. These forces include: *the genetic material* – the chromosomes – inherited from you and your partner, which directs development towards one sex or the other; *the part played by hormones*, before birth, during childhood and in adolescence; and *the part played by society*.

Chromosomes

Your adolescent's individuality depends to some extent on the actions of chromosomes. Each of the millions and millions of cells in the human body contains twenty-three pairs of chromosomes. Each chromosome contains genes, up to a thousand or more, which control development and determine individual characteristics. The colour of your child's eyes, whether they are right- or left-handed, tall or short, are all determined by the genes.

Sex chromosomes One pair of chromosomes – the sex chromosomes – is important for sexual development. The sex chromosomes of girls and women are different from those of boys and men.

A woman has a pair of sex chromosomes which, under the microscope, look like an X. So the female sex chromosomes are called XX chromosomes.

A man has a pair of sex chromosomes, one of which looks like an X and the other like a Y. So the male sex chromosomes are called XY chromosomes.

How does this come about? The only cells in the body which are not made up of twenty-three *pairs* of chromosomes are the egg cell, produced in the woman's ovaries, and the sperm cell, produced in the man's testes. It is these which fuse together at conception to produce the embryo.

Egg cells and sperm cells each have twenty-three *single* chromosomes. In both men and women one of these is the sex chromosome. In men this can be an X chromosome or a Y chromosome. About half of sperm cells carry Xs and half Ys. In women the egg cell always has an X chromosome.

At conception, when the sperm cell fuses with the egg cell, the single chromosomes of the egg cell and the single chromosomes of the sperm cell pair up together. So the fertilised egg has twenty-three pairs of chromosomes.

If the sperm cell has a Y chromosome, this will pair with the woman's X chromosome to produce an XY, a male chromosome pair. If the sperm has an X chromosome, this will pair with the woman's X chromosome to produce an XX, in other words a female chromosome pair.

Prenatal hormones

From conception, the embryo is genetically either XY – male – or XX – female. To begin with, development is the same for both sexes. Then, from the sixth week, rudimentary testes develop in the XY embryo and ovaries develop in the XX embryo. The other minute structures which will eventually develop into male and female genitals are still identical for both XY and XX embryos.

During the second month, hormones start to play their part in determining the sex of the embryo. Without the action of these hormones, all development would be female.

At this time the male embryo produces male hormones, some of which stop female sexual development and others of which promote male sexual development. If, as happens in some cases, the male hormones are not produced, the embryo will go on to develop physically into a female, although remaining genetically XY.

The female does not need hormones, at this stage, to continue developing as a female. But it can happen, for various reasons, that an XX (female) foetus is exposed to male hormones. In such cases the foetus may develop genitals which are neither clearly male nor clearly female, and at birth a difficult decision has to be made about the baby's sex.

There are other reasons why some children are born without a clear sexual identity. These cases are distressing for parents, quite apart from the children themselves. Being a boy or being a girl is part of a person's identity. It is almost unthinkable that a child should be brought up without knowing, or without other people knowing, its sex. The usual practice is therefore for the child to be assigned a sex, given a boy's or a girl's name, and brought up as such. Later, hormone treatment and plastic surgery both play a part in helping the child to develop in accordance with the assigned sex.

These conditions are rare, but, as we shall see, the treatment can teach us about the acquisition of sexual identity in our society (see page 53).

Biological influences on sex roles

Children are born male or female for complex biological reasons, as we have seen. But is it 'natural' for boys to behave like boys and girls to behave like girls because of their biological make-up? The answer to this question is not entirely clear.

There is some evidence that different hormonal balances can affect behaviour.

■ If, for example, mothers are given a certain drug in pregnancy, it results in less androgen (see page 7) being produced than usual. A group of boys whose mothers had taken this drug were, therefore, less androgenised than is normal. In adolescence, these boys spent less time in physical, rough-and-tumble play than others.

- Studies of girls who have been exposed to unusually high levels of androgen, prenatally, find that they are more likely to play with boys and to enjoy rough-and-tumble games than other girls.[1]

Learning to be male or female

In contrast, other research has shown that biological factors, while they have some importance, are not paramount in determining a person's gender. This research was carried out on children who were born without a clear sexual identity and who were assigned a sex. In some cases this did not match their chromosome sex. Nevertheless these children were brought up by their parents as members of their assigned sex, called an 'appropriate' name and given 'appropriate' toys and clothes. They grew up quite at home in their assigned sex and behaved like other members of that sex. These youngsters had taken on the gender that they had been given, the characteristics which go with being male or female, masculine or feminine in our society (see pages 54–5).

Your own son or daughter has also, over the years, acquired a gender identity. They have their own experience, their own particular awareness of what being male or female means for them personally. This understanding of their gender has a long history which has developed over the years of childhood.

Parents' wishes

Before a baby is born, parents think in terms of the child's sex. They choose names for a boy and names for a girl and often have a preference for a child of one sex rather than another. Parenting a girl and parenting a boy are seen to be different experiences and from the earliest days people treat boys and girls differently and see them in a different light. One research experiment that showed this clearly was carried out with fathers who were visiting their newborn infants in hospital. Even though they had only seen them for a few moments through a glass screen, they described the boys in such terms as 'mischievous' while they spoke of the girls as being 'pretty' or 'cute'. The fathers were projecting on to their children socially acceptable qualities which fit in with the stereotypes we have about boys and girls in our society.[2]

Not only do adults think of boy babies and girl babies in different terms; there is also a mass of research which shows that they treat boys and girls very differently. The research includes experiments where the adult is introduced to a strange baby and either not told the infant's sex, or misled about it. The results are always the same. The adults play in a more exciting way with the 'boy' and in a more soothing way with the 'girl'.[3] This is one of the ways in which children learn what is expected of them. It happens before they have any understanding that they belong to one sex rather than the other and before they have learned that they will remain the same sex for life; their only experience is of being treated consistently as though they are a certain sort of person.

In various other ways children learn how members of the two sexes 'should' behave.

- Adults reward them for behaving in a way that is appropriate to their own sex. For example, little girls are praised and have more attention paid to them when they wear pretty clothes or when they behave like 'little mothers' with their dolls or with real babies. The strength and adventurousness of boys is also commented on favourably. By contrast, children who behave in a way that goes against how they are 'supposed' to behave are either ignored or told off. The classic case is when boys are told that 'boys don't cry'. Other children are quick to comment and to make fun of those who do not conform to sex stereotypes.
- Children constantly observe how members of both sexes behave; these are models for them to imitate and learn from. In two-parent families, boys and girls alike learn that mothers mostly look after the children and the house (even those who go out to work) while fathers are the 'breadwinners'. Television also offers an endless stream of images of men and women which are highly stereotyped.

Eventually children come to internalise their ideas about what girls do and what boys do, what men do and what women do. They know which toys are for girls and which toys are for boys; what girls should wear and what boys should wear; how boys and girls should behave. By the time they are aged about six or seven these inner 'rules' have a strong moral force for them.

When they reach adolescence, however, they are capable of realising that some of these rules are more a matter of convention than of morality. In England, for example, males never wear skirts (except for priests and judges!) but in Scotland they may. Although they can understand this anomaly at an intellectual level, for many adolescents one way of adjusting to their newly acquired physical appearance may be to become more intensely 'male' or 'female'. Together with friends of the same sex they find new ways of expressing their gender identity. These can include a greater interest in clothes or zealous support for a football team, in accordance with what is seen to be desirable for teenagers of their sex.

They may not yet be fully aware of the force of certain stereotypes, which to some extent control the behaviour of the sexes. An important example of sex stereotyping is the different roles undertaken by men and women in Western society: how mothers give more time to childcare and men to paid work; how it may seem more usual for women to be in supportive or caring jobs, like being secretaries or nurses, than men – although some men do go into nursing and there are more women working in the top and middle management of companies than was once the case. Stereotyped ideas about how the sexes are supposed to behave too often go undisputed. Many of us have been brought up to believe that girls and women are expected to be gentle and to consider other people. Men, on the other hand, are expected to be brave and adventurous and not to cry.

It is very difficult to step outside these conventions and to see them for what they are: means of social control rather than natural ways for the two sexes to behave. But a look at society in the past, or in other parts of the world, shows how differently the sexes can behave from the way they are expected to do in our society today.

- In Victorian England men were 'allowed' to cry in public: Gladstone wept openly in Parliament; in the same era the idea of women wearing trousers was morally reprehensible, as was women studying and practising medicine.
- In some societies, including our own, girls are treated as though they are more vulnerable than boys, and generally not allowed the same independence as their brothers. Refreshingly, however, a classic study of three traditional societies by the anthropologist Margaret Mead found that in one of them boys were socialised to be passive, emotional and dependent while girls were brought up to be aggressive, independent and rational.[4]
- In some societies it is the males who wear flamboyant clothes and decorations, not the females. Even in our own society there have been great changes since the Second World War in what is acceptable clothing and decoration for men. At certain times over the decades long hair has been the fashion for men, earrings and other male jewellery have become commonplace and cosmetics and colognes are now available for men.

As these findings show, typically male and typically female behaviour depends to a greater extent on the society someone lives in than on chromosomes and hormones.

Psychologists are not the only people who concern themselves with the issue of sex roles; this is of equal importance to teenagers and their parents. We shall see later how sex roles relate to, and affect, various areas of adolescents' lives: how they can influence choices made at school (see pages 210–11); how girls may be less ready to admit to their own sexuality than boys and therefore unwilling to take practical steps with regard to contraception, although it is they, and not boys, who risk pregnancy (see pages 81–2); how the two sexes do not participate to the same extent in sport; how girls can be more confined to the home and more taken up with domestic chores than their brothers (see page 252); how a desire to be acceptably slim, according to the female stereotype, may lead to excessive dieting and to anorexia nervosa (see pages 117–19).

Some young people, of either sex, may experience sex roles as restricting and not all young people conform to the stereotypes. American research shows that between a quarter and a third of teenagers actually combine masculine and feminine qualities. In addition, youngsters who do so have higher self-esteem, do better at school, have better relations with the opposite sex and are more self-reliant and independent than those who incline towards being more 'masculine' or more 'feminine'.[5]

For parents, the most important task is to bear with their adolescent children as they explore and find their own sexual identity. Whatever the turmoil a young person is going through, they need your backing. When their behaviour does not conform to the stereotypes, when a teenage boy cries with disappointment, or a girl seems to be more interested in a career than the prospect of marriage and motherhood, they need to feel accepted. The challenge for other parents may be in accepting children who follow totally conventional patterns, the completely macho boys and the ultra-feminine, dependent girls, when they would prefer less stereotyped behaviour.

Adolescents are as they are and they need their parents as allies, sometimes in the background, at other times openly supportive, as they come to terms with their sexual identity.

You may feel that other people are trying to mould, and perhaps limit the scope of, your adolescent's life, according to the prevalent stereotypes. This can happen in school, where there may be restrictions on academic choices, or in the family if another adult – or a brother or sister – is critical of a young person who does not conform. In these cases your adolescent needs your encouragement and perhaps your intervention on their behalf.

Sexuality

The expectations that people have of boys and girls, and men and women, can also have an effect on how adolescents feel about their sexuality. Sexuality is a dimension of human life from the beginning. Boy babies have erections while they are still in the womb; the vaginas of girl babies lubricate from birth onwards; babies and toddlers find pleasure in exploring their genitals; sexual activity goes on through adult life and into old age. During adolescence, sexual maturation, the increase in hormonal activity, and social customs all lead to a greater awareness of sexuality. Now comes the realisation for many adolescents that they are people who experience sexual urges, longings and pleasure. The possibility of relating to another person sexually becomes a reality.

The awareness of their own sexuality is more central for some adolescents than for others. For boys the pleasures – and embarrassments – of erections and nocturnal emissions can be a fairly frequent reminder of physical sexuality. Research suggests that girls differ as to how they experience their sexuality: some experience strong and identifiable physical feelings, for others these may be more diffuse and more linked to emotions like love and affection than local physical responses.[6]

Why the sexes differ in this way is not yet clear. Various factors play their part and these include the difference in upbringing of boys and girls. This can be seen in an extreme form if we turn to the past. In the nineteenth century only immoral women were supposed to enjoy sex and men often separated their sexual feelings, which could be expressed towards prostitutes, from their feelings of love, which were reserved for their wives. Since then attitudes towards sex, and towards female sexuality, have changed, but echoes of earlier attitudes persist which, by many subtle means, are conveyed to children and young people. It is beyond doubt that today women do enjoy sex. Recent research suggests that their capacity for sexual response is greater than that of men.[7] Nevertheless women seem in many ways to be less free to experience and express their sexuality than men.

Importance of sexuality for adolescents

Although sexual maturity is a notable aspect of adolescents' lives, it is not one on which young people always focus strongly. There are many tasks to accomplish in adolescence, including studying and making decisions about work. Housework has to be done; money is earned and spent; family visits and outings are planned; what to watch on television is discussed. There are also friendships to enjoy. Girls often have 'best friends' with whom they can share their secrets and talk over their hopes and fears. For boys, especially in early adolescence, friendships are less intimate – the focus is more on group interests and activities.

All of these can be a matter for conflict or co-operation with a teenager and play a larger part in everyday life than sex.

Parents and adolescent sexuality

In many areas of life young people claim, and are given, greater independence in adolescence and this is as it should be. As you come to control fewer of the details of your children's daily life, there are changes in your relationship. When they were babies, this was tremendously close. You could probably give a detailed daily account of exactly how much they had eaten, how many dirty nappies they produced, how long they slept. Throughout childhood this close monitoring of your child grew less as he or she became more capable of taking responsibility for their own well-being. Now, in adolescence, your son or daughter reaches the point where they need adults less and less to manage the ordinary business of life.

This increasing independence can show itself in relation to their developing sexuality as well as in other matters. Boys and girls who never cared about nudity, or locking the bathroom door, can become self-conscious at this stage. Not all youngsters need this sort of privacy – much may depend on the habits of your own family – but if they do, their feelings ought to be respected. You may be able to sympathise if you remember similar feelings you had yourself. Respecting an adolescent's wishes for privacy is not the same as promoting puritanism or distrust or shame about their body; it is a matter-of-fact recognition that they want more privacy now than they did a few years ago.

In adolescence young people increasingly claim their own space and an identity which is increasingly distinct from that of their parents. They still need your support, acceptance and love, but they need it as a separate person whose needs and wishes may be different from your own. It is at this time that many youngsters become interested in boyfriends and girlfriends and form warm attachments to them. This is part of loosening the ties to parents in preparation for adult partnerships. Eventually most people find someone for whom they feel a real commitment and with whom they can enjoy an intimate physical relationship. Until then, during adolescence, come the pleasures and pains of falling in and out of love, of dating, going steady, and all the emotional upheavals of attachments, lost and won.

Boyfriends and girlfriends

Friendships with members of the opposite sex were quite rare during childhood when sex stereotyping meant that many – not all – boys played only with boys and girls only with girls. But in adolescence the attraction of the opposite sex overcomes this earlier prejudice. Young people may, for the first time, spend their time in friendship groups of both sexes. Some adolescents start to 'go out' with a girlfriend or boyfriend and this may give them high status among their friends. But not all young people share this view. One survey among English teenagers found that only about a quarter considered it important to have a boyfriend or girlfriend.[8]

In Britain the whole business of dating is much less formal than it is in the USA. In America many parties and school social events are built round the idea that teenagers, and even younger children, will attend as a pair. This can lead to pressure on young people to start dating before they would otherwise do so. In Britain the conventions are different but pressures to pair up can still occur among teenagers. These pressures can range from enquiries from relatives whether they yet have a girlfriend or boyfriend, to pressures to start dating because friends have started and it is part of school ethos to do so.

In a recent survey 43 per cent of the young people interviewed said they thought there was pressure to have a boyfriend or girlfriend. More of the older teenagers felt this than the younger ones. Most of them thought that the pressure came from other teenagers. A fourteen-year-old boy said: 'If you haven't got a girlfriend they get you down about it and say that you're ugly and a lot of other rubbish ...' and a sixteen-year-old girl said: 'I think it makes you desperate because you think everyone has got a boyfriend except me, and you think "What's wrong with me? Nobody wants me ..." '[9] It is easy to see that having a girlfriend or boyfriend can be important for reasons of self-esteem in some teenager groups.

As a parent, it is advisable to be aware of these pressures and to fend off those that come from other members of the family. When they are ready, teenagers will find a girlfriend or boyfriend for themselves. Some youngsters may need your reassurance that this will happen in due time, that there is no need to look for something they do not feel ready for yet, and that there is nothing wrong with them because they feel the way they do.

Falling in love

Whatever 'falling in love' means, it is fairly obvious that when it happens people do not have much control over it. Most of us can remember what it is like to fall in love, when feelings and thoughts revolve around one person. And this is a state that many adolescents are in at any one time. In a survey of twelve- to eighteen-year-olds in the USA, more than half of those questioned said that they had been in love. Girls were more likely to be in love (and to have been in love) than boys. Not unexpectedly, the older adolescents (sixteen- to eighteen-year-olds) were more likely to be in love than the younger ones (twelve- to fifteen-year-olds). Sixty-nine per cent of the older girls compared with 49 per cent of the younger girls said they were currently 'in love' and 43 per cent of the older boys, compared with 38 per cent of the younger ones.[10]

Although being in love can be idyllic, it is not always a happy experience for a young person. The object of their love may not reciprocate it – may not even notice that someone is in love with them. The person who is in love, meanwhile, plans their day so that paths cross; they find opportunities to introduce the beloved's name into conversation and daydream that one day their love will be returned. Even established romances have their ups and downs and relationships between adolescents frequently do not last. When they finally break up, there may be anguish and a sense of deep loss, bereavement even, for one member of the couple (see pages 177–9).

Young people do not usually confide in their parents when they fall in love. 'I am someone who falls in love' is a new component in their identity; they need to get used to it for themselves first. It is rather easier to admit to having a boyfriend or girlfriend, or 'going out' with someone – although this, too, may make them feel self-conscious. As a parent you may never know about the emotional upheavals that your son or daughter is experiencing. Parents have to be ready to accept their adolescents' confidences if they offer them, to listen, support and give advice if asked; but parents should also acknowledge that their children's feelings are their own and that they are not necessarily able to share them.

If there are real signs that a teenager is becoming depressed about a friendship (see pages 191–3), then they need help. Some youngsters may be experiencing serious problems in other areas of life and finding it difficult to cope generally. For them the loss of a boyfriend or girlfriend can be the last straw and make them feel that life really isn't worth living. But most adolescents seem to cope with falling in and out of love for themselves with no more than temporary upsets. Often they confide more easily in a close friend than in a parent.

At any rate it is important to be sensitive towards a teenager who appears to be in love – whether they are heart-broken or on top of the world. Although adults may see a funny side to the situation, teenagers are particularly sensitive on these issues and making jokes only convinces them that they are not properly understood. We need to remind ourselves that they will recover and that their normal sense of humour will one day be restored.

'Going steady'

As well as the highs and lows of falling in love, relationships between the sexes have other things to offer. It is good to have someone to talk to, to confide in, to enjoy being with. For boys this can be a special bonus if their own male friends are perhaps less sensitive and less likely to be good listeners than girls.

But entering a serious relationship too young can interfere with the other important tasks of adolescent life. Settling down with one partner at this stage may mean neglecting friends and so not learning the lessons which come from mixing with other young people who are going through the same stage of life (see pages 282–3). Also, teenagers who are having a serious relationship may be less concerned with schoolwork and their future career prospects than other youngsters.[11]

Romeo and Juliet

Sometimes you may, for many reasons, wish that your adolescent did not have a boyfriend or girlfriend, or at any rate not that particular one. But putting up opposition to a relationship can make it more romantic and long-lasting. This 'Romeo and Juliet' effect was shown in research with dating couples over a period of six to ten months, where it was found that the stronger the parental interference the more intense the romance. Less parental influence in the relationship was linked to 'love' which eventually cooled down.[12] It is very difficult, if not impossible, to control young people's feelings; they need to be acknowledged rather than dismissed or argued away.

You may have a vague feeling, or even a distinct worry, that a boyfriend or girlfriend is having a bad influence on your adolescent. If this is so, try to become more aware of what your worry is about; discuss it, if possible, with your partner or with a close friend. Try to focus on specifics: what in particular bothers you about the relationship? It may be that your son or daughter comes home late or does not concentrate on schoolwork as before. Perhaps you are worried about their involvement with a group of people you do not know, who may have a lifestyle that, generally speaking, causes you concern. It is these specific problems which you need to talk over with your teenager, explaining how you feel about them, seeking a solution rather than trying to undermine their feelings. Criticising an absent boyfriend or girlfriend on vague grounds can lead to divided loyalties, so do not express your worries by blaming them; instead, say what is on your mind and then concentrate on listening to your son or daughter's point of view. You may be surprised to find that he or she shares some of your feelings. Whether or not this is so, establish between you acceptable rules for the relationship: for example, not going out until homework is done and returning at an agreed time. And, remembering the 'Romeo and Juliet' effect, do not ban a boyfriend or girlfriend from the house. Later in this book there is a more detailed section on how to be constructive when there is a possible source of conflict between you and your adolescent (see pages 183–90).

Sexual intercourse

Your own attitude towards sexual morality may have changed since you yourself were in your teens, from being more to being less permissive or vice versa. We live in a society where people hold very different values and readers of this book will not all think alike. But whatever their views about the morality of sex outside marriage, or outside long-lasting relationships, many parents are anxious about their adolescents having sexual intercourse because of the risks of pregnancy and of sexually transmitted diseases (see pages 81–97).

For most young people, entering a sexual relationship is not the most important item on their agendas. In a study of a thousand New York teenagers, girls placed 'having sex' at number thirteen in order of importance and boys put it at number eight compared with other goals in life. It followed such items as 'getting a job', number one for both sexes, and 'getting along with my family' which was fifth for the girls and sixth for the boys.[13] There is a similarity here with the English research which found that only a minority of teenagers (less than 30 per cent) thought that having a boyfriend or a girlfriend was important or very important. Nevertheless, sexual intercourse, although it may not be their most important goal in life, is certainly becoming more common among young people. Many surveys show that teenagers begin to have sex younger than they did twenty or thirty years ago, and that the trend is continuing.[14]

This same trend can be seen in many Western countries. For example, a study carried out in Britain in the mid-1970s found that half of the single women and two-thirds of the single men had had intercourse by the age of nineteen,[15] and a similar ratio was found in the USA.[16] Some of these teenagers had had sex only once, and many of them had had sex with only one partner. Most were not promiscuous, they did not 'sleep around' but stayed with one partner.[17] Some of these relationships break up, of course, and then the young person may move on to another sexual relationship.

There are many different factors, some of them interlinked, which can explain this. One is that youngsters are becoming sexually mature at an earlier age; another that attitudes towards sex have changed in the population as a whole, leading to greater 'permissiveness' in sexual morality. Studies both in Britain and the USA show that teenagers are more 'permissive' than adults about sex outside marriage.[18] This may in part be due to lack of experience; teenagers are not as aware as their parents of possible emotional and physical problems. Nevertheless, there seems to be a genuine difference in beliefs between the generations about what is right and what is wrong. Most teenagers believe that there is nothing wrong with sex between people who care for one another. They take the view of one English teenager who said: 'I think sex before marriage is all right as long as you don't just sleep around with anyone, if you've been going steady with someone for a long time – but just to sleep with anyone I think is wrong.'[19]

It may be very hard for parents to accept that they have no control over the sexual activities of their son or daughter, especially in late adolescence and young adult life. This can be distressing for some parents whose religious or personal beliefs are strongly against sex outside marriage. Parents hope, throughout the years of childhood, that children will share their own beliefs and standards and to a large extent they do. Perhaps it is in matters of sexuality, above all, that young people most clearly show their individuality and distinctness from their parents. It is through their sexual attachment to others, together with the autonomy they now have over their own bodies, that parents learn to let go of them as children and to accept them as adults.

This is not to say that parents have no role to play in seeing that teenagers come safely through the hazards of adolescent sexuality. The support of parents, and the secure framework they can provide, will make it less likely that adolescents will want to have sexual relationships before they are ready for them. Later in this book there is a section dealing with the emerging independence of adolescents (see pages 262–4), emphasising the importance of parents knowing where teenagers are going, who they are with and what time they will be home. In this way they are providing them with a structure which they may grumble about occasionally but which also gives them a sense of security.

There is also the need to be open with them about your own feelings, to be sensitive towards their relationships, but not over-inquisitive, to welcome their friends home without being intrusive, and, of course, to be ready to listen (see page 38). The skill lies in being able to walk the narrow line between encouraging sons and daughters to be independent and giving them an acceptable level of security.

Accepting sexuality

It is also important for parents to acknowledge that there is a sexual dimension to their adolescent's lives, and not to ignore it. The last chapter explained the necessity for young people to be informed about sex, pregnancy, contraception and sexually transmitted diseases before they start to have boyfriends and girlfriends. To prepare them in this way is to accept their developing sexuality and, in so doing, to help them to accept it for themselves. Without this acceptance, their sexuality will remain outside their control and they will not behave in a sexually responsible way.

In a British study of teenage pregnancy a problem for one young woman was that of keeping contraceptives at home. Because her sexuality was not acknowledged by her mother, she felt she could not bring contraceptives into the house in case her mother found them. She therefore did not use them and subsequently became pregnant.[20]

It may be difficult for parents to accept their children's sexuality because they want to protect them from premature sexual experience. They worry in case a teenager is being pressurised into a sexual relationship before they are ready, that they are growing up too soon. In a recent survey half of the parents of teenagers thought that there was pressure on teenagers to have sex. Although the percentage was not so high, a substantial number of teenagers thought so too, especially girls and teenagers in the sixteen-year-old age group.[21]

An important piece of information that parents can pass on to teenagers is that it is quite permissible to say 'no' if they do not want sex. This in itself is a good enough reason and the same goes for boys as for girls. Some boys not only put pressure on their girlfriends to have sex but they encourage other boys to have sex as well. They do this by boasting about their own sexual prowess and also by taunting boys who are inexperienced. An important part of sex education is that teenagers should resist pressure to have sex until they themselves feel ready for it. It is only then that they will be able to take it seriously and to understand the possible consequences of sex both for themselves and for their partner. Having sexual intercourse is not just an easy step on the road to being grown up, like going to a first disco; it is a serious matter that calls for thought and preparation and knowing a partner well enough to be sure that they also really want it and are prepared for it, having discussed it with them in advance.

In some cases, however, young adolescents do have sex before they are emotionally ready or properly understand the possible consequences. They do it to claim independence from their parents, to show that they are grown up, or because they think that it will make their partner love them. When young people have sex for reasons of this kind, it is an indication that they are already unhappy and sex may add to their emotional and practical problems rather than the reverse.

Whether or not your own adolescent is involved in a sexual relationship, if you have reason to think that they are persistently unhappy and rebellious, and the approaches suggested in this guide have not proved useful (see pages 183–90), try to find help from outside the family. They really need an opportunity to talk about what is troubling them and to sort out their problems.

Sex and the law[22]

The 'age of consent' for sexual intercourse with members of the opposite sex is sixteen. Until that age young people are not held, in law, to be able to give informed consent to a sexual relationship.

- At the age of sixteen, young men and women may marry with parental consent (this is not needed in Scotland). At eighteen they may marry without parental consent.
- It is against the law for a man to have sexual intercourse with a girl under the age of sixteen.
- It is an absolute offence for a man to have sexual intercourse with a girl under the age of thirteen – that is, an offence for which no defence is allowed.
- A man can offer a defence where sexual intercourse takes place with a girl aged between thirteen and sixteen if he believes that he is married to her (for example, if the marriage took place abroad) or if he believed her to be sixteen or over at the time of the offence.

This law forbidding sex with young women under the age of sixteen applies to all men who are aged fourteen and over. In practice, prosecutions are rare where sex is between young people of a similar age.

- A girl or woman having sexual intercourse with a boy under the age of sixteen could, in theory, be charged with indecent assault.

Heterosexuality and homosexuality

Part of adolescents' discoveries about sex is the realisation that they are sexually attracted – and attractive – to other people and some may feel that they are especially attracted to people of their own sex. At one time people thought that homosexuality and heterosexuality were quite distinct, that people were clearly one or the other. In the light of a great deal of research carried out since the Second World War the picture is rather less clear. Many people have some sexual experience with those of the same sex, especially during childhood and adolescence, but are basically heterosexual. Others – bisexual people – feel attracted to both sexes during adult life, or may have phases of being attracted to one sex or the other. Some people are completely heterosexual. A small group is totally homosexual during adult life.[23]

For parents, the question of homosexuality can arise if they find that their adolescent – or pre-adolescent – child is experimenting sexually with someone of the same sex. Or it may happen that a son or daughter confides in parents that they think they are gay or lesbian.

Sex play and experiments in childhood and adolescence

Sexual play between children and adolescents of the same sex is quite common. It may consist of exploring each other's body, out of pleasurable curiosity. Sometimes it involves playing doctors and nurses. Adolescents may take part in group masturbation, sometimes of a competitive nature, and may masturbate each other. Different researchers have found different proportions of young people, both boys and girls, who have these experiences. One survey of homosexuality found that half of older boys and men, and a third of women remembered this sort of play.[24] Another found that 5 per cent of thirteen- to fifteen-year-old boys, 17 per cent of sixteen- to nineteen-year-old boys and 6 per cent of girls in both age-groups had had homosexual experiences of some sort.[25]

Young people who have erotic fantasies about people of the same sex, or crushes on people of the same sex, or take part in sex play and masturbation with people of the same sex, do not necessarily become homosexual adults. And some people who are homosexual in later life have had no homosexual experience in childhood or adolescence.

If parents discover their adolescent to be involved in sexual play with another person of the same sex they should not panic. It is probably best to ignore the incident unless their son or daughter wishes to talk about it. It is certainly unhelpful for the adolescent's fragile self-esteem to blame them or to label their behaviour as homosexual or lesbian. For the most part, this will not be their adult sexual orientation so such terms are misleading. Growing up is often about experimenting, trying things out, and at this stage of life childhood play is still close. Sexual behaviour in adolescence has aspects of both experimentation and play and should be considered as such. Adolescents need love and acceptance; they need to feel that whatever they do, their parents' feelings for them will not change.

'Coming out'

The situation is rather different when a son or daughter decides to confide in their parents that they are gay or lesbian; that they believe their permanent sexual orientation is towards members of the same sex. Whatever other feelings this arouses in parents, they should also take it as a mark of great trust. It is not an easy statement to make to parents. Young people who 'come out' to parents may have gone through a lot of heart-searching about their sexual orientation and about whether or not to confide in their parents.

For parents, the problem may in part be that they are unsure about what homosexuality entails. People who are homosexual have a strong and enduring preference for others of the same sex. They are not necessarily effeminate men or masculine women, although some people do express their orientation in this way. People who are homosexual have no problem about their *sexual identity*: gay men do not feel that perhaps they are really female or lesbians that they are really male. (People who think that their sexual identity is the opposite of their biological sex are known as transsexuals.) Gay men regard themselves as men who prefer other men as sexual partners and lesbians see themselves as women who prefer other women as sexual partners. For radical feminists, lesbianism can be a chosen political identity which does away with the need to relate to men in personal relationships.[26]

The 'causes' of homosexuality

Parents who learn that a son or daughter is homosexual may wonder why their development has worked out in this way and whether they are in some way 'to blame'. At present nobody knows why some people are homosexual and others heterosexual. Whatever theory or body of research is looked at to provide explanations, nothing very clear or satisfactory emerges. Biological and hormonal explanations do not provide any answers: homosexual men are biologically and hormonally male and lesbians are biologically and hormonally female. Neither can it be said that certain types of childhood experience lead to homosexuality. For example, while some homosexual people have had poor relationships with their parents, virtually all research has found that significant numbers of homosexual people have had *good* relationships with them.[27] On the other hand, significant numbers of heterosexuals have not had good relationships with their parents.

Homosexuality has been common throughout history and in some societies has been seen as a normal way of life. This was the case in ancient Greek civilisation. Many people of genius have been homosexual including the philosopher Plato and the artists Leonardo da Vinci and Michelangelo. But there is no need to romanticise the situation; most homosexuals are and were ordinary people who get on with their work and everyday life.

In Western society, however, with its strong Judaeo-Christian base, homosexuality has not been tolerated. From a religious point of view, homosexual acts have been seen as sinful and from a legal point of view, as criminal. Neither the religious nor the legal prohibitions against homosexuals are as strong today as they were in earlier times; there are various religious support groups for homosexuals, which offer a positive identity and one that is not thought to be in conflict with religious beliefs. Legally the restrictions on homosexual behaviour are not as stringent as they were in the recent past, when private homosexual acts, between consenting adult men, were criminal offences.

Nevertheless, quite apart from religious and legal considerations, being a homosexual is not an easy identity to hold in our society because of the prejudice that exists against homosexuals. For example, there are still people who believe that to be homosexual is to be mentally sick, although research has shown that homosexuals are as well-adjusted as heterosexuals. Being homosexual can affect job prospects and the chances of finding housing. There are also all the negative stereotypes to contend with: the jokes about camp men and butch women which betray the feelings, ranging from unease to hatred, which many heterosexuals feel towards gays and lesbians. What matters most for the emotional well-being of homosexuals, as for everyone else, is that they come to terms with their sexual identity and are accepted by the most important people in their lives.

For young people who 'come out' there is great relief if their parents can accept them as themselves, just as they would accept a son or daughter whose orientation was heterosexual. This means parents being as loving towards them as always, including continuing to express affection physically. It also means accepting their homosexual friends in the same way that other friends would be accepted, and being prepared to listen to their confidences. If they have no adult to confide in, young homosexual people can feel very isolated and depressed, for there may be few, if any, friends they can trust. Other teenagers can be very cruel to gays and lesbians, especially at school.

The parents of homosexual children therefore have a specially important part to play in their well-being. But their child's disclosure that they are gay or lesbian can be a very difficult experience to cope with. Much depends on parents' own past experiences, on whether they have known other gay people and how they have felt about them. In some places there are mutual support groups for parents where they can talk over their feelings and learn more about homosexuality. There are also many books which may help (see pages 299 and 300) and some parents might find counselling useful. A young person who is worried or unsure about their sexuality and wants to talk about it may also find that a counsellor would help (see pages 292 and 295 for addresses). Parents may feel too involved to be able to offer the sort of non-judgemental, calm listening that their child needs, or they may feel that they do not understand enough about homosexuality to be of use.

Homosexuality and the law

The Sexual Offences Act 1967 refers to homosexual acts between men. In Britain, homosexual acts conducted in private are legal between consenting men aged twenty-one and over. This means that for adolescents, homosexual acts are illegal.

Homosexual acts between women of any age are not illegal. However, if the act was against the will of one of the women concerned, then the other could be charged with indecent assault.

CHAPTER FOUR

CONTRACEPTION, PREGNANCY AND SEXUALLY TRANSMITTED DISEASES IN ADOLESCENCE

WHEN TEENAGERS ARE properly educated about sex, and feel secure about themselves, they are less likely to stumble into the problems which occur for young people who are less well prepared and who exercise their sexuality carelessly.

The first part of this chapter covers the important subject of teenage fertility: how youngsters can become mothers and fathers before they are ready for parenthood, and the information about birth control that is necessary for young people who decide to have sexual intercourse. This is followed by information about teenage pregnancy and a discussion of the options that are open when a young woman becomes pregnant – keeping the baby, adoption or abortion. The last section of the chapter is about diseases which can be transmitted by sexual intercourse, sometimes called venereal diseases, and how the risk of becoming infected can be reduced.

Taking sex seriously

Some young people, although by no means all, have sexual intercourse whatever their parents' wishes, or the religious background of the family. This is a possibility which can worry parents, especially if they suspect that their own adolescent is not as well informed as might be. Parents know about the risk of sexually transmitted diseases, including AIDS, and the risk of pregnancy. Your adolescents need information about these subjects *before* they begin to have close relationships with boyfriends and girlfriends, and certainly before any relationship develops into a sexual one.

If you give your adolescent this sort of information, it does not mean that you are encouraging them to be sexually active before they are ready for it.[1] Education about contraceptives, for example, does not have this effect. Through sex education, talking things over with you and with other people they trust, young people learn that entering a sexual relationship is an important decision which needs to be made thoughtfully and with preparation. Sex education should also assure them that there is no reason for any young person to be rushed or pressured into 'going all the way'.

Taking sex seriously is a move forward from attitudes which were common in the 1960s and 1970s. For many complex reasons repressive public attitudes towards sex were relaxed at this time. For young people, sexually transmitted diseases were no longer a serious threat, because antibiotics provided a readily available cure. The new birth control pill meant that women felt safe from unwanted pregnancy; and men, if their partner was on the pill, did not need to take any contraceptive precautions.

Many parents of adolescents were themselves young adults during the 1960s and 1970s and will have their own opinions about the sexual climate of that time. Whatever these may be, those years do not provide a good model for sexual relationships today. With the arrival of AIDS (see page 94), a carefree attitude to sex is a careless attitude to sex, and people who are careless are a physical danger to themselves and a source of danger to others.

And, as always, there remain the risks of unplanned pregnancies for teenagers who have sex without any practical preparation.

Young people need to be aware of the responsibilities they take on when they enter sexual relationships. Grown-up behaviour leads to new, adult obligations. If a young woman or a young man has sexual intercourse, they should be ready to look after their own physical and emotional well-being and that of their partner. Two major responsibilities for anyone involved in a sexual relationship are to avoid unwanted pregnancy and to avoid sexually transmitted diseases.

The two young people concerned must be able to talk to one another about sex, and, if they are agreed that they both really want this sort of relationship, about the precautions which need to be taken. This means that each one, the boy and the girl, must be prepared to raise the subject of contraception and protection against AIDS, if the other does not do so. If they have had the opportunity to take part in school discussions about sex, and if they have been able to talk openly at home, then they may find it easier to raise such issues with their partners.

Contraception

Unfortunately many young people do not use contraceptives until they have been having a sexual relationship for several months. During this time it is quite possible for the young woman to become pregnant and many do so. Young people do not use contraceptives because:

- Their first experience of sexual intercourse may be quite unplanned, so they have not had any chance to take precautions. Pregnancy may still follow.
- They may not understand the risks involved or may be misinformed about them; for example, they may think that 'you can't get pregnant the first time' or 'if you do it standing up' or 'if it's the girl's period' – all of which are, of course, untrue.
- Taking practical steps about contraception means admitting their own sexuality to themselves; they may not yet feel ready for this.
- They may feel that if they take responsibility for contraception, or want to discuss it, this suggests to their partner that they are more experienced than in fact they are.
- Some youngsters are not too shy for sex but they may be too shy to talk to one another about taking precautions – it is a shyness that can have disastrous results.
- If they come from a religious background which is against sex outside marriage, then they may feel guilty about their behaviour. This guilt may not stop them from having intercourse but it can stop them from using birth control – which needs thinking about and preparation in advance. Again they are taking a huge risk.
- They may feel that using contraceptives takes away from the spontaneity of sex, that it's not very 'romantic' – but then neither is an unplanned pregnancy!
- They may know about using contraceptives in theory but not know which kind to use or how to go about getting them. They may feel too shy to buy them or to go to a clinic or doctor.

- They may be careless and take precautions on some occasions but not on others.

If any of the above circumstances apply, they should be taken by adolescents as signs that they are too young for sex and should wait until they are able to take on the responsibilities involved. Having said this, people are not invariably rational about sex; it is not an activity where, in the excitement of the moment, sensible decisions are always made. This is all the more reason for discussion and preparation about contraception before any need arises.

Advice for young people about birth control

If a teenager is thinking about having a sexual relationship, then they need – in advance – not only information about contraception but vital, practical advice about it. This applies to both boys and girls. It does not put any pressure on them to have sexual intercourse; it simply ensures that if they decide, with their partner, that this is the right thing for them, then they are prepared.

There are various places where young people can get advice. They may approach their family doctor if they feel at ease with him or her or a family planning clinic or a Brook Advisory Centre (see pages 292–3 for addresses).

Under-sixteens

In Britain it is illegal for a man to have intercourse with a girl under the age of sixteen. But although her boyfriend is acting illegally, the girl herself isn't breaking the law. So a doctor can give her contraceptive advice and treatment without aiding and abetting an illegal act. The doctor can advise her and treat her without her parents' knowledge or consent, provided certain conditions apply:

- She is capable of understanding the doctor's advice.
- The doctor is unable to persuade her to tell her parents or to let him tell them.
- She is likely to have sexual intercourse, whether or not she gets contraceptive advice or treatment.
- Unless she gets advice or treatment, her physical or mental health, or both, are likely to suffer.
- Her best interests require the doctor to give her advice or treatment without her parents' consent.[2]

Different types of birth control

If your son or daughter comes to you for advice and information about contraception, the next few pages may be helpful. They describe the different types of contraceptive available for men and women, explain how they are obtained and describe any advantages and disadvantages.

Three important points about contraception should first be made:

■ No form of birth control is 100 per cent safe and, for the most part, using contraceptives needs some advice and care if they are to be effective.

■ Couples need to be able to talk to one another about what is acceptable for each of them. Sex involves two people and what suits one partner may be less satisfactory for the other, so each needs to take responsibility for letting the other know if, for any reason, they are not happy about contraception.

■ A couple should always consider both the risk of pregnancy and the risk of sexually transmitted diseases in making a choice of which contraceptive to use. Some contraceptives are highly effective in preventing pregnancy but give no protection against AIDS. So some couples may choose to use, for example, the pill as a contraceptive, but also use a condom as a protection against AIDS.

TYPE OF CONTRACEPTIVE

The *condom*, also known as the sheath, Durex, French letter.

Used by man or woman

The condom is used by the man.

How it works

A condom is made of very fine rubber and is worn by the man, over his penis, during intercourse. It stops the semen produced during intercourse from entering the womb and making the woman pregnant.

It should be worn before there is any contact between the man's penis and the woman's vagina: there may be semen in the drop of moisture produced by the penis as soon as it is erect.

Each condom is supplied in its own packet and is rolled up, ready for use. At the end is a small teat which expands when it is filled with semen. The condom is put on when the penis is erect. The man pinches the teat flat between the finger and thumb and rolls the condom down over the glans to the base of the penis with the other hand. After the man has ejaculated, or 'come', he should hold the condom firmly in place while the penis is withdrawn from the woman's vagina. A condom should only be used once, then thrown away.

How it is obtained From chemists, family planning clinics and slot machines. Condoms should not be used after the 'sell by' date. Those which meet the standards of the British Standards Institution carry a 'kitemark'.

Success rate 85–98 per cent with careful use.

Advantages Protects the woman against cancer of the cervix. Gives protection against AIDS (see pages 94–5) and some other sexually transmitted diseases – *unless both partners are totally sure that neither has had sex with someone else or injected drugs intravenously with a shared needle,* **sex without a condom is not safe – even if some other form of contraceptive is used.**

Disadvantages Some couples dislike using condoms because they feel that putting one on is an interruption to love-making.

TYPE OF CONTRACEPTIVE

The *diaphragm* and the *cap*. These are rather similar, dome-shaped, rubber contraceptives. Both need to be used with spermicide – a cream or jelly which kills sperm.

Used by man or woman They are used by the woman.

How they work The cap (or the diaphragm, whichever is used) stops sperm from getting through to the womb. It is spread on both sides with a layer of spermicide cream, which is an added precaution, and put high up in the vagina so that it covers the cervix – the entrance to the womb. The cervix can be felt as a firm 'bump' underneath a cap (or a diaphragm) when it is properly in place. It should be left in place for six hours after intercourse, then removed and washed.

How they are obtained Caps and diaphragms can only be obtained from a doctor or at a clinic. A doctor makes an internal examination of the vagina to decide on the right size and type of contraceptive needed. The woman is shown how to use it and can then practise putting it in place correctly. She should return for a check-up every six months.

Success rate 85–97 per cent with careful use.

Advantages	May protect against cancer of the cervix and some venereal diseases.
Disadvantages	Does not protect against AIDS.
	TYPE OF CONTRACEPTIVE
	The *sponge*. This is round and made of polyurethane foam with a small loop to aid removal. It already contains a spermicide when it is bought.
Used by man or woman	The sponge is used by the woman.
How it works	The woman puts the sponge into the vagina before intercourse so that it covers the cervix, and leaves it in place for at least six hours afterwards, then removes it and throws it away. It works by stopping sperm from getting through to the womb. The spermicide also kills sperm.
How it is obtained	It can be obtained at some clinics and at chemists.
Success rate	75–91 per cent with careful use.
Advantages	It is easily obtained.
Disadvantages	It is less reliable than the diaphragm or cap and a woman may need advice about putting it in place properly. It does not protect against AIDS.
	TYPE OF CONTRACEPTIVE
	Intrauterine Device (IUD). These are small objects made of plastic and metal which come in a variety of shapes.
Used by man or woman	The IUD is put into the woman's womb by a doctor and left for between two and five years.

How it works	It is not certain exactly how the IUD works, but it probably prevents a fertilised egg from settling in the wall of the womb.
How it is obtained	It is fitted by a doctor.
Success rate	90–99 per cent.
Advantages	Once it is successfully in place it needs no further attention.
Disadvantages	It is not recommended for women who have not been pregnant. It gives no protection from disease. Some women using the IUD have cramps and nausea and sometimes their periods are longer and heavier. It does not protect against AIDS.
	TYPE OF CONTRACEPTIVE
	The *combined pill* – contains two hormones: oestrogen and progesterone (see page 7).
Used by man or woman	The pill is taken by the woman.
How it works	The woman takes one pill a day for twenty-one days, at the same time each day. She then stops for seven days. Among other effects, the combined pill stops eggs being released each month, making fertilisation impossible.
How it is obtained	It is prescribed by a doctor.
Success rate	99 per cent if taken as prescribed.
Advantages	Easy to use; regularises periods.
Disadvantages	There may be physical side-effects ranging from nausea to weight gain. If these persist, the doctor may prescribe a different sort of pill. More rare, and serious, side-effects can include thrombosis, stroke and raised blood pressure. The risks are greater for some groups of people including smokers, people who are overweight,

	diabetic patients and women with a family history of strokes, heart attacks and blood pressure. The pill gives no protection against sexually transmitted diseases, including AIDS.
	TYPE OF CONTRACEPTIVE
	The *mini-pill* – contains one hormone only: progesterone.
Used by man or woman	The woman takes one pill a day, at the same time each day, continuously.
How it works	The mini-pill may stop eggs being released each month; it causes changes in the mucus at the neck of the womb which makes it difficult for sperm to enter and prevents eggs from settling in the womb.
How it is obtained	The mini-pill is prescribed by a doctor.
Success rate	98 per cent if taken as prescribed.
Advantages	Easy to use; less risk of thrombosis or raised blood pressure than there is with the combined pill.
Disadvantages	There may be physical side-effects including irregular periods and weight gain. The mini-pill gives no protection against sexually transmitted diseases, including AIDS.
	TYPE OF CONTRACEPTIVE
	Contraception by *injection of a hormone* – progesterone.
Used by man or woman	The hormone is injected into the woman, every two or three months.
How it works	The injection works in a similar way to the mini-pill (see above). It is meant for women for whom other contraceptives are unsuitable.
How it is obtained	The hormone is injected by a doctor or at a clinic.

Success rate 99 per cent.

Advantages There is disagreement about its benefits.

Disadvantages These can include weight gain and loss of periods. In addition, once a woman has been injected she must put up with any side-effects for some months, unlike the pill which she can come off at any time she chooses. There is no protection from sexually transmitted diseases, including AIDS.

TYPE OF CONTRACEPTIVE

Natural family planning or the 'safe period'.

Used by man or woman Natural family planning depends on both the man and the woman.

How it works With natural family planning both the man and the woman agree to abstain from sex at the time when the woman is thought to be fertile. Three methods can be used to find out when this is and all need to be taught by a specially trained teacher. The three methods should be used together.

1 The woman keeps a record of the number of days between her periods, every month, for six months to a year. With this information she can then be taught how to calculate when she is likely to be fertile.
2 The woman learns how to examine and understand changes in mucus discharge from the cervix. She can be taught how to recognise when an egg is released into the womb.
3 The woman takes her temperature every morning before she gets up and records it on a chart. A specially trained teacher can instruct her how to know when sex is 'safe' by interpreting changes in the chart.

How it is obtained More information about natural family planning, and people who teach it, may be obtained from the addresses on pages 292–3.

Success rate 85–93 per cent when the mucus and temperature methods are combined but this depends on the woman being trained and keeping careful records and observations.

Advantages	Couples can feel very responsible for each other; there are no physical side-effects and some couples prefer it because it is 'natural'.
Disadvantages	It needs great care on the part of the woman and the willingness of both the man and woman to abstain from sex during the fertile period. It offers no protection from sexually transmitted diseases, including AIDS.

For the sake of completeness it is also necessary to add 'withdrawal' and sterilisation to the list, although withdrawal is not a reliable method of contraception and sterilisation is not a choice which most young people would make.

Withdrawal

The man withdraws his penis from the woman's vagina before he ejaculates ('comes'). This is much less safe than other methods and needs self-control on the part of the man. Also there may be sperm present in the drop of moisture produced when the penis first becomes erect; this can be enough to cause pregnancy.

Withdrawal offers no protection from sexually transmitted diseases, including AIDS.

Sterilisation

Both men and women may be sterilised – a permanent method of birth control which is carried out surgically. People who decide on sterilisation must be absolutely sure, for one reason or another, that they do not want children (or that they want no more children).

Sterilisation of women The Fallopian tubes are closed so that an egg cannot travel down them and become fertilised. The operation needs a general anaesthetic. There are occasional failures (one in three hundred).

Sterilisation of men The tube from the testes to the penis is blocked or cut, so that sperm cannot get from the testes into the semen. Without sperm, the woman's egg cannot be fertilised. This is called a *vasectomy* and involves a local anaesthetic.

Teenage pregnancy

Although information about contraception is much more available than it used to be, every year many adolescent girls become pregnant, and adolescent boys father children.

As we saw earlier (see pages 10 and 17), adolescents are often fertile in their early teens, and almost always by their mid-teens, so, at a physical level, they are ready to reproduce, to become parents themselves. Alongside their biological maturity they are acquiring a more adult understanding of the world and can look after many of their own basic needs. In some less advanced societies, and at other times in history when life was less complex, there was no reason why young people should not become parents in their teens. All that was necessary was that they should be capable of supporting themselves and their offspring.

In our society, however, most teenagers remain financially dependent on their parents for many years: they need education and training to fit them for life in a highly developed society and they need their parents' support, at least until they leave school. Until they can stand on their own feet they are not in a position to support children of their own.

The percentage of teenagers who become pregnant differs from country to country. An indication of how many teenagers become pregnant can be found in official records of live births and of abortions.

Why do teenagers become pregnant?

Of the many teenagers who become pregnant each year, there are some who actually want to be pregnant because having a baby may seem to be preferable to school or unemployment. But usually pregnancy is unintended. Young people have sexual intercourse, they do not use contraceptives and sooner or later the girl becomes pregnant. Younger teenagers, especially, are less likely to use contraceptives: they do not acknowledge that their actions can have long-lasting effects on the rest of their lives and some of them, unrealistically, believe 'it can't happen to me'.

Also, if a girl decides to seek information about contraception, she is, as one researcher points out, admitting to herself that she is a sexual being, and, furthermore, admitting the same to a doctor.[3] This can be difficult. Young women who cannot acknowledge their sexual feelings are those who are least likely to use contraceptives. When mothers discuss contraception with their daughters this seems to bring the subject out into the open and helps the young woman to accept her own sexuality and take responsibility for it. Daughters whose mothers talk to them about contraception are more likely to take precautions than those whose mothers are not open with them.

Are some teenagers more likely to become pregnant than others?

Research undertaken in Britain and the USA points to a link between social factors and teenage pregnancy. The young women who become pregnant are more often – but not always – those who belong to a lower social class and who may also be socially disadvantaged in other ways. One possible reason for this is that the major role open to under-privileged young women is that of being a mother. For many, education and the prospects of a career are both less interesting and more demanding than they are for young women from higher social and economic backgrounds. To those who hope to leave education as soon as possible, an unplanned pregnancy may seem less serious than it would be to someone embarking on a career. They may, therefore, be less careful than other teenagers.

Social differences have also been found to influence whether or not young women continue with their pregnancy. Both in Britain and the USA, more working-class teenagers go on to give birth, while more middle-class teenagers have abortions.

Teenage fathers

Very little research has been done into teenage fathers and so little is known about them. However, the fact that a mother is in her teens does not mean that her partner is also of the same age; the likelihood is that he is rather older than herself.[4] Overall, there are fewer adolescent fathers than adolescent mothers and even these may not learn that they have become fathers if the young women concerned choose not to inform them.

Sometimes teenage fathers are not informed that they have become fathers because parents advise their daughters to have no further contact with the young man concerned. In other cases the baby's father can be a real source of support to a young mother and, if they wish it, the baby can be registered in both their names. There is, however, evidence that involvement in pregnancy and parenthood is stressful for young fathers.[5] They are worried about their relationship, about becoming a father, about the health of the mother and child and about their own education and career and the effect the pregnancy would have on it.

Problems of teenage parenthood

There are many reasons why teenage parenthood is not advisable:

■ Becoming a mother, paradoxically, can increase a young woman's dependency on her own parents at a time when she should be becoming, year by year, more capable of standing on her own feet. Under the age of sixteen, or until her education is complete, a teenage mother has to handle a contradictory set of roles. She is legally a child and dependent on her parents, but at the same time responsible for her own child's welfare.

■ Having a child can be a major disruption to education. This is true for girls and, in cases where the father is involved in parenting, for boys.

■ Lack of resources – young people do not have enough money to be able to bring up children easily. This can be true even where there is a father as well as a young mother, who can both share the responsibility. Children are expensive to clothe, feed and house. The earning power of young people, especially when they have cut their education short, is limited.

■ Sometimes marriage is seen as a way forward. But it can leave the teenage mother somewhat cut off from the support she would otherwise have received from her own family and more teenage marriages end in divorce than marriages between older couples.

■ The younger the mother, the greater the risks of childbearing to her own health and that of the baby. It is possible that this risk is shared by other disadvantaged groups of women and is caused by factors other than age. For example, disadvantaged women are less likely to attend antenatal clinics and their diet may be poor – both of which factors can undermine the health of mother and baby. But over and above these disadvantages it seems that there are real risks for very young mothers.

■ Bringing up a baby can be a lonely business. Although some young couples may live together, with or without marrying (and the trend is away from marriage), young mothers can suffer from the social isolation experienced by older mothers but which the latter may be better able to cope with. Without close emotional support many mothers suffer from depression.

■ While many young mothers welcome their new babies they may not be emotionally mature enough to cope with the demands they make, especially if they have little support from other people and from the community. Research evidence suggests that with young mothers there is a greater risk of child battering and neglect.[6]

Having pointed out all the disadvantages, it should be said that, against the odds, some young women make a real success of motherhood. This is more likely to be the case if a girl has the full support of her own mother[7] and can call on the resources of her family to help support the child. Some grandparents actively enjoy their new role, coming at a time when they thought their family was complete, and others, who initially have mixed feelings, would not be without their grandchild after he or she is born.

Counselling about pregnancy

When a teenager finds that, without planning to be so, she is pregnant, there are three main options open to her: she can continue the pregnancy and keep the baby; she can continue the pregnancy and put the baby up for adoption; or she can decide to end the pregnancy and have an abortion.

Her decision may be influenced by many factors, including how she feels about being a mother; the emotional and material support available to her, from the baby's father and from her parents; her wishes for the future, including education, training and work; and her feelings and beliefs about abortion.

It is very important for a pregnant teenager that her parents let her make up her own mind about which option she chooses.[8] This does not mean holding back advice if she asks for it but it does mean making clear that the decision is finally hers and that her parents will support her in it. This can be very difficult for parents to come to terms with. They, after all, are more experienced than their daughter and understand better than she can all that is involved in bringing up a child. In addition, especially with a younger teenager, her decision will have far-reaching consequences for them too. They may find themselves worrying about her future, asking themselves 'Where did we go wrong?' and making practical arrangements which change the pattern of life they were accustomed to.

Nevertheless the decision must be made, in the end, by the pregnant girl herself; this is most important for her life, both at present and in the future. If she does not take responsibility for the decision herself, she will never be truly content with it. If she is pressurised to go against her own wishes there can be real dangers for her own well-being and, in some cases, that of the child.

A helpful way forward can be to talk things over with someone outside the family. The young person could go to one of the pregnancy advisory agencies or to the Family Planning Association (FPA) to talk to a trained counsellor (see pages 292–3 for addresses). She should make clear, however, that she wants the opportunity to sort things out for herself, not to be directed to take one decision or another.

In cases where a social worker has been allocated to a young mother (via her school or at the hospital), they may be able to help in what can be a difficult decision.

Trained counsellors, because they are not personally affected by the pregnancy in the way that close families are, are in a better position to listen without their own emotions getting in the way. They can help a young woman to come to a decision which is right for her at a time when her feelings may be very mixed. She may feel pleased to be pregnant but worried about how she is going to manage at a practical level. She may be full of regret and self-blame. She may be angry with her boyfriend, anxious about her parents, guilty at even thinking about abortion, may feel wretched about adoption – and also be unwilling to accept her new identity of mother, or pregnant woman. An outsider can, if the young woman wishes, help her to sort out what she herself most wants from the situation more easily than family or friends.

Continuing with pregnancy

If a teenager wishes to continue with her pregnancy, whether she is going to keep her baby or offer it for adoption, then there are health and educational services which she can make use of during this time.

Health services

Antenatal care provided by the family doctor or at a hospital clinic is available for all mothers, including teenagers. Some young mothers may not start antenatal visits until late in their pregnancy, for a variety of reasons. They may not at first realise that they are pregnant, especially if their periods have only recently begun and not yet settled into a regular pattern. They may be misled into thinking that their period is delayed and not give its absence very much thought. Some delay having a pregnancy test, or visiting a doctor, because they do not want to admit to the possibility that they may be pregnant, and for a time try to ignore their suspicions.

It is important that young mothers have antenatal care as soon as possible after their pregnancy is confirmed and also that they attend regularly. This is true for all mothers but especially for the youngest group, who need particular care from the beginning of pregnancy. Statistics show that teenage mothers are particularly likely to run into difficulties[9] – although it is not easy to pinpoint exactly why this should be so. It may be in part because they are more often poorer than others; more likely to be inadequately fed and less likely to use antenatal services.

Visits to the antenatal clinic are monthly to start with and more frequent towards the end of pregnancy. Over the course of her visits, the young mother may be X-rayed, and blood and urine tests will be carried out to check for infection and diabetes. Her blood pressure is monitored regularly so that if there are any problems she can be given extra attention. The foetal heart is listened to and its position checked.

During her antenatal visits she will have an opportunity to talk about the birth and about whom she wants to be with her during her labour and delivery – whether her mother, a close friend or the father of the baby.

At each visit she is weighed and her weight recorded. This is of significance because steady weight gain is a sign that at least she is eating enough. A mother-to-be needs some extra calories for the baby and, if she herself is still growing, her own food requirements may be higher than that of older mothers. But most important of all, she needs a nourishing, well-balanced diet at this time (see page 101). As well as giving her advice about diet, the hospital may give her vitamin and iron pills as a supplement.

Educational Services

The less her pregnancy interrupts her education the better it is for a young mother and, incidentally, for her child. Early pregnancy, together with curtailed schooling, can affect a woman's future income – and therefore the future health and well-being of herself and her child. (Someone who has her first child when she is fifteen is twice as likely to live at the poverty level than someone who has a first child at nineteen, and three times as likely as someone who is twenty-two when her first child is born.[10])

Until a young person is sixteen the local education authority has an obligation to provide education for them. Sometimes pregnant schoolgirls wish to stay at school as long as possible, but teachers may discourage them from remaining at school once pregnancy shows. Most pregnant girls are excluded from school at some stage. If this happens, the young mother needs advice about the best way to continue her education and it is vital that she gets it. There are two main questions which she needs to ask: how can she go on studying until the baby is born and what are the educational opportunities open to her afterwards?

Before the baby is born

If the young mother is preparing to take examinations, then it is a good thing for her to carry on, rather than try to pick up the theads later, after a long break. She should talk to one of the pastoral care teachers at school (see page 203) and decide what is possible for her, taking into account the time when her baby is due.

Different local authorities have different schemes to provide education for pregnant schoolgirls, but in some places there may be little choice.

- *Home tutors* In some areas a special tutor can come to her home to teach her and a girl may like this individual attention. She may be missing all the social contacts she had at school, and be bored at home all day.
- *Day centres* There may also be an education day centre where she can go with other teenage mothers but these are not provided everywhere. A positive feature of such centres is that the students are all in the same predicament and can offer one another support. As well as allowing the girls to continue their education, the centres run courses in childcare and prepare the mothers for the birth. They may go together to attend the antenatal clinic.

Sometimes the centres have a crèche and after the birth the mother can take the baby to the centre with her. The baby is looked after during the day while she continues her studies. The timetable is arranged so that she can feed and play with her baby.

After the baby is born

Once the baby is born, the biggest problem for mothers who want to continue their education (except for those fortunate enough to attend a centre with its own crèche) is finding someone to look after their baby during the day. If it is not possible to get help within the family, then the mother should go to the local social service department and ask what day care is available in the neighbourhood. Day nurseries are few and far between but the social worker will know of any that exist, and will also know about any local childminders. In some cases social service departments meet the costs of a day nursery or a childminder.

If the young mother does not wish to return to her old school, and has by this time passed the statutory leaving age, another possibility is to find out about full- or part-time courses at a college of further education. Such colleges prepare students for various public examinations and provide vocational training courses.

Abortion

Abortion is the ending of a pregnancy and, in medical terms, this word is used to cover miscarriages as well as terminations of pregnancy. The word is used here in this last, more usual sense.

People have very different feelings and opinions about abortion and this is true not only of individuals but also of countries. In a very few places abortion is totally forbidden, but for the most part it is legal, though with various restrictions.[11] These include the permitted reasons for abortion and the stage of pregnancy at which it is carried out.

There are three main attitudes towards the issue of abortion. There are those who believe that the rights of the woman are more important than those of the foetus and that it is the woman's right to choose what she does with her own body, at whatever stage in a pregnancy. Directly opposed to this view are people who campaign for the rights of the unborn child, over and above all other considerations, and who believe that abortion is always wrong. The middle body of opinion holds that, in certain circumstances, abortion is the lesser of two evils and therefore justifiable.

You will have your own opinion about abortion, based on your background and upbringing, and all the experiences which have helped to form your personal beliefs and values. Whatever these may be, you may find the following facts and information about abortion helpful in answering teenagers' questions.

How are abortions carried out?[12]

Abortions are carried out in different ways, according to the stage of pregnancy.

The morning-after pill

The morning-after pill is used to end a pregnancy, or suspected pregnancy, within three days of intercourse. It is not strictly speaking a form of abortion because the woman does not in fact know whether she is pregnant when she takes it, so legal regulations governing abortion do not apply.

The pill contains strong hormones which change the balance of the woman's hormonal system (see pages 6–7) and make pregnancy very unlikely. The pill is specially prescribed by a doctor and is taken in two doses, twelve hours apart. It is used for emergencies only, for example, in cases of rape or when a woman has had intercourse without using contraception. It is not a substitute for regular contraception.

It is not suitable for everyone. The high dose of hormones can make the woman feel sick.

Abortion in early pregnancy

During the first three months of pregnancy – that is, twelve weeks from the date of the last menstrual period – and after a positive pregnancy test the usual procedure is to stretch the opening of the womb and scrape the lining to detach the foetus, which may then be removed by a vacuum pump. This is carried out under anaesthetic. The patient may experience cramps, low down in the pelvis. She may go home the same day or shortly afterwards, and should rest and take care of herself until she has recovered. Her doctor will tell her when to return for a check-up.

There is some risk of complications. The instruments used may cause damage to the wall of the womb, which can result in bleeding (haemorrhage). This also occurs if there is some foetal material left behind. There is also the risk of infection if care is not taken in the weeks following the abortion. The risks are much less, however, than the risks associated with a normal birth.

Late abortions

After fifteen weeks of pregnancy, a similar operation to that described above may be performed, according to the practice of the surgeon. Or a pregnancy may be terminated by injecting a hormone called prostaglandin directly into the womb. This causes the woman to go into early labour, which lasts for several hours. The womb contracts, the neck of the womb dilates and the foetus and placenta are expelled. The patient is given pain relief.

She stays in the hospital or clinic for a further day. She should rest and take care of herself until she has recovered. Her doctor will tell her when to return for a check-up.

This sort of abortion has more risks associated with it than abortions that are done earlier in pregnancy and it can be more distressing for the woman. For women with certain medical conditions, like diabetes or asthma, special monitoring is necessary.

Abortion and the law

At the time of writing, a woman is, under the terms of the Abortion Act 1967, allowed an abortion during the first twenty-eight weeks of pregnancy if two doctors agree that the following would be at greater 'risk' if an abortion were not performed:

- the life of the pregnant woman, *or*
- her physical or mental health, *or*
- the physical or mental health of any child she already has, *or*
- the mental or physical health of the expected child.

The Abortion Act 1967 does not apply to Northern Ireland where abortion is illegal.

Adolescent abortion and the law

For a teenage woman who has an unplanned pregnancy, a possible option is to go to her family doctor or to an abortion agency and request an abortion. What does the law have to say about this? And, while her parents may have a very important part to play in supporting her and advising her, what legal right do they have to be involved in her decision?

Women over sixteen

There is a difference in law between the position of young women over the age of sixteen and those who are under sixteen. The law assumes that anyone over sixteen, who is not mentally impaired, can give *informed consent* to medical treatment: they are given an explanation of the treatment, they understand what is going to happen and they agree to it. So the decision to apply for an abortion is one which, in law, a young woman over the age of sixteen is allowed to make for herself. And if two doctors agree that there are grounds for an abortion she can herself sign the necessary consent form.

For a woman with mental disability, under the age of eighteen, consent to medical treatment must be given by parents or by a court of law. After the age of eighteen she can give her own consent to treatment, unless she is incapable of doing so.[13]

Women under sixteen

It is clear from the ruling in the Gillick case (brought to the House of Lords in 1985)[14] that a young woman under the age of sixteen is legally entitled to talk to a doctor and seek confidential advice and information.

When it comes to giving treatment, as opposed to advice, the situation is rather different. If the young person presented legal grounds for an abortion and wished to go ahead with it, the most usual procedure would be for the doctor to approach her parents for their consent. If, for various reasons, it was impossible to approach the parents, and if the doctor had the informed consent of his young patient, then her consent would be sufficient to proceed with the abortion.

In some cases, such as when parents withhold their consent despite medical advice and the wishes of their daughter, it is possible to make the girl a ward of court. In these circumstances the court is permitted to give consent if it is considered that abortion is in the young woman's best interests.

Should a young woman under sixteen be in the reverse situation – where it is she who wants to carry on with her pregnancy and her parents who want her to have an abortion – her wishes count for most with the law. Parents cannot force their daughter to end her pregnancy; her consent is necessary in order to do so. Terminating the pregancy against her will would be very upsetting for her and the risks to her mental well-being would be greater than those incurred by giving birth.

Adoption

Some pregnant young women feel that they cannot keep their baby but, for their own reasons, do not want to have an abortion. For others, abortion is not an option because the pregnancy is too advanced. These mothers can, if they wish, put their baby up for adoption.

Sometimes grandparents, or other close relatives, feel that they would be happy to have another child and are willing to take on the responsibilities that this entails. In these cases they can legally adopt the baby, who is then brought up as its real mother's brother or sister, nephew or niece. In circumstances like these, the young mother needs to be very sure that she agrees to the arrangement and fully accepts the fact that she will have no more rights towards the child than if the adoptive parents were complete strangers.

In law, mothers are only allowed to arrange the adoption themselves if the adoptive parents are close relatives. There are also various voluntary agencies who will arrange an adoption either before or after the birth, as can the local social services departments. In such cases the mother is not told the identity of the adoptive parents. The final decision about the adoption cannot be made until the baby is six weeks old and the mother signs the form giving her consent to the adoption. Until this time she can change her mind.

When the adopted child reaches the age of eighteen, he or she has the right to know the identity of their biological mother and there is the possibility that, understandably, the child might wish to make contact with her. This possibility may not be easy for the mother to live with. She can long to see her child again but without any guarantee that this will happen, for not all adopted children try to find their mothers. On the other hand, she may prefer that there is no contact, but the decision must be made by the child, not by the mother.

There are many parents who would like to adopt a child and social services departments and adoption agencies follow careful procedures to find people who would give a child a good home and bring it up as their own. Even so, giving up her child can be a painful experience for a young mother. She will need the opportunity to talk over her decision so as to be sure that what she is doing is best both for her and for the child.

Sexually Transmitted Diseases[15]

Sex is a normal, healthy part of life and as with other normal human behaviour – like eating or going to work – there are health risks associated with it. In particular there is the risk of becoming infected with a sexually transmitted disease. Today we understand these risks and know how to avoid them or reduce them.

As they grow up, your son or daughter will also need this information but, unfortunately, it is an issue which can easily be left out of sex education. People who find that they can talk openly about other sexual matters are less comfortable when it comes to the subject of disease. Some parents find it difficult enough to accept their child's sexuality and passing on information about VD is going one stage further. It is admitting that an adolescent son or daughter may have a sexual relationship with someone who is sexually experienced, and that a son or daughter may become infected and may pass that infection on.

The rate of sexual infection among teenagers, compared with other groups in the population, is not low, which suggests that some teenagers do pass on sexually transmitted diseases to one another. Teenagers therefore need to have an understanding of these diseases and how they can be avoided, or the risks reduced, in order to decide how to exercise their own sexuality. With this awareness they will be better equipped to take responsibility for their own health and that of their partner if, at any time, they choose to enter a sexual relationship.

There are three names used for the illnesses which can be passed by sexual contact from one partner to another:

- *VD (venereal diseases)* A term which everyone seems to know but which is less used by doctors now than it used to be. It means diseases to do with love – the word 'venereal' comes from the name of Venus, the goddess of love. Venereal diseases are passed on through sexual intercourse with an infected partner and they affect the genitals and parts of the urinary system.
- *GU (genito-urinary diseases)* Diseases which affect the genitals, the bladder and the outlet to the bladder. These are usually, but not always, passed on sexually. Clinics which specialise in these diseases are often called GU clinics.

■ *STD (sexually transmitted diseases)* As the name implies STD are diseases which are transmitted from one person to another in the course of sexual activity. This includes genital intercourse, anal intercourse and oral sex.

For the most part this last term, sexually transmitted diseases, or STD for short, will be used in the following pages, even though some of the conditions discussed may also be passed on by other means. This section describes symptoms which would suggest STD, explains how they can be avoided, or the risk of infection lessened, and ends with a short description of the main diseases (see pages 94–7) and their treatment.

Sexually transmitted diseases include: AIDS, genital warts, genital herpes, hepatitis B, gonorrhoea, non-specific urogenital infections, pubic lice, thrush and syphilis. Some of these may also be passed on non-sexually.

■ Some sexually transmitted diseases, like syphilis, although potentially dangerous if they are not treated, can be cured fairly easily.
■ Others, like genital herpes, are less serious but can be persistent and troublesome.
■ In the case of AIDS, there is as yet no cure and the disease is fatal.

People catch STDs through sexual contact with someone who is already infected. Sexual contact includes oral and anal sex. No one would, knowingly, allow themselves to be infected with an STD and all would avoid sexual contact with someone who is already infected. Unfortunately, the infected person may have no obvious symptoms and they may not know that they are infected and a danger to their partner. In other cases they may not want to admit that they are infected. Sexual relationships need to be based on mutual trust and understanding, and this includes knowing a partner well enough to be sure that they would not deliberately conceal a sexually transmitted disease. Obviously it is essential for young people to avoid sexual intercourse with people they do not really know.

There is no risk involved where two people have had no sexual partners but each other. With each new sexual partner the risk increases.

The more partners anyone has, the greater the likelihood that they will catch a sexually transmitted disease, treatable or untreatable. A person can be infected on the first occasion they have sexual intercourse, if their partner is infected.

Reducing the risk of catching a sexually transmitted disease

The only guarantees against catching an STD are abstaining from sex, or staying with a single partner who has had no other sexual relationship.

The following precautions reduce the risk of catching an STD:

- Avoiding casual sex with unknown partners.
- Staying with one partner, long term.
- The man using a condom.
- Washing the sex organs before and after intercourse.
- Urinating after intercourse.
- Not having sex with a partner who is showing any of the symptoms of an STD.

Symptoms of sexually transmitted diseases

More details of symptoms for each disease are given below; in some cases an infected person may have no apparent symptoms. The following are general symptoms which suggest an STD:

- Any sores or rashes on or near the sex organs.
- Unusual discharge from the penis or vagina.
- Irritation and soreness in the area of the penis or vagina, including when urinating.

Treatment

These symptoms should not be ignored, even if they appear to clear up by themselves. They may be the first indications of a disease which could develop further, so anyone who has them should seek medical advice. If necessary a doctor will refer the patient to a special clinic which may be called a GU clinic, or a VD clinic or an STD clinic. If preferred, it is possible to bypass the family doctor and go straight to a clinic for tests and, if necessary, treatment. Most hospitals have a VD department and addresses are listed in telephone directories under Venereal Diseases; the Family Planning Association also provides information (see page 293 for address). The people who work at the clinic treat patients in a straightforward, unembarrassing way. If it is found that there is an infection, the clinic will want the patient to tell his or her sexual partner(s) that they should also have tests.

AIDS or Acquired Immune Deficiency Syndrome

This is an illness caused by one of the HIV viruses and is caught from someone who is already infected. A person can carry the HIV virus but not suffer from the disease or know that they are infected. Others may develop the disease in a different form – ARC – the AIDS Related Complex, which is itself a serious illness. Still others develop AIDS.

The AIDS virus attacks the body's own defence system so that the sufferer cannot fight off infection. As a result, he or she suffers from a syndrome, or set, of uncommon infections and cancers. The symptoms include prolonged fever, rapid weight loss, diarrhoea, a dry cough and skin cancers.

Catching AIDs The HIV virus is passed from someone who is a carrier, into the bloodstream of another person. People catch AIDS in the following ways:

- By having sexual intercourse – anal or vaginal – with someone who is carrying the HIV virus or is suffering from AIDS. *Both men and women can be AIDS sufferers and HIV carriers.*

  There may be small cuts on the penis or in the vagina or anus through which the virus from the infected partner may enter the body. Neither partner may be aware of these cuts.

- By sharing needles with someone who injects drugs into their veins. After injecting, a little blood is pulled back into the syringe. If the blood is infected with HIV, then the next person to use the syringe injects the virus directly into their own bloodstream (see pages 164–5).

- By receiving a blood transfusion which is infected with HIV. In the UK, all donated blood is tested for the HIV virus.

- A woman who has AIDS can pass on the virus to her baby.

Avoiding AIDS As yet there is no cure for AIDS, nor any way of immunising people against it, but it is an avoidable disease.

As always with sexually transmitted diseases, the fewer the sexual partners the lower the risk.

Unless a couple knows for certain that neither partner has had sexual contact with anyone else, and that neither has injected drugs, they should never have sexual intercourse without using a condom. This is a protection for both partners.

If a young person has a drug problem, and is injecting (see pages 164–6) they should always use a new needle, never one which has been used by someone else.

Hepatitis B

There are three sorts of hepatitis – A, B and C. Hepatitis B is caused by a virus which is passed on by sexual contact or contact with body fluids such as blood, saliva and urine.

The virus causes inflammation of the liver. The illness can last for several months and involve weakness, pain in the joints, tiredness, loss of appetite and weight, and jaundice.

There is a vaccine available to prevent people who are at risk – including the partners of patients with hepatitis B – from being infected.

Genital herpes

This is an infection caused by a virus related to the cold sore virus. It is passed on by direct contact with the herpes sores of an infected person.

The herpes virus causes painful blisters on and around the genitals. These last for a week or two but can recur at other times. If a woman has herpes blisters at the time of giving birth, these can infect the child. A pregnant woman with herpes should therefore tell her doctor in case a Caesarean delivery is advisable.

There is no cure for herpes but there are creams which can be used to relieve the symptoms.

Genital warts

Genital warts are caused by a virus which is passed on by direct contact with the genital warts of an infected person.

They are contagious and can block the vagina or the anus.

They can be treated by burning them off with a special ointment, or, if necessary, by removing them surgically.

Gonorrhoea

Gonorrhoea is caused by a bacteria and passed on by sexual intercourse with an infected person.

Many women and some men have no symptoms but some women have a discoloured discharge from the vagina and irritation and a burning feeling when urinating. Men have discharge from the penis and pain when urinating. If gonorrhoea is not treated it can lead to sterility, arthritis and blindness. It can cause eye disease in a baby born to a woman who has the disease.

Gonorrhoea is treated with antibiotics.

Non-specific urogenital infections

These infections are most often caused by bacteria, passed on by sexual intercourse with an infected person, but they can also occur without any sexual contact.

Many women have no symptoms. Where there are symptoms, they are similar to those of gonorrhoea (above). Untreated, these infections can lead to infertility in women.

They are treated with antibiotics.

Pubic lice These are parasites, lice and nits which live in the pubic hair. They are passed on by skin-to-skin contact with an infected person, or by immediate contact with an infected object.

They cause intense itching around the genitals.

They can be got rid of with a specially prescribed lotion.

Syphilis Syphilis is passed on by sexual intercourse with an infected person.

The first symptom is a painless sore on the penis or near the vagina. This is followed by a rash and flu-like symptoms. Untreated syphilis can lead to serious complications including damage to the heart, paralysis and insanity. It can infect an unborn child. Until a cure was discovered it was as much feared as AIDS is today.

Syphilis is treated by antibiotics.

Thrush Thrush is caused by a microscopic fungus, *Candida albicans*, which is frequently present in the body without giving any trouble. If the fungus increases, it causes 'thrush'. The infection can be transmitted by sexual intercourse with an infected person, but thrush can also have other causes.

Men do not usually show symptoms; in women there is a thick white discharge from the vagina, together with irritation. The baby of an infected mother can get mouth and throat infections during delivery.

Thrush is treated with antibiotics.

CHAPTER FIVE

ADOLESCENT HEALTH CARE

WHILE IT IS QUITE difficult to define good health, it is easy to recognise it when you see it. Being healthy certainly includes the absence of disease, but it is more than that. Healthy adolescents have the energy required for their stage of life; not only do they have the resources to cope with the physical changes of adolescence; they can also cope with increased study, examinations and career choices and with expanding independence. Healthy adolescents have the physical and psychological potential to deal successfully with everyday stress, whether the stress incurred in schoolwork, the ups and downs of romantic friendships or the physical stress caused by minor infections. One aspect of psychological health for adolescents is the self-esteem which can accompany having a healthy body.

Much can be done to promote young people's health and prevent illness during adolescence while, at the same time, laying the best foundations for the future so that, in adult life, they will be able to make a positive contribution as workers, citizens and, in their turn, parents, unthreatened by the avoidable major diseases of our time.

In earlier chapters we saw that adolescents' developing sexuality raised important health issues. This chapter will look at further subjects which are of vital importance for youngsters' health, both now and for the future. The first section looks at the areas of responsibility for adolescents' health; the second and third examine the related subjects of food and exercise; the fourth is about miscellaneous 'care' topics, including hygiene and the care of the skin, acne, footcare, eye and dental care, and immunisation. The final section covers drugs, starting with tobacco and alcohol.

Responsibility for adolescents' health

When it comes to the matter of adolescents' health it is necessary to understand where responsibilities lie. Parents certainly have a part to play but they do not have total responsibility.

In the teenage years, young people take on increasing responsibility for their own lives and responsibility for health is part of this. As parents, you are no longer in full charge of their health needs. You cannot monitor everything they eat, force them to take exercise if they do not want to, nor stand over them each time they clean their teeth, encouraging them to do it properly. In any case, close supervision is not appropriate for teenagers: it goes against the whole process of growing up. If you want them to take responsibility for their own health care, you need, increasingly, to stand back as they progress through the teenage years. This is not always easy. Parents can feel guilty when an adolescent son or daughter needs to have precious second teeth filled; they wonder if they have reminded them enough about the dangers of eating sugary foods or the importance of cleaning their teeth properly. One of the hardest lessons for parents in this and in other matters is that they cannot live their teenagers' lives for them and are sometimes forced to watch them make mistakes. For teenagers, like parents, are not perfect; they do not always act wisely and in their own best interests.

Although your teenage children's lives are not under your tight control, there are still areas where you have an influence and can give practical help. They need the motivation to take health seriously and to make choices which maintain and promote good health, and here you can certainly help. But there are also many outside influences which, for good or bad, can have an effect on adolescents' health.

Outside influences

Some outside influences are direct and some are less so. Friends can have a direct influence. For example, teenagers, at the stage when they like to go around in groups, often enjoy meeting in local snack bars and pubs. Here consuming 'junk' food and alcohol can seem an integral part of social life and hard to resist. Similarly, smoking a first cigarette may be the direct result of being offered one by a friend. But the influence of friends need not be negative; friends can encourage one another to take part in sport and be a positive influence against unhealthy habits like smoking.

Other influences come from the larger adult world:

- *The school* plays a part through the priority it gives to health education and how this is put into practice. These decisions are themselves influenced by central government policy which is currently to leave health education as an option, outside the national curriculum (see pages 206–7).
- *Central* and *local government*, and *the school* itself, can all influence the quality of food provided in school meals.
- The *local authority* may or may not have a high priority towards sport facilities for young people.
- The *snack and fast food industries* can be persuasive in encouraging young people to buy their products, irrespective of health hazards.
- *Central government* can influence your teenager's health in a less direct way by the control it chooses to exercise – or not to exercise – over the food industry and those who supply alcohol. Recently the law about serving alcohol to under-eighteens was tightened up (see page 151). On the negative side, there is no legislation insisting that food manufacturers label their products in a complete and uniform way so that consumers are well-informed about what they are eating (see page 113).

It is more difficult for parents to have an effect on those influences which come from outside the home; nevertheless, the following sections suggest a number of possible courses of action which parents can take to improve matters for young people.

Food and health

Parents have their own ideas, about what constitutes a healthy diet and what adolescents should eat, and not eat, to keep healthy. In some respects these may be well-founded but in others parents may be unaware of the latest findings on what makes a healthy diet.

A comparatively recent survey carried out by the Department of Health and Social Security suggests that schoolchildren do not suffer from food deficiencies.[1] On average, they seem to be getting all the nutrients they need. But there are also the exceptions among young people who, for one reason or another, do not get enough of the different nutrients for a healthy diet. These will include very faddy youngsters, those who are obsessed with losing weight and those where the family income is very low.

The main health hazard for most young people is not that they get insufficient nutrients but that they eat far too much of the wrong sorts of food, and through this some of them are laying the foundations of ill health in later life.

What follows sums up recent recommendations and gives some advice on how to put them into practice. We shall also look at the question of how much food youngsters need and what happens when they eat too much or too little.

Eating for health

The main recommendations are:

- to eat a healthy, varied diet;
- to cut down on fat, sugar and salt;
- to increase the amount of fibre in the diet.[2]

A healthy varied diet

Dietitians are agreed that people need to eat a variety of foods and especially fresh foods. In this way they are more likely to get the various nutrients which their bodies need. The essentials include:

Protein builds and maintains the body. It is found in eggs, fish, bread, meat, cereals, cheese, beans and milk.

Fat provides us with a concentrated form of energy; fat not used to provide energy is stored as body fat. It is found in many foods including oil, butter, margarine, cheese, meat, eggs and nuts. It is a main ingredient in made-up foods like biscuits and cakes.

Carbohydrates provide energy and are found in the following forms:

Sugar: a large component of cakes, sweets, jams and many soft drinks; also found in fruit and honey.
Starch: found in cereals, bread, pasta, rice, beans and potatoes.
Fibre: found in the cell walls of plants; it gives them structural support. Rich sources include wholegrain cereals, peas, nuts and beans.

Vitamins help to regulate bodily processes. They are chemicals which are found in minute quantities in a variety of foods. For example, vitamin D, obtained from fish liver oil and other sources, is necessary for building bones; vitamin C, found in fresh fruit and vegetables, including the often maligned potato, helps to keep body tissues healthy and is needed for the absorption of iron.

Minerals Very small amounts of minerals are also needed. For example, calcium, found in milk, is used for building bones and iron, found in dried beans, dark green vegetables, liver and meat, eggs and dried fruit, maintains the necessary level of red blood cells. Without enough iron people suffer from anaemia.

If your teenager eats a varied diet, comprising, over the course of each week, many different sorts of food, then it is likely to contain everything he or she needs for good health. It will provide the nutrients needed for growing muscles and bones and, for girls who have started their periods, it will make good the loss of iron.

Vitamin supplements There is no need for young people to take vitamin supplements unless their diet is very restricted, consisting mostly of processed food – pies, sausages, crisps, sweets and so on, and lacking in fresh foods. If they are very fond of 'junk' food, to the exclusion of other foods, it would be a good idea to see if, between you, you can work out ways of improving their diet, perhaps following some of the suggestions found later in this chapter.

Cut down on fat

The DHSS survey found that many young people eat a lot of fatty foods like crisps, chips and cakes. There are many good reasons why adolescents should not eat too much fat.

Staying slim Fat is concentrated energy. Weight for weight, it contains many more calories than other forms of food so eating less fat is a good way to avoid getting fat. Obesity increases the risk of heart disease – it means the heart has to work harder and, of more immediate concern for adolescents, it does not look good.

Keeping cholesterol low Cholesterol is a waxy fat which is made in the liver and is necessary for our bodies to function healthily, but we do not need too much of it. If there is a high level of cholesterol in the bloodstream there can be a build-up of fat on the artery walls. This results from eating food which is high in cholesterol – like dairy fats, eggs and meat – and food which is high in saturated fats (see next page).

Signs of a diet high in cholesterol may already be present in adolescents. Deposits of fats have been found, for example, in the coronary arteries of young teenagers[3]. In middle age these may build up to such an extent that they block the supply of blood to the heart, causing a heart attack.

The age at which people suffer from heart disease is younger than it used to be and it is now not uncommon in early middle age. Heart disease causes much unnecessary suffering both to individuals and to their families.

Different types of fats

Although it is good to cut down on total fat consumption, there are some types of fats which it is more important to avoid than others. The foods to cut down on are those which are high in saturated fats.

- *Saturated fats* are contained in large proportions in animal fats. For example, butter, cheese and full-cream milk all contain saturated fats. Some vegetable oils, notably coconut oil and palm oil, and margarines also contain high levels of saturated fats.

Saturated fats stimulate the liver to make more cholesterol, so a diet high in saturated fats increases the risk of heart disease. Many ready-made bought foods are high in saturated fats. These include biscuits, cakes and pies.

- *Unsaturated fats* are found at high levels in many vegetable oils and in some margarines. Soya, corn and sunflower oils and margarines are all high in unsaturated fats of different sorts.
- *Polyunsaturated fats* are types of unsaturated fat which some scientists believe lower the level of cholesterol in the blood. This could protect people against heart disease. Again soya, corn and sunflower oils and margarines are all high in these.

What parents can do about fat in the family diet

It is now recommended that only a third of daily calories should come from fats but most people eat more. Youngsters, especially, eat snacks which are high in fat – crisps, chips, hamburgers, cakes – at school and on the way home. There is a part to be played in explaining to adolescents the dangers of eating too much fat, and saturated fats in particular, and warning them about the high fat content of much 'fast food'. There are also practical things you can do to keep fat consumption low, by taking care about the sort of foods you buy and how you cook them at home.[4]

Adolescents can be very conservative about food so if you want to change the family diet there are two lines of approach. There are some things you can do to change the family diet for the better which the family will hardly notice. Other beneficial changes are more obvious and might need to be introduced gradually. Some of the suggestions below may appeal to you as things you can do immediately while you could introduce others by degrees. *Whatever you do to cut down fats is really worth while for the sake of your adolescent's health.*

If you want to improve the family diet, any of the following could help:

Choose unsaturated fats

It is better to use unsaturated fat or oil for cooking and salad dressings, and margarine high in polyunsaturates for spreading on bread.

Manufacturers like to advertise the fact that food is 'healthy' and you should look for information on the label. 'High in polyunsaturates' and 'low in saturated fat' mean that there is less of the risky saturated fat in a product. Look out for these phrases particularly on margarine and oil labels.

If the manufacturer gives no information, then it is likely that the margarine or oil is high in saturated fats and should be avoided. Oils labelled 'blended vegetable oil' are often high in saturated fats.

Take care how you cook

- Grill meat and fish rather than frying it.
- Grill bacon, sausages and hamburgers until the fat runs out.
- Use a non-stick frying pan with a minute amount of fat or oil for frying.
- Cut visible fat off meat.
- Choose minced meat labelled 'low fat' or 'lean' – or skim off any fat that comes to the surface when you are cooking.
- Gradually cut down on the number of days each week you eat red meat – beef, lamb and pork.
- Serve fish, chicken and turkey more frequently.
- Remove the skin from chicken and turkey – that is where most of the fat is.
- Substitute low-fat versions of sausages, if your food store stocks them.

Select dairy products

- Gradually introduce low-fat milk – first of all semi-skimmed and eventually skimmed milk – for use in drinks and with cereals. It is not easily detected when used in cooking.
- *Either* cut down on the amount of cheese you give your adolescent or choose cheese which is lower in fat than other cheeses such as Edam, Brie and cottage cheese, *or* look out for, and request, low-fat versions of other cheeses. Again some manufacturers give helpful labels.

- Choose low-fat yoghurt.
- Sorbets, home-made or bought, have no fat, unlike ice cream (but they can be high in sugar!).
- If your family enjoys home-made cakes and pies sometimes, substitute polyunsaturated margarine for other margarine and butter in your baking.

Reduce snacks See if you can cut down on biscuits and crisps if these figure to any extent in your weekly shopping list and gradually substitute healthier snacks: fresh and dried fruit, raisins and unsalted nuts are possibilities.

Cut down on sugar Sugar presents two health hazards. First, eating too much sugar can make adolescents fat, with all the health hazards attendant on obesity. Second, it is the main cause of tooth decay.

Sugar provides energy but it does not contain any other forms of nourishment – none of the vitamins and minerals, nor the fibre, which are necessary for health. A healthy diet can supply enough energy without including sugar. Young people who have a lot of sugar in their diet, at the expense of a variety of fresh food, miss out on essential nutrients. It is not difficult for youngsters to have too much sugar. Apart from the sugar they spoon on to cereals and into drinks, many consume large quantities of sugar-rich colas and other soft drinks as well as sweets and chocolate bars, biscuits and cakes, not to mention the sugar which is hidden in unlikely savoury foods like ketchup, pickles and baked beans.

A recent health report[5] has recommended that we should cut the use of sugar by a half, and especially between meals when it is most dangerous for teeth (see page 139). Sweets and soft drinks are often part of the teenage social scene. As a parent you may have been fighting a losing battle against them for many years; however, even at the younger end of the age-range, adolescents are becoming more sensible and responsible. It is worth explaining to them why it is a good idea to limit eating sugary foods to meal-times and suggesting – or providing – alternatives for between meals. These could include drinks with permitted artificial sweeteners and nuts.

Unfortunately, it is quite easy to be misled into thinking that many 'wholefood' snacks – cereal bars, for example – are good alternatives to sweets between meals, when this is not so. Anything made with sugar – be it white, brown, or in the form of honey – causes tooth decay. Indeed, all simple sugars can cause decay, including the 'natural' sugar found in cereal bars, fresh and dried fruits and fruit juices. It may be that these foods are less harmful than others because they are less sticky and they also contain valuable nutrients not present in confectionery, cakes and sweets.

Cut down on salt

Two recent reports have concluded that we eat too much salt in our diets and recommended that we should cut it down.[6] The reason for this is that in countries where a lot of salt is eaten there are more people with high blood pressure than elsewhere. High blood pressure – a raised level of the pressure with which the heart and arteries push blood around the body – is linked to heart attacks and strokes and can also damage the kidneys.

It seems a reasonable precaution for adolescents as well as other people to cut down on salt in their diets. Many foods on your weekly shopping list already contain salt, including sausages, meat pies, ham, bacon, butter, margarine, tinned vegetables, stock cubes, crisps and salted nuts.

In some cases low-salt products are available and it is worth looking out for these. However, it is you who have most control over the amount of salt used in your household. One way of cutting down on the family's salt intake is by gradually reducing the amount used in cooking. People soon become used to food which is less salty and you can provide extra flavour with herbs and lemon juice, if you wish. Another way is to cut down on salt used at table, but wait until the family is used to food which is cooked with less salt before suggesting that they reduce the amount of salt sprinkled on food at meal-times.

Increase fibre content of diet

Alongside advice about what not to eat, recent reports also provide positive encouragement for everyone to eat more fibre in their diet. There are many foods, both sweet and savoury, that are rich in fibre. Whole-cereal foods like Shredded Wheat and wholemeal bread, pulses such as baked beans, kidney beans, peas and so on are all good sources of fibre, as are dried fruit and nuts. There is also a useful amount in other fruit and vegetables, including potatoes. Given all these fibre-rich foods, there is no need to resort to eating pure bran!

Foods which contain no fibre include sugar, and foods made from it, fats, butter, cream, meat and cheese.

Eating sufficient fibre is good for health in several ways:

- Too little fibre is linked to bowel disease, including irritable bowel syndrome, constipation, diverticulitis and cancer of the colon.[7] A high-fibre diet, on the other hand, makes for bulkier, softer faeces which pass through the gut more quickly and with less strain.

- A diet which is high in fibre is satisfying without containing too many calories, so adolescents who eat high-fibre food are less likely to put on unwanted weight.
- High-fibre foods are mostly low in sugar, fat and salt, all of which should be reduced for healthy eating.

It is not difficult to get your adolescent to eat enough fibre. It just means providing wholemeal bread, a wholewheat breakfast cereal, potatoes and plenty of vegetables and fruit.

Feeding adolescents

The principles of healthy eating are: *eat less fat, sugar and salt* and *eat more fibre*. Perhaps the best way to start improving your adolescent's diet is to continue serving food they like while introducing changes that bring meals more into line with health recommendations. It is not easy to alter family eating patterns overnight. Shopping and cooking are based on years of habit and family preferences which we take for granted. Feeding the family is a lot of work and changing eating patterns means changing meal-planning, shopping and food preparation. It may be preferable to take gradual steps towards a healthier diet rather than trying to achieve everything at once. After a month or so you can introduce further improvements.

Some of the tips given earlier may help (see pages 100–6). Here are some suggestions for meals, some of which could appeal to your family, whether you do the cooking yourself or adolescents take their turn. Giving them the experience of preparing healthy, tasty food, and explaining the principles behind it, can help lay the foundations for healthy eating later in life.

The ideas that follow are built round the foods which adolescents like and which contain a high proportion of fibre, like potatoes, wholemeal bread and brown rice. Many people are more used to planning a meal round meat but the menus below redress the balance in favour of eating for health. Families do not always sit down together for every meal, so there are also some suggestions for individual servings, and light meals, which can be eaten as required.

Fibre source: potatoes

Potatoes have had bad publicity in the past, but they can play a significant part in a healthy, varied diet. They are satisfying and a good source of fibre and vitamin C.

Jacket potatoes It can take under ten minutes to bake one jacket potato in a microwave – quick and easy enough for an impatient teenager. The ordinary oven may be more convenient for three or four potatoes and will produce a crisper skin.

The only thing to be cautious about is serving potatoes plain with butter, which is high in saturated fats and which an unfilled potato soaks up. Have any of the following fillings available instead:

Grated low-fat cheese – mixed with chopped onions, if liked.
Cottage cheese, either plain or mixed with chopped, crunchy vegetables, like celery, peppers or onion.
Baked beans Some stores stock beans which are low in sugar and salt, compared with others.
Coleslaw Either buy the low-calorie version or make your own with shredded white cabbage, dressed with a vinaigrette made from a little polyunsaturated oil, vinegar and mustard, adding a sprinkling of raisins, peanuts or grated carrot for sweetness.
Beef chilli Minced beef, browned and the fat drained off, simmered with onion, cooked red beans and chilli powder to taste.
Ratatouille Tomatoes, courgettes, peppers, aubergines and herbs simmered together with olive oil.

Jacket potatoes, served with any of the above fillings, make a substantial light meal. You can also serve them as a main meal, perhaps adding a hot vegetable, or a salad or a piece of baked chicken. Fruit and yoghurt would complete the meal.

Mashed potatoes Potatoes mashed with skimmed milk and a little polyunsaturated margarine are filling and can be used as a topping.

Fish pie Steam, poach or microwave the fish. Make a white sauce, using polyunsaturated margarine (you can use about a quarter less than in a conventional recipe) and skimmed milk. Remove any skin and bones from the fish, flake it and mix with the white sauce. Put the mixture in an oven-proof dish. Top the mixture with mashed potato, roughen the surface with a fork and brown lightly under the grill.

Shepherd's pie Heat a frying pan – do not use any fat – and, when it is hot, brown some minced meat in it. Drain off the fat which runs out of the meat. Simmer a finely chopped onion in a cupful of water. Add the meat to the simmered onion and its water, together with herbs to taste and a pinch of salt. Simmer the meat for about twenty minutes, until tender. Thicken with wholemeal flour and top with mashed potato. Finish under the grill.

Serve either of these with salad or a hot vegetable.

Roast potatoes and chips Home-made chips can be an occasional treat. Use polyunsaturated oil and cut the chips fairly large. A pound of potatoes cut into large chips absorb less oil than a pound of potatoes cut into small chips.

Successful roast potatoes can be cooked with very little fat. Parboil the potatoes. Melt half an ounce (15 g) of polyunsaturated margarine – or use a similar oil – in a roasting tin. Roll the potatoes in the margarine until the surfaces are covered and roast in a hot oven until they are done.

Fibre source: wholemeal pasta

Because it is made from wholemeal flour this sort of pasta is high in fibre. It is also filling! Here are two ideas which may suggest others to you:

Spaghetti with meat sauce Make this in the usual way, but remember to drain any surplus fat from the mince when you have browned it. Increase the fibre and vitamin content by adding a tin of tomatoes and some chopped green pepper to the mince and simmer them together. Toss the cooked and drained spaghetti in olive oil or a polyunsaturated oil. Serve with a green salad.

Pasta shells with tuna Cook the pasta. Meanwhile chop an onion and lightly cook in a little polyunsaturated oil. Add green peas and/or sweetcorn kernels and stir-fry briefly; add the drained tuna, broken into chunks. Drain the pasta and mix in the fish and vegetables. Serve with salad. This is good cold and can be packed for a school lunch.

Fibre source: wholemeal bread

Wholemeal rolls and sliced bread A satisfying light meal can be made from wholemeal bread and soup. Lentil soup is particularly nutritious; or grate some low-fat cheese on to home-made onion soup or minestrone. A salad and fresh fruit or yoghurt turns it into a full meal.

Contrary to previous health beliefs, sandwiches can be a good component of your son or daughter's diet. Use a polyunsaturated margarine for spreading lightly on the bread. Possible fillings are mashed tuna or sardine, with cucumber; peanut butter with something crunchy like celery; low-fat cheese, chicken or ham with salad.

Pitta bread Wholemeal pitta breads are particularly useful. Split them and pack with salad, low-fat cheese, or chicken, or sliced ham from which the fat has been removed. They are good to put in school-lunchboxes. Also serve pitta breads with humous and salad.

Wholemeal pizza Make a scone dough using wholemeal flour and polyunsaturated margarine. Pat it out into a pizza-sized circle. Top it with tomato purée, mixed with a spoonful of olive oil and some marjoram. Cover with slices of vegetables to your own taste – onions tomatoes, mushrooms, for example, and then some grated low-fat cheese. Youngsters like to suggest their own toppings. This can also be sliced for school lunches.

Fibre source: brown rice

Brown rice has more fibre than refined rice. It can be a base for curries of various sorts, including vegetable curries and curries made with pulses like lentils, dried beans and chickpeas, which can be served with low-fat yoghurt and salads.

Baked chicken goes well with brown rice, especially when accompanied by a home-made tomato sauce and served with salad or fish and meat can be cooked with rice, as in a risotto.

Caribbean risotto uses boiled rice, cooked red beans, chopped spring onions, garlic and ginger root served with chicken.

Texan hash uses brown rice mixed with minced meat, cooked until the fat can be drained away, cooked onions and tomato purée. It is flavoured with chilli powder.

Puddings

Many home-made puddings are fairly high in fat and sugar. The following may provide some useful alternatives:

Low-fat yoghurt with fresh or stewed fruit, or fruit salad made with dried fruit.

Apples cored and stuffed with dried fruit and baked in the microwave or regular oven.

Bananas baked in their skins, in a moderate oven, for about fifteen minutes or until the skins are black. Serve in their skins. Open and sprinkle with lemon juice or cinnamon, if liked; or eat with yoghurt or *fromage frais.*

Jellies made with fruit juice (not pineapple, which does not set) and gelatine; the instructions are on the packet. The flavour can be sharpened with lemon juice, if needed, and fresh fruit, or fruit canned in juice (not syrup) can be added before the mixture sets.

Breakfast

Many of us were brought up to think that a cooked breakfast is a good breakfast. In the case of the traditional British breakfast this is just not so: fried eggs, bacon, sausages, together with fried bread, are loaded with fat. But some youngsters like doing a fry-up for themselves from time to time. If this is the case with your son or daughter show them how to grill bacon until it is crisp and how to fry an egg using a non-stick pan, perhaps with a smear of polyunsaturated oil. Or let them learn how to poach an egg or to scramble it using polyunsaturated margarine and skimmed milk; and substitute wholemeal bread or toast for fried bread.

In fact, a breakfast of wholemeal cereal, like Shredded Wheat, Weetabix, or muesli, fits in better with present-day recommendations for health. The muesli should be sugarless and if eaten with fresh or dried fruit – sliced banana, apples or raisins – you may find that teenagers need to sprinkle less sugar on top. Substitute skimmed milk or low-fat yoghurt for full-cream milk.

Wholemeal bread or toast with polyunsaturated margarine is also good for breakfast. Have peanut butter or bananas available as a substitute for jam.

Unsweetened fruit juice or fruit make a good start to the day.

Going without breakfast

Not all youngsters want to eat breakfast before they go to school. If they do not eat breakfast, however, they are quite likely to drop off at the shop, en route for school, and buy sweets, drinks or crisps, so it is worth having some wholesome snacks available for them to take with them to eat before school or at break-time. Sandwiches, nuts and fruit juice are possibilities.

Packed school lunches

If your son or daughter takes lunch to school every day, involve them in the planning and preparation until eventually they can take over for themselves and produce healthy and tasty meals.

Think about the main fibre content of the lunch first. Is the meal going to be based on wholemeal bread, rolls or pittas, with tasty fillings? Options include chicken, turkey, low-fat or cottage cheese, ham, mashed-up sardine, tuna, the occasional egg, together with salad.

Or is the main fibre ingredient going to be in the form of a salad? It is worth cooking extra brown rice, wholemeal pasta or potatoes for an evening meal in order to have some left over to form the basis of a salad to be packed in a container for lunch the following day. Keep the rice, pasta or potatoes in the fridge overnight and add other ingredients in the morning. These could include a variety of fruit or vegetables – peas, sweetcorn, red beans, chopped celery, radishes, apple, nuts and other foods like chopped chicken or ham, fish or cubes of low-fat cheese. These can be dressed with low-fat yoghurt, or a little dressing made from polyunsaturated oil or vinegar and flavoured to taste.

The meal can also include fruit-flavoured low-fat yoghurt, nuts, dried fruit and fresh fruit and fruit juice to drink. If you can find low-fat, low-salt crisps, these could be an occasional addition.

What else can parents do about food?

At home, parents can have a direct effect on what young people eat, but there are also some measures which parents can take in the local community and in the wider community to help young people towards a healthier diet. As poll taxpayers and electors, you have the right to try to influence public policy. This is not easy and, because earning a living and bringing up young people are demanding occupations in themselves, not all parents have the time available to get involved. But if you feel strongly enough about it, and you have the time, you can take action outside the home to promote your adolescent's health. Three areas which present possibilities for change are:

- *The school* Does the school your son or daughter attends educate its students about healthy eating and does this include providing a healthy and attractive choice of food at lunch-time?
- *Labelling of products* How do manufacturers label the ingredients present in food? Could improved labelling help parents and adolescents to make informed choices about what they eat?
- *Agricultural policies* Do these encourage the availability of certain foods rather than others?

School lunches

The midday meal can provide a substantial part of adolescents' different nutritional needs, so school lunches have an important part to play. A DHSS survey in 1986 found that schoolchildren obtained 30 per cent of their energy requirements from school meals.[8] At one time standards were laid down by the Department of Education and Science to ensure that school meal services provided a set meal which, according to the understanding of the time, was balanced and nutritious. In recent years, however, public policy on school lunches has changed.

Since 1980, local authorities have been left to decide on their own standards; they are also allowed to tender out school meals to private caterers. Nowadays these are often served cafeteria-style, rather than as a set meal. This puts the responsibility for choosing a healthy meal on to children and adolescents who, again according to the DHSS and other surveys, prefer food which is high in fats and sugar, if it is available. This is hardly surprising given that advertising aims to influence them to choose these foods. In addition, students now have ready money, provided by parents, to buy their food in the school cafeteria or elsewhere. They do not have to book, or pay for, a set meal in advance, as used to be the case. So some young people patronise local fast-food outlets in the lunch hour. For various reasons they do not want school meals; perhaps the choice available when it comes to their turn is limited, or the atmosphere of the dining hall may not be attractive.

Often the foods they choose in local take-aways do not provide a healthy, varied diet.

Fortunately, some schools make an effort to inform youngsters about how to choose a healthy diet. They give information on food in the classroom, whether in health education, biology or home economics. They also encourage the students to apply the information to their own eating and help to motivate them to make wise choices. Boys and girls are taught to cook and prepare food that meets nutritional requirements, rather than the sort of meals which eventually undermine health. The efforts of the teachers are backed up by school meals staff who provide attractive, nutritious food. There are also posters and displays reminding students about how to pick a well-balanced meal.

This has implications for choosing a suitable school for your son or daughter. If you are still at the stage of making this choice, find out what sort of policy the schools you are considering have about food. Do all the pupils learn about the importance of healthy eating for a healthy life? Is this education carried through into the dining room so that what has been learned in the classroom can be put into practice? Is the dining room fairly comfortable? What is the noise level like? Does the atmosphere suggest that the students are too rigidly organised, on the one hand, or chaotic, on the other?

Food labelling

The days when parents produced and prepared much of the food their families ate belong to the distant past. We buy a large proportion of all the food we eat ready-prepared: bread, biscuits, margarine, cornflakes, tinned vegetables and fruit, dairy products, sausages and pies, sweet and savoury snacks. But it is difficult to really know what we are buying because of inadequate labelling and, therefore, whether we are meeting the current guidelines to cut down on fat (especially polyunsaturated), on sugar and salt and to increase the amount of fibre in family meals. Improvements in labelling depend on the voluntary action of manufacturers or on legislation.

Agricultural policies

Food production is often interlinked with politics – a matter of priorities being given to certain types of food rather than to others. The Health Education Council's Committee on Medical Aspects of

Food Policy (1984) pointed out that some aspects of the European Common Agriculture Policy could discourage families from eating a healthy diet.

- Farmers may be encouraged to produce fat, rather than lean, animals, for example, because they are now paid to produce fewer animals per hectare of land. This means that food which is high in saturated fat and cholesterol will be more widely available.[9]
- The EC also subsidises the production of sugar and butter, with the consequent lowering of world prices – and comparative cheapness – of substances we should be cutting down on.

Seeing that young people have a healthy diet is the responsibility of the wider community as well as of parents.

Vegetarian adolescents

Some people become vegetarian in their teens even when there are no other vegetarians in the family. They may do so for political or moral reasons: adolescence can be a time of idealism of various sorts (see pages 26–9) and becoming vegetarian can be a sign that a young person is establishing their own values and way of life rather than following those of the rest of the family. If you are a vegetarian yourself, then you will not find it difficult to supply your vegetarian son or daughter with a healthy diet. But if you are a meat-eater, whose teenager unexpectedly announces that they no longer wish to eat meat, you may feel you do not know how to give them the food that they need.

A vegetarian diet can be perfectly healthy, but there are some points over which you need to take care. You also need to explain these to the young person concerned who, to an increasing extent, is responsible for his or her own health and, therefore, diet.

Vegetarian adolescents need to eat a good variety of foods to obtain the nutrients they require.

- A vegetarian should not simply cut out meat, that is, have the same meals as the rest of the family except for the meat. To do so would be to miss out on protein and calories which growing adolescents, especially, are in need of.
- Vegetarians should eat more beans, pulses, nuts and cereals to substitute for meat. It is especially useful to combine two of these in the same meal – for example, hummus (made with chickpeas) with wholemeal bread, beans on toast, brown rice and bean curry. This provides a wider range of protein.
- It is not healthy to turn frequently to eggs and cheese as a meat replacement. These have a place in a vegetarian diet but they are high

in saturated fat so they should not be eaten in large amounts, either by vegetarians or by meat-eaters. Nuts, cereals, grains and pulses are better.

■ Vegetarians should also eat plenty of fresh fruit and vegetables. It is especially important that they have enough vitamin C to help with the absorption of iron from other foods.

Basically the guidelines for healthy eating are the same for vegetarians as for meat-eaters: *cut down on fat, sugar and salt* and *eat food which is high in fibre*.

A sound approach is to suggest to a vegetarian adolescent that you take joint responsibility for seeing that they eat properly. If they are encouraged to help prepare some of their own meals, or cook them for themselves, they will, with your assistance, learn something about healthy eating as a vegetarian.

It may be convenient to plan some completely vegetarian meals each week – for example, vegetarian lasagne, where minced walnuts, peanuts and wholemeal breadcrumbs can substitute for meat in your usual recipe. Also recommended is to cook large batches of suitable food – chickpeas in tomato or onion sauce, nut rissoles, lentil curry – and freeze them in single-person portions. (See page 293 for the address of the Vegetarian Society.)

The vegan adolescent

Vegans do not eat any food which comes from animals. This means no eggs, milk or cheese and no meat. If an adolescent becomes a vegan, it is particularly important for them to understand about the foods they need to eat to keep healthy. They should be aware that they can easily miss out on vitamin B_{12} and calcium, if they do not eat adequate replacements for the animal-derived foods.

In some health food shops, soya products – milk, cheese, yoghurt – can be obtained which are specially fortified for vegans. They should also eat almonds and other nuts, dried fruit and dark green vegetables. Sometimes vitamin supplements are necessary.

The Vegan Society can give advice (see page 293 for address), or you could ask your family doctor if it would be possible for your son or daughter to talk to a dietitian to find out about healthy eating for vegans.

Over-eating and under-eating

So far we have concerned ourselves with what makes a wholesome, varied diet for adolescents: a balance of food that makes for good health and well-being. The next question to consider is how much food an adolescent needs and the problems of eating too much or too little.

How much food?

Throughout life, the amount of food a person needs is related to the amount of energy that person uses up. Not surprisingly, people need more energy from food in adolescence – a time of rapid growth (see pages 9 and 14) – than at any other stage in their lives. An adolescent who is always on the move needs more calories than another youngster who is more sluggish. Energy intake and energy output are linked together so it is not really possible to say how much food any one teenager requires. The sort of food they eat is important, as we have seen, but the amount they eat can be left to them unless they are either overweight or underweight.

Obesity

If people are overweight, it means that the balance between energy output and energy input has gone awry. There can be a vicious circle of not wanting to take exercise, to dance, swim or change into sports clothes because of feeling miserably fat and self-conscious. And feeling miserable can lead some teenagers to seek consolation in more food – often of the high-fat, high-sugar, high-salt, low-fibre variety. Other overweight adolescents deny that anything is wrong and over-eat, in a spirit of rebellion.

If your son or daughter is fat it is important to realise that they need to be highly motivated in order to lose weight. Nagging will not make things any better, nor will making jokes – however well meant – about their size.

You can, of course, share your worry with them, tell them that you have noticed that they are overweight and that it is not good for their health, now or in later life. Or you can pick up on anything they say that indicates that they are not happy about being fat. They may be very glad to talk about their feelings if the right opportunity arises and if you listen in a supportive way without being judgemental. Do what you can to encourage them and to strengthen their motivation to lose weight.

You may, however, feel that there are other people who are better placed than you are to talk to your son or daughter about their weight. Between parents and children, food can have an emotional history – think of those times when children have been off-colour and had a poor appetite, and how eating is a sign that they are on the mend, or when you have gone to a lot of trouble to prepare a meal, only to find that they are not hungry, for one reason or another; how a child who 'eats everything up' is praised for being a good boy or girl; how nice food is given as a reward for good behaviour – or even denied, as a punishment. An older brother or sister or aunt or uncle might be more successful in helping to encourage them to lose weight.

At a practical level you can provide the sort of diet that follows the recommendations about healthy eating described earlier. A youngster who keeps to this is less likely to put on weight than someone who eats in an unhealthy way. But you cannot control their eating when they are away from home, nor force them to take exercise if they are not inclined to.

A young person who is overweight and who has decided that they want to reach a more normal weight needs to eat a healthy and varied diet. This may mean a change of eating habits, cutting out snacks that are high in fat and sugar and, therefore, calories – cakes, chocolate, biscuits, crisps and sugary drinks – and eating more fresh vegetables and food that is high in fibre (see page 106).

'Crash' dieting is not advisable. It is easy to regain lost weight quickly once the diet is over, and to fall into a pattern of dieting, followed by weight gain, followed by further dieting.

The aim should be to establish a way of eating that is nutritious and satisfying and that can become a lifelong habit. Together with extra exercise, this should be enough to get down to a healthy weight. Above all, the overweight adolescent, who is trying to eat sensibly, needs all the support that the family can offer. They need admiration for keeping to their resolution and encouragement if they backslide.

Eating disorders

Most overweight adolescents will be realistic about their decision to eat less in order to keep in better shape. However, there are conditions – anorexia nervosa and bulimia nervosa – in which adolescents and young adults who are not at all overweight become obsessed with a need to lose weight. They have a totally unrealistic phobia about weight gain and go to desperate lengths to avoid it. These conditions are eating disorders which have only been brought to the public's attention within the last ten years or so.

Anorexia nervosa

People who suffer from anorexia are mostly, but not always, adolescent girls. There are many theories about what causes anorexia. We live in a society in which a slim, boyish shape is often put forward as ideal by the media and the fashion industry, so it is not surprising that many young women, whether they need to or not, try to lose weight at some time or other. Anorexia (and bulimia) may be an extreme response to the social pressure for young women to be slim. It is held in some quarters that adolescents become anorexic in order to regain their childlike shape and thus to escape from their developing sexuality. Another theory is that the anorexic youngster is trying to achieve control over his or her life by a strict control of diet and weight. They may have an intense desire to be 'perfect', which shows itself in the obsessional pursuit of slimness. Whatever the roots of the condition, it is one which is very distressing for parents and other members of the family.

Anorexic adolescents appear to be less distressed about their condition than other people. It is very unlikely that they will admit that anything is wrong even though they are, day after day, systematically starving themselves. They go to great lengths to hide this from the family. They may take their food away from the table, supposedly to eat alone but in fact to hide it or throw it away. Or they may make excuses about not eating, because of real or pretended stomach aches. On occasions they may refuse to sit down to family meals at all, saying that they are not hungry, or will eat later. Many youngsters behave in this way at some time, but an anorexic avoids eating as often as possible and their loss of weight is, eventually, obvious. Some may do what they can to disguise losing weight by wearing layers of garments, or baggy clothing to disguise their shape.

People with anorexia are never content with their weight loss. They set themselves lower and lower weight targets and are convinced that anything they eat results, immediately, in an unsightly weight gain. Their body image is totally unrealistic, so that they think they are fat when in fact they are skeletally thin. They are obsessive in pursuing what they see as perfection and their perception of themselves has become completely distorted. In their attempt to constantly lose weight, some anorexics also exercise frantically, or, on the occasions when they do eat, they may later take doses of laxatives to avoid digesting the food properly and to hurry it through the system. In some cases they eat in order to pacify other people, but vomit immediately the meal is over (compulsive vomiting is a feature of bulimia, see next page).

When parents realise what is happening, the ensuing conflict is most painful. The young person denies that there is a problem, convinced that he or she is hideously fat and seeing each mouthful of food as a disaster. They remain secretive and make excuses. Sometimes they become very ritualistic in exactly what they eat, how much and in what way. Meanwhile the parents cajole, reason and threaten. In the early stages some anorexics are, apart from their food phobia, quite cheerful and not lacking in energy. They may spend time and care cooking for the rest of the family but not eating anything themselves.

Eventually, as the process of starvation and emaciation continues, they become weary and weak. A fine downy hair may grow on their bodies and face and, in young women, their periods stop. Nevertheless they refuse to admit that they are in any way ill and persist in deliberate self-starvation.

Treatment If a young person behaves in a way that suggests they are anorexic, tell them about your concern and seek help as soon as possible. Cases are known in which the patient recovers spontaneously, but anorexia nervosa is a severe condition that can result in death and risks should not be taken.

The names of associations which can offer help and information are on page 293. The family doctor is also a source of help but he or she may have had little experience of young people with this condition. It may be necessary to spell out to the doctor the young person's anorexic symptoms, including details about weight loss, food intake, excessive exercise, obsessive routines and loss of periods.

Changing eating habits can be a lengthy process and can involve the whole family. Parents can feel bewildered and guilty but it is very important for them to realise that the condition is not their fault. Living with an anorexia sufferer calls for love and patience and family members need to share their feelings and to listen to one another (see pages 38–43).

It is sometimes necessary for a person with anorexia to be hospitalised in order to learn new eating habits and for nursing and medical care. Psychotherapy, including group and family therapy, are also sometimes advised.

Bulimia nervosa

Bulimia nervosa is an eating disorder which has some features in common with anorexia nervosa and affects young women in their late teens and early twenties. It also affects young men.

Again there are various theories about the causes of the condition. People with bulimia may appear to be perfectly competent on the surface while inwardly suffering from anxiety and doubts about their own worth. Like anorexics, they are also preoccupied with a profound fear of becoming fat. An adolescent or adult with bulimia has a habit of 'bingeing and vomiting'. They eat compulsively until there is no food left, or they can no longer continue because they are too full. Often this eating is in private, or late at night, and it may happen every day or at weekly intervals. After bingeing, the youngster can feel deeply depressed and guilty about eating in this way and resort to vomiting to get rid of the food. They may also use laxatives for the same purpose.

Various signs suggest that an adolescent is bulimic. Large quantities of food may inexplicably disappear from storecupboards or the freezer. The bulimic teenager eats huge amounts of food but always remains thin. At the end of a meal they rush away from the table, in order to get rid of their food by vomiting, although this may not be apparent to parents. In the end vomiting becomes an irresistible habit.

Bulimia can cause physical problems ranging from the loss of tooth enamel and subsequent tooth decay to, in some cases, damage to the heart and kidneys.

As with anorexia, advice should be sought if parents suspect that a young person is suffering from bulimia. It may be very difficult to do anything about it without outside help. The names and addresses of support groups for parents and for adolescents can be found on page 293.

Physical activity and sport

That there are connections between exercise and health is now well known. For example, taking regular exercise has been linked with reducing the risk of developing high blood pressure, with improving the way the body handles cholesterol, with controlling weight and with giving a feeling of well-being, all of which can have an effect on the likelihood or otherwise of someone developing coronary heart disease.[10]

Having an active lifestyle is enjoyable and keeps people in good spirits and better able to cope with life. Unfortunately the level of activity among young people tends to drop off as they grow older. Among pre-school children it seems quite natural that they are always on the move. And in primary school, playgrounds are full of children running around and playing games. This sort of informal game-playing tapers off as children grow into adolescence. But even at this stage many youngsters take part in games and sport whenever there is the opportunity. There are also the physical education lessons in school which play some part in keeping young people fit. But only half of school-leavers continue with any sort of sport and women take part less than men.[11]

The challenge for both parents and school is to help adolescents to establish the *habit* of taking exercise. This involves giving them the opportunity to find out the sort of exercise they enjoy and also to introduce them to activities which are easy to continue when they have left school. Team sports – like football and hockey – are less likely to be continued into adult life compared with individual activities like swimming and cycling, and pair sports such as tennis. Team games have a lot to offer, but there is little encouragement or opportunity for adults to take part in them after leaving school or college. For this reason it is worth giving particular encouragement to your son or daughter to take part in individual sports and pair sports, as well as team sports.

For adolescents to enjoy sport is very important. They are more likely to take part in activities because they enjoy them than because they will be done good by them. Coronary heart disease may seem such a distant threat as not to be worth worrying about. There is such a variety of sports and activities for adolescents to take part in that it should not be impossible for them to find something that they enjoy. As well as the traditional sports there are many other activities to consider (see page 127). Canoeing, orienteering, dancing, acrobatics, for example, all provide their own particular satisfactions. There is the challenge to do something really well, for young people to discover their own potential and to set their own goals and targets. There are the moments of excitement and adventure and the friendships that can grow out of sharing them with other young people.

Of course, parents cannot force adolescents to take part in exercise, no matter how beneficial it may be, but boys and girls just entering their teens may be more open to suggestion than older adolescents. Once reluctance has set in it may be more difficult to encourage them to play games and take exercise. It is much more fun to do so with other people than alone and youngsters really appreciate your presence and support at games and competitions. You can find what is on offer at local sports centres and suggest family outings to which they can invite their friends. You may want to join in yourself, perhaps, and there are family holidays which incorporate sport and other opportunities for both parents and children; for example, a teenager could have tennis coaching while a parent took part in a photography class. For some sports there is also the possibility of special coaching during the school holidays, whether by day or residentially. The school physical education staff can supply information, as can the national bodies of the various sports and the Sports Council (see pages 293–4).

Older teenagers will probably not look to you for suggestions and involvement in the same way. Your role is rather to give them encouragement to take part in various activities. They may want your help with transport to matches or other events, and financial assistance to buy equipment. By providing help of this kind you are also giving support.

Intensive training

In some cases, where adolescents are very talented, there may be a risk that a parent over-identifies with a son or daughter, and puts too much pressure on them to train, until it reaches the point where there is no more pleasure in the sport. Parents whose adolescents are talented athletes should be aware of the risk of stress for the teenager, and for themselves, if training demands a great deal in terms of time and resources. The situation may need to be reassessed if a youngster is spending all his or her time in training, going to school and doing homework, and is isolated from ordinary social activities, or if one parent is under some strain, spending long hours driving their adolescent to training facilities, waiting around, perhaps getting up very early each morning.

Girls and sport

Girls and young women do not take part in sporting activities to the same extent as boys and young men. The reasons for this are connected with women's gender identity (see pages 53–5) in our society. Yet over recent years women have improved their performance in competitive sport to an extent which would have been incredible a few decades ago. In many sports the records men set at the beginning of the century are constantly surpassed by women athletes.

There is only a short tradition of girls taking part in competitive sports at an international level. Show jumping, for example, has not long been open to women in the Olympics. And women's sporting events do not raise the same interest as occasions like the Football Association Cup, where the players are all men. In the community girls and women are less likely to meet members of their own sex who take part in sport than men who do so. Local sports centres may not make a particular effort to help women to feel at home; activities, posters and advertising may be more directed at men than at women, and the atmosphere at the centres may be 'male' rather than inviting for everyone. It is also difficult for women to participate in sporting activities because of their responsibility for looking after children and housekeeping as well as, in many cases, going out to work. This would explain why young women do not have many role models to encourage them to see sport in a positive way. On the contrary, for a girl to be good at sport may be viewed as suspiciously masculine.

It may also be more difficult for girls to exhibit the open self-assertion that is necessary in competitive games. There is much in girls' upbringing which leads them to back off, rather than to go for success. Taking part in sport may also make it more difficult to maintain, for the duration of the game at least, a well-groomed, 'attractive' appearance, of the 'ideal' sort which is constantly put before women by the media and which girls often try to emulate. Healthy sweat and hair in disarray may be a real disincentive for some youngsters. So girls need more encouragement and support than boys if they are to take part in activities which they will carry into adult life and which will promote their health. In some places educational authorities are aware of the inequalities faced by women in the field of sport, and schools and the local youth service are trying to meet the needs of adolescent girls in this respect. Some of these opportunities are described below.

School physical education

The school can make a big contribution towards introducing adolescents to a life-long enjoyment of healthy physical activity.

Some questions involving exercise which you may want to ask when you are choosing a secondary school for your son or daughter include:

- Does the school include awareness of the value of exercise in its curriculum – whether in health education or in some other subject?
- Is the emphasis, in physical education, on competitive team games or is there also plenty of opportunity for youngsters to try out a variety of individual and pair activities? Research has shown that young people do not necessarily confine themselves to one sort of activity for months at a time.[12] They like to try many different sports, given the opportunity. In this way they find out what is on offer and what they enjoy.
- What are the links between the school and local sports centres and clubs? Are there visits to local centres so that young people, boys and girls, find out what is available locally and feel more confident to use them in their spare time, and to carry on using them when they leave school?
- What is the policy towards girls? Are there mixed PE classes, as well as a variety of 'girls only' games?
- Are school sports facilities open to the community – including teenagers – outside school hours? (Eighty per cent of secondary schools are available for sport and recreation out of school hours, but usually only in term-time and for limited periods.[13])

These are questions which can also be raised with school governors (see pages 200–1). The PE staff will inform you of opportunities for sport that are open to your teenager, both at school and locally.

Youth service

Sporting facilities and classes are also available through the local youth service (see pages 284–6), with some offering coaching in certain sports during the school holidays. If you have an adolescent daughter you could make enquires about local policy for girls and sport. What special opportunities are there, not just for talented athletes but for the enjoyment of all girls? Are sports centres equally inviting to boys and girls?

What sporting activities are available?

Different forms of exercise and movement promote different aspects of fitness:

- *Suppleness* People who are supple can bend and stretch, twist and turn. Being unsupple means stiffening up.
- *Strength* People with strength can push, pull and lift without straining themselves.
- *Stamina* People with stamina can keep on the go, running, walking, dancing, without getting out of breath. Stamina is developed in 'aerobic' activities – energetic dancing, walking and games which need sustained effort and which use the large muscle groups in a repeated, unstrained manner. Activities which develop stamina protect people against heart disease.

Team sports

Most team games are very good for developing stamina and strength, and are good for suppleness too. For teenage boys who so wish, including school-leavers, there should be no difficulty in getting involved in a club or team where 'mainstream' team sports are involved – football, rugby, cricket, hockey.

There are certain to be local clubs only too eager to accept a young, enthusiastic, and possibly skilled player. A visit to your local leisure centre, or YMCA, should provide information. If there is neither in your area, information should be available at your public library or even at the editorial offices of your local newspaper (it will, after all, be covering local sporting events). Failing this, it is always possible for the dedicated enthusiast to start his or her own team.

An advantage of 'mainstream' team sports is their relative cheapness. You will probably find that appropriate footwear is the most expensive item. In the case of cricket or hockey it may be necessary or desirable for the player to provide his or her own kit – protective clothing, and bat or stick. However, you may find that your local club or team is prepared to provide all or part of it.

One clear disadvantage of 'mainstream' team sports is that they are largely seasonal. But the cricket enthusiast may be lucky enough to join one of the two thousand clubs up and down the country which have facilities for indoor net practice and even indoor matches, while the only requirement for informal all-the-year-round football is a group of people willing to play, and a ball. Even so, it is a good idea for adolescents to participate in more than one sport – for example, cricket in the summer and indoor swimming in the winter, or tennis for the summer and football for the winter. The latter arrangement has the advantage of combining a team sport with an individual or pair sport.

There are, of course, many other team sports which involve the player, or his or her parents, in no great expense, and some of these are listed below. Should you find it difficult to locate your nearest club or team, the best thing is to write to the national association for information (see pages 293–4 for addresses):

Baseball a minority sport in the UK, but an increasingly popular one.

Basketball a local YMCA will certainly have the information you require; the game was, after all, invented by and for the YMCA.

Handball perhaps the simplest to learn of all team sports, yet the second fastest (ice-hockey is the fastest).

Netball still regarded primarily as a sport for women.

Volleyball there are four versions of the game and size of teams can vary according to requirements (the Olympic game is six versus six). It may be played indoors and outdoors.

Water-polo bears no resemblance to polo, and has been more accurately described as 'football in the water'. It needs both strength and stamina.

There are other team sports in which opportunity of joining may be limited by location and expense.

Ice-hockey until recently a male preserve but now open to both sexes. As with water-polo, strength and stamina are essential requirements. Some clubs assist with the protective clothing required, but helmets, face-shields, gloves and padding are needed, in addition to skates, and would-be players will find more often than not that they must supply their own.

Rowing an ideal sport for building up and maintaining stamina and endurance, and one available to disabled people.

Sailing there are, of course, many varieties of sailing, some of which – such as windsurfing (board-sailing) – are relatively cheap. It can be wholly non-competitive, as with sailing barges on the old canal systems or cruising on the Norfolk Broads, or even rowing on a lake in the local park. Where racing is involved, however, skills must be acquired and practised, and the expense of mooring a boat, let alone acquiring one (or even a share in one), is likely to prove considerable.

Pair sports

These have the obvious advantage that the player only needs to find one other person with whom to play and, as time goes on, age will prove no bar to enjoyment. Most of the popular pair sports can be played during all seasons of the year, and are inexpensive.

The probability is that the teenage or school-leaver enthusiast already knows of potential opponents and venues for playing. If not, enquiries may be made to the same sources of information as for team sports, and failing them, the national associations will be able to help (see pages 293–4 for addresses).

Badminton a very fast game. Although the shuttle can float gently in the air, it can also reach 200 mph when struck properly. It requires lightning reflexes and staying power.

Fencing the three types of weapon used – foil, épée, and sabre – each require a particular skill, but all lead to an improvement in speed, reflexes, co-ordination, balance, concentration and general fitness. Clubs will initially provide protective clothing, masks, and weapons, but serious participants will eventually be expected, and indeed would wish, to provide their own, and this could prove expensive.

Lawn tennis because of the provision of courts in public parks and gardens, lawn tennis is accessible to anyone who can afford a racquet. It is an all-the-year-round game which can be played indoors as well as out, on hard courts as well as grass.

Squash one of the fastest-growing sports of the present time, it has grown during the past twenty years from a minority sport to one played regularly by over 3 million men and women.

Table tennis probably the most accessible and inexpensive of all pair sports. Facilities are easy to find in most places.

Individual sports

These may be competitive or just for pleasure, setting one's own standards or trying to improve them.

Archery the most familiar and popular form is target archery. It stimulates (and calls for) muscular strength, poise, and concentration. It is particularly suited to certain types of disablement, and many clubs now actively encourage membership by the disabled. It is, unavoidably, a rather expensive sport: the equipment required, arrows and quiver, bracer and tab, and above all the bow, have become a great deal more sophisticated than their historical counterparts.

Athletics a multi-faceted sport with running, jumping, and throwing as its basic elements. It is necessary to join a club, both to obtain the variety of equipment which is needed and, of course, to find competition.

Canoeing a popular sport and one which is relatively straightforward to take up, simply by buying a canoe of the kayak, general-purpose recreational variety, and finding some water in which to use it. For the sake of safety, canoeists must also be swimmers and it is essential for youngsters to receive skilled instruction and to be supervised when they first start to canoe.

Cross-country running essentially a winter sport and an excellent means of keeping fit when bad weather precludes other outdoor exercise.

Cycling can be enjoyed by all ages separately or together. It is simple, cheap, can be purely recreational, or – as with road- or track-racing, touring or speedway – intensely competitive.

Exercise movement and dance classes are widely available in sports and leisure centres, and community centres. There are also many private dance schools and health and fitness centres. Information on these, as well as on **yoga** classes should be readily available from your public library or your local authority's leisure and recreation department.

Golf has the advantage of being able to be enjoyed by all ages while the system of handicapping allows a young or inexperienced player to compete against a highly skilled and experienced veteran. The need to belong to a club and to acquire the necessary equipment, however, does make it one of the most expensive among popular sports.

Gymnastics a very demanding if immensely popular sport, it requires a high level of agility, strength, and physical fitness, and shoul always be practised under supervision in properly equipped spor centres.

Horse-riding can be enjoyed both recreationally and as a spor Horse-riding purely for recreation needs protective clothing whic can be hired, as can a mount. Competitive riding demands that th competitor owns (or has a part share in) his or her mount, and bot the purchase and stabling of a horse or pony is relatively expensive

Riding is recognised as an activity for people with physical an mental disability, and there is a Riding for the Disabled Associatio which you can contact either through the British Equestrian Cent or the British Sports Association for the Disabled (see page 294 fc addresses).

Ice-skating an excellent way of keeping fit as well as one of th most sociable forms of individual sport. As rinks are indoors, it is a all-the-year-round activity. Virtually all rinks have skates for hire, s there is little expense involved, and you will be able to obtai information there regarding coaching in your locality, should yo require it.

Skiing a sport that can be taken up for pleasure or competitivel Learning to ski is no longer reserved for winter holidays. There ar plenty of opportunities all over the country for learning the basi techniques on artificial slopes. In summer, grass-skiing, with speci roller skis, is an excellent way to practise.

For mountain skiing, proper training, protective clothing and equip ment are essential and there should always be responsible adu supervision for young people.

Swimming an excellent way to achieve and maintain overall fitnes and to strengthen a wide range of muscles. Facilities are widel available, and the expense minimal. Your local swimming-pool shoul provide all the information about coaching that you require. It particularly suited to youngsters with certain physical disabilities an your local swimming-pool or public library should be able to provid you with the necessary information about suitable activities.

Sports for disabled people

Many sports, apart from those mentioned specifically above, are ope to disabled adolescents. Many sports organisations welcome peop with disabilities and provide coaching facilities. Some offer speci arrangements to facilitate participation, for example, the governin associations in angling, archery, basketball, bowls, camping, fencing, golf, judo, movement and dance, riding, sailing, swimming, tennis, and water sports. Local authorities or the British Sports Association for the Disabled (see page 294 for address) should be able to provide the necessary information.

Hygiene and skin care

The physical changes of adolescence bring with them new concerns about personal cleanliness. Shaving (see page 17) and coping with periods (see page 12) are two of these. Hormonal changes also affect the skin and hair, which become greasier. Sweat glands are more active, especially on the feet, under the arms and around the genitals.

Teenagers are obviously of an age to manage their own hygiene needs with little support from you. They may need to be reminded, sometimes, about changing their clothes and not letting dirty clothes pile up in their bedroom. Some may find that life is so interesting that they do not seem to have time to bath or wash regularly. If this is the case, then let them know that they have BO as directly as you can without hurting their feelings (see pages 187–90). They also need toilet items which they did not need before – razors and sanitary towels are obvious examples. You could increase their pocket money to cover such necessities (see page 254) or have a family supply always available.

Keeping clean

A daily bath, shower or an all-over wash is the best way for an adolescent to keep clean and sweet-smelling, especially after taking vigorous exercise. They also need to have a ready supply of clean clothes so that they can change pants, shirts, socks and tights every day. Some of them still need reminding about this and about elementary hygiene, like washing their hands after they have been to the toilet, or before eating, while others are almost fanatical about washing.

Antiperspirants and deodorants

If your son or daughter is self-conscious about sweating and having wet patches under the arms, then an antiperspirant or deodorant can be used.

Deodorants should not be used in the genital area, whatever advertisements suggest, because they could irritate delicate skin.

Hair care

Because the pores on the scalp, as well as elsewhere, produce more oil in adolescence, hair can become greasier than in childhood. Dirt clings to greasy hair so it needs frequent washing, remembering, however, that washing it each day may be counter-productive because this may actually stimulate the oil glands and make the hair still greasier. If your adolescent feels that daily hair-washing is necessary, then he or she should use a really mild shampoo.

Shampooing also gets rid of dry skin from the scalp, which falls away in scales as dandruff. It is sometimes necessary to use a medicated shampoo to control heavy dandruff and, if this does not work, obtain a prescription from the family doctor for a more effective remedy.

Lice

Like children, adolescents sometimes catch head lice. This is not a sign that they do not wash enough or that they come from a dirty home. They have just been in close contact with someone who is already infected and the louse has walked from one head of hair to another. The first sign of infection is irritation and scratching because the louse has been feeding on the scalp, biting and sucking blood. It has also been laying eggs, or nits, at the rate of sixty a month, attaching each egg firmly to a hair.

Ordinary shampooing will not kill the nits; a special lotion is needed from the chemist. This is applied to the hair and left to dry naturally; it can then be shampooed out. A second application may be necessary.

Skin care

Acne

Acne is so closely associated with the teenage years that having spots is included in most people's stereotype of an adolescent. A few lucky youngsters escape but between the ages of thirteen and twenty-five the majority suffer from acne at some time, whether mildly or more severely. Many teenagers have just a few spots, mostly on the face, but sometimes inflamed areas of skin appear on the chest and shoulders and, in severe cases, elsewhere on the body. Acne occurs on the areas of skin where the sebaceous glands – the oil-producing glands – are larger and where hair is fine.

The trouble starts in a hair follicle, the pore in which a hair grows. Each follicle is lined with the tough, but very fine, horny outer layer which covers all the skin. This outer layer can form a plug – a blackhead – which blocks the pore. The blackheads are not dirt; the dark colour is due to the natural pigment of the skin.

If the pore is blocked, its contents – the sebum, bacteria and outer skin cells – build up and spill into the surrounding skin which becomes inflamed and raised. This is an acne spot, which in some cases can be tender and painful.

What causes acne?[14] It is not yet known why some young people suffer from acne and others do not, but these are some of the factors associated with it:

- Acne sufferers have greasy skins (but not everyone who has a greasy skin develops acne).
- The 'male' hormone testosterone plays a part. This is produced by both boys and girls (see page 7) and its increase in adolescence is linked to an increase in the oil sebum produced by the skin.
- The harmless bacteria which are present on everyone's skin are also involved. In acne their numbers increase.

What can be done about acne? Acne can be a great nuisance, not least because youngsters feel very self-conscious about it. There is no quick and easy answer for acne sufferers but there are treatments which help, and things to do and others to avoid so as not to make matters worse.

Some effective lotions and creams are obtainable from the chemist but they may make the skin feel rather sore. Treatment can take some weeks to work, so teenagers need to be patient. If, after two months, there is no improvement, and the condition is distressing, or if the treatment actually seems to be making it worse, they should go to the doctor for help. The doctor may be able to prescribe lotions and antibiotics which are more effective. Treatment obtained early on can reduce the risk of scarring, although the scars are usually insignificant and tend to improve with time.

Self-help

- *Sun* Teenagers should get out into the sunshine whenever possible as this seems to have a beneficial effect. They should use an oil-free high-protection sun cream or lotion. (Sun lamps should not be used without a doctor's advice.)
- *Clothing* Youngsters who are prone to acne should avoid heavy, tight clothes and clothing made of irritating materials. Greasy work clothes can make matters worse, as can close-fitting hats and helmets. In general, clothing which makes young people hot and sweaty is to be avoided.
- *Environment* A steamy, greasy environment can exacerbate acne, as can work which involves getting the hands greasy. Teenagers with bad acne should think about this when they choose a job or if they take on part-time work at weekends; working as a mechanic or in a restaurant kitchen is to be avoided.
- *Washing* There is no need for adolescents with acne, or blackheads, to wash more than usual: too much washing can make sensitive skin

sore. If the skin is sore, use a mild soap, rinse well and pat dry.

Washing with an anti-bacterial, detergent-type lotion may help mild acne.

- *Cosmetics* If teenagers want to use cosmetics they should use light, non-greasy products; the same applies to night creams and hair oils which, if they are greasy, can make spots worse. If any cream or cosmetic has a bad effect, then teenagers should try something else.
- *Camouflage* Some treatment creams are coloured to camouflage spots and inflammation and are available for people of different skin colours. Some of these have to be bought on prescription and others can be obtained from the chemist without a prescription.
- *Hair* Hair which falls over the forehead may cause spots in this area.
- *Shaving* Boys need to avoid affected areas when they are shaving. They can let the beard grow or cut it back (carefully!) with scissors. An electric razor may be kinder than wet shaving.
- *Picking spots* can cause bleeding and infection.

Living with acne Some adolescents can take a few spots in their stride, but for others, especially in severe cases, acne can make life a misery. Although, as a parent, you realise they will eventually grow out of acne, that the spots will erupt more rarely and will have disappeared by the time they reach their mid-twenties, this is small comfort for a self-conscious youngster. Perhaps the most useful advice you can give, if they are really depressed and worried, is that they should go to the family doctor to get a more effective treatment.

It is also important to give your adolescent encouragement and to help them over the bad times. If necessary, or if they are being teased about it, reassure them that acne is not infectious and that their friends are not going to catch it from them. Listen to them (see page 38) and let them know you understand how they are feeling. Do not blame it on their diet, or on not washing, or nag them about picking their spots. If they feel – irrationally – guilty about their acne, nagging will only make them feel worse. Encourage them to enjoy themselves, to see their friends and to take part in interesting activities – not to hide themselves away, bored and depressed, at home.

Ear-piercing

If your son or daughter wants to have their ears pierced and asks for your advice about it, the following should be borne in mind:

Where to have ears pierced

Ear-piercing should be done professionally and by a reputable practitioner. Your adolescent could ask friends if they have had their ears pierced, where they had it done, if it was painful and if there were any problems afterwards. A large department store, a well-known jeweller or a registered beautician may be a good choice. High standards of hygiene and sterilised equipment are essential.

Type of earring The earring worn immediately after piercing should be made of gold. Non-precious metals can lead to allergic reactions. Even silver, which may contain some nickel, can cause contact dermatitis.

Small gold hoops are easier to keep clean than the stud type of earring. After the ear has been pierced, the wound 'weeps' and sediment can built up in the hole around the earring, but hoops can be turned around in the hole and properly cleaned without being removed from the ear.

Later, when the ear has healed, it is better to keep to gold earrings for ordinary use because of the risk of reactions. If an adolescent wants to wear a non-gold earring sometimes, it should not be kept in for longer than about six hours.

Large, heavy earrings should be avoided for everyday use because wearing them frequently, or for long periods, can stretch the hole. There is also the risk of damage to the ear lobe if they are accidentally pulled during games.

Hygiene After ear-piercing and until the lobe is healed, the ring and the ear lobe should be cleaned twice a day with surgical spirit, dabbed on with clean cotton wool. The earring should subsequently be removed and cleaned every five days.

Possible problems

■ *Soreness and infection* There is always some soreness after ear-piercing but this should get progressively better until the lobe is completely healed. If the ear does not seem to be healing, or if it is becoming infected, the family doctor can give advice.

After the initial healing there are sometimes allergic reactions and rashes, particularly if non-gold earrings are worn. If this happens, the adolescent should return to gold earrings and keep both lobe and ring clean with surgical spirit.

If there is any swelling while the wound is still healing, the 'butterfly' that holds a stud in place may become embedded in the lobe and an abscess can form. Should this happen or if you, or your son or daughter, are worried about any soreness, rash or swelling, consult your family doctor.

■ *Scarring* Afro-Caribbean people are at greater risk of developing scar tissue after ear-piercing than other ethnic groups. Young people with an Afro-Caribbean background should be made aware of this risk if they are of an age to make up their own mind about ear-piercing and want to have it done.

Tattooing

Tattooing anyone under the age of eighteen is an offence under the Tattooing of Minors Act 1969. Tattooing can obviously cause problems in that a tattoo can be difficult to remove or disguise, and a message or design that pleases a fourteen-year-old may be a source of great embarrassment in later life. Tattooing which is not carried out under hygienic conditions carries the risk of infection.

Foot care

Toenails should be cut straight across to avoid them ingrowing.

Sweaty feet

If your adolescent has a sweaty foot problem, they should be advised to wear socks made from natural fibres like cotton or wool, or mixtures that contain these, and change them daily, more often if necessary. Socks made of artificial fibres, like acrylic and nylon, are not absorbent and so the feet get sweatier. Encourage teenagers to wear sandals and go without socks in warm weather.

After washing their feet, adolescents should make sure to dry carefully between the toes. Warm, soggy skin is a perfect environment to encourage infections like athlete's foot and verrucae. Young people can be especially prone to these if they use communal changing rooms where foot infections are easily picked up.

Athlete's foot

Athlete's foot is the name given to a fungus infection which usually occurs between the toes or under the arch of the foot, causing a rash or flaking and peeling. It can be very irritating. If careful drying between the toes does not solve the problem, there are a number of foot powders and creams which your chemist will recommend. If these are not effective, a young person should consult the doctor or make an appointment to see a state registered chiropodist (see page 295 for addresses).

Athlete's foot can easily recur, but the chance is lessened if adolescents do not walk about barefoot in changing rooms and around public swimming-pools, and keep their feet clean and dry.

Verrucae

This is another name for warts which infect the feet. Like other warts, they are caused by a virus and they are very contagious. They can be painful if they press against the shoe, but are easily removed by the doctor. Someone who has a verruca should not go barefoot because of passing the infection on to someone else.

Choice of shoes At the time when adolescents grow most quickly they soon outgrow their shoes. There should be half an inch (1 cm) space between the end of the shoe and their longest toe, and the shoe should be wide enough to allow the toes to wriggle. Because ill-fitting shoes squash the growing bones, leading to bunions and foot trouble in later life, teenagers frequently need money for new shoes. Socks which shrink also constrict the foot and these need to be replaced.

Fashionable shoes cause no harm so long as they fit properly and do not have very high heels. High heels throw the weight forward on to the toes and also put strain on the spine.

Eye care

Because adolescence is a period of rapid growth, it is also a likely time for the onset of short-sightedness (*myopia*), and the chances of this will be greater where there is short sight in the family. Myopia classically sets in between the ages of thirteen and fifteen.

In myopic adolescents the length of the eye – that is, the distance between the *cornea* and the *retina* – increases, but the lens does not lengthen proportionately. So, while reading and writing cause no problems, a short-sighted adolescent is no longer able to focus on objects in the middle and far distance.

There are many reasons why myopia, if it is not corrected by using glasses or contact lenses, is a nuisance, or worse. First of all, a short-sighted adolescent cannot appreciate the world to the same extent as someone with good sight. Details, such as the leaves on trees, are lost, many sports become impossible and friends may not be recognised in the street. Riding a bicycle is hazardous and, by the time a young person is old enough to learn to drive, uncorrected short sight is a disqualification. In school, uncorrected short sight is a serious handicap to progress at a time when adolescents should not be held back. At secondary level teachers use the board, large maps and diagrams more frequently than at the primary stage and short-sighted youngsters can miss important details displayed in this way without being aware of it.

Eye tests Short-sightedness does not come on overnight; the person concerned hardly knows it is happening and the problems it is causing. The everyday lives of some teenagers provide natural eye tests when they try to read bus numbers or station indication boards and realise that they are now having problems. Others do not have these naturally occurring tests, so if there is a history of short sight in the family then teenagers should have their eyes routinely tested. It is also worthwhile to have eyes checked in the event of an adolescent's performance at school falling off for no apparent reason. (For details of the provisions of the National Health Service for young people, see page 147.)

Glasses or contact lenses?

Once an adolescent is responsible enough to look after contact lenses properly, the question of whether to have glasses or lenses is purely a matter of choice.

Glasses These may be preferred by some teenagers. Within the National Health Service, and commercially, teenagers can choose the sort of frame that pleases them most, in a variety of colours and styles. Fine, strong metal frames have the advantage of giving a clearer field of vision than heavier frames because they do not cause blind spots and youngsters prefer these for sports.

Adolescents should have their sight checked regularly to be sure that the prescription is still appropriate. Those who need glasses should wear them every day, and clean them every day, to obtain full benefit from them. Parents need not be afraid that wearing glasses all the time will in any way weaken the sight; this is not so.

Contact lenses These are small plastic lenses that float on the surface of the eye and correct vision in the same way that glasses do. There are lenses which are suitable for most types of sight defect. There has been great development in contact lenses in recent years and the original hard plastic lenses are hardly ever used now. For most people, getting used to the newer, soft lenses presents no problem; in fact they are soon unaware that they are wearing them.

Contact lenses can be worn all the time, including for sport, although they have to be removed for cleaning. Some types can also be worn during sleep.

Youngsters have to be responsible enough to take care of their contact lenses as instructed; they have to clean them, store them in the container provided and wash their hands before putting them in or taking them out. They should also go for regular check-ups according to the optician's advice.

Contact lenses have two great advantages over glasses: they give a clear field of vision at all times and they are virtually undetectable in wear. Although they are suitable for most youngsters there are some medical conditions, including diabetes, which make the eye too sensitive to cope with them comfortably.

The biggest disadvantage of contact lenses is that they are more expensive than glasses, although National Health vouchers may be used to cover part of the cost (see page 147). Find out what they are going to cost before the prescription is made up and check up on insurance schemes which are available in case of loss or damage.

Soft lenses can scratch, so they need replacing about every one or two years.

Care of teeth

Good teeth make their own contribution to well-being. Teenagers can be self-conscious enough without having to worry about unsightly teeth or about the possibility of bad breath. Teeth which are not looked after can result in agonising toothache and abscesses. If they are neglected, sooner or later they may have to be removed and false teeth fitted. No one wants to have to confess to dentures, especially a young person who is romantically involved.

By educating your adolescent to take responsibility for their own dental care, and with the help of the dentist, teeth can be preserved into old age. National Health dental treatment is free for people under the age of sixteen or in full-time education. A list of NHS dentists is available at the post office, the public library or from the family practitioner committee (the address is in the local phone book).

Dental disease

Dental decay Very few teenagers escape dental decay. Surveys show that by the age of fifteen, 97 per cent of young people have had some caries (cavities).[15] The rot sets in, literally, when sugar comes into contact with plaque – a film which adheres to the teeth and contains bacteria and which we all have. When sugar enters the mouth, these bacteria produce acid which softens the enamel surface of the tooth. To some extent this acid is washed away naturally with saliva or neutralised by other foods eaten at meal-times. But if sugary foods and drinks are taken frequently, especially between meals, then the acid has more chance to eat into the tooth. In time a cavity appears.

The most important weapon against this acid attack is fluoride, which strengthens children's and adolescents' teeth as they are formed. If the water supply in your area contains a low level of fluoride, the dentist may prescribe a flouride supplement (see page 141). The fluoride in toothpaste also plays a useful part in making the softened tooth surface strong again.

Unfortunately, brushing the teeth will not prevent decay – this is only possible by avoiding food and drinks which contain added sugar, especially between meals – although the fluoride in toothpaste and drinking water will help to minimise it. There are places in the mouth which the toothbrush cannot reach – fissures on the surface of the tooth which bristles do not penetrate and tight spaces between the teeth. This does not mean that teenagers should give up tooth-brushing! Brushing their teeth will prevent gum disease which is just as serious as decay.

Gum disease (periodontal disease) Plaque is also the main cause of gum disease. If it is allowed to build up at the base of the teeth where they meet the gums, the gums become red and puffy and bleed when teeth are brushed. The plaque accumulates in the narrow crevice where the tooth meets the gum, forming a pocket. This is called gingivitis and it often starts in childhood. Unless it is treated it progresses down into the bone and the fibres which support the tooth, leading to a condition called periodontitis. This causes the tooth to loosen, abscesses may form and teeth may need to be removed.

To prevent gum disease, adolescents should keep plaque down to a minimum. This can be done by thorough brushing of teeth at least once a day and by having plaque removed regularly by the dentist.

To cure gum disease while it is in its early stages, thorough, gentle tooth-brushing helps. This should include brushing the gums where they meet the teeth. There may be some bleeding at first but this stops after a few days' brushing. In the later stages of gum disease a dentist may be able to save the teeth, but with regular check-ups and treatment this should not be necessary.

To sum up, dental science is now advanced enough to give sound advice about how teeth can be preserved:

- Avoid foods and drinks containing sugar especially between meals.
- Clean teeth properly every day.
- Use a fluoride toothpaste.
- Have regular check-ups and treatment.

Any young person who follows this advice will have sound teeth and a pleasant smile. They will not be numbered among the 30 per cent of the population (39 per cent in Scotland) who have had all their teeth extracted.

The fact that the incidence of dental disease is declining in developed countries is partly due to the introduction of fluoride into water supplies and toothpaste. This is encouraging but still people are suffering unnecessarily. One of the problems is that when young-sters leave school they do not have regular check-ups as they did during school years, when appointments are arranged by their parents or through the school dental service. So it is important for parents to help teenagers to get into the habit of booking their own dental appointments and understanding why they are essential.

Fluoride in drinking water

There is a great advantage if you live in an area which has a high enough level of fluoride in the water – whether this is natural or added locally. Water supplies in certain parts of the country have been fluoridated since 1945 with no harmful effects. In Britain 5½ million people drink fluoridated water and major cities like London, New York and Moscow all have fluoridated water. Studies have shown that when fluoride is introduced it can cut the level of tooth decay in the local community by anything from 40–70 per cent.[16] If your water supply is not fluoridated your dentist will be able to advise if it is necessary for your son or daughter to take a fluoride supplement.

What can parents do to help preserve adolescents' teeth?

Avoid sugar Keep sugar in the family diet to a minimum. It is sugar which causes tooth decay.

Buy suitable tooth brushes Until teenagers start to look after themselves parents need to buy their toothbrushes for them. A new toothbrush is needed as soon as the bristles of the old one start to splay out – after a surprisingly short time if the brush is used properly.

The head of the toothbrush should be small enough to get round the mouth and into nooks and crannies easily. A toothbrush with nylon tufts is best; these should be soft to medium – not hard – and packed close together.

Buy fluoride toothpaste Buy fluoride toothpaste for the family. Most, but not all, toothpastes contain fluoride nowadays.

Arrange check-ups Make appointments for regular six-monthly check-ups – or encourage teenagers to make their own when you think they are ready to start doing so. You may need to remind them, or even to make occasional appointments for them when you make your own, but the aim is to help them to take on responsibility for their own health needs as a matter of course.

What can adolescents do to preserve their teeth?

Avoid sugar Teenagers should remember that tooth decay is caused by eating foods containing sugar. To keep their teeth healthy they should therefore cut down on foods and drinks containing added sugar, especially between meals. They should choose snacks with no added sugar – like nuts and drinks with permitted artificial sweeteners.

Clean their teeth every day Young people should clean their teeth regularly and thoroughly with fluoride toothpaste.

- Brushing helps to remove the plaque which causes gum disease. Gum disease leads to tooth loss; brushing prevents it.
- When people have eaten food or drink containing sugar, the bacteria in plaque feed off the sugar and break it down into acid which softens the tooth. Fluoride toughens up the surface of the tooth when plaque has moved in on the attack.

How to brush teeth Teeth need a thorough daily brushing. Some people give their teeth a quick brush two or three times a day because it feels fresh. This is well and good so long as teeth are brushed really well – for about three minutes – at least once a day.

- Place the brush next to the edge of the tooth where it meets the gum. Use very short, horizontal movements which dislodge plaque from the area adjacent to the gum and between the teeth.
- Apply gentle pressure and clean all the surfaces in turn – both on the inside and on the outside.

Adolescents may find disclosing tablets helpful and intriguing. When sucked, these tablets colour any plaque on the teeth and show which teeth need more attention than others. This can lead to more efficient brushing. You can buy disclosing tablets at the chemist.

Check-ups As they grow up, teenagers should start to make their own appointments for six-monthly check-ups, to have plaque removed and for any necessary treatment.

What can the dentist do for adolescents' teeth?

Good dentists do much more than fill teeth and take them out. They also want to promote dental health and there is much that they and the dental hygienist (employed in some dental practices to carry out non-surgical work) can do:

- *Give advice about diet* They can explain the importance of avoiding food and drink containing sugar, especially between meals, for dental health.
- *Advise about keeping teeth clean* They can give advice about how to brush teeth properly and how to use dental floss or tooth picks, if necessary, to clean between the teeth. They can show your son or daughter how to use disclosing tablets (see above).
- *Remove plaque* Even though your son or daughter clean their teeth every day they should also have them cleaned regularly by the dentist. This is one of the reasons why it is important to have regular check-ups.
- *Seal fissures* The biting surfaces of the back teeth are not smooth;

they have grooves or fissures which are difficult to clean. Your dentist can seal fissures with a plastic coating, before any decay sets in, and it can be renewed as required. (This is not available under the NHS.)

- *Give fluoride treatment* Sometimes, especially in parts of the country where water has a low level of fluoride, dentists apply fluoride directly to the surface of the teeth.

You, or your son or daughter, can ask the dentist about any of these services.

Dental treatment

If your dentist finds tooth decay, treatment depends on how extensive this is. Regular check-ups mean that cavities can be detected and filled at an early stage, before there is too much damage. If necessary an injection can be given – and the gum itself can be made numb by dabbing on a special liquid before the injection.

The dentist can also treat gum disease.

Extraction is a last resort when a tooth cannot be saved.

Orthodontics Some adolescents have crooked or protruding teeth which can be a problem for the obvious reason that adolescents can be very self-conscious about their appearance. In addition teeth may be difficult to clean if they are packed close together or crossed and, because of this, they can be more prone to gum disease and decay. If teeth protrude, there is the danger that they are more easily broken in a fall.

Crooked or protruding teeth may need to be straightened by orthodontic treatment.[17] Your dentist will advise if this is necessary, and, if so, whether they will carry out the treatment themselves or if your adolescent should be referred to an orthodonist.

Orthodontic treatment is usually carried out between the ages of eleven and thirteen, while mouths are still growing. Sometimes a dentist may decide to wait a little longer, until more of the second teeth have come through.

The dentist may decide to remove some teeth, to make more room for the rest, and will then fit a brace. Where the problem is slight this will be made of plastic and can be removed every day for cleaning. In more serious cases, a brace made of stainless steel is fixed in position until the treatment is finished. The brace is attached to the teeth which it gradually draws into a better position.

Dentists need to be sure that your son or daughter will co-operate with the treatment by wearing whatever braces are necessary and by being especially careful about cleaning both the braces and their teeth. It is easy for plaque to build up around orthodontic braces.

The treatment can take from a few months to about two years. In older adolescence and for adults the treatment takes longer than it does while the mouth is still growing. So this is one good reason why it is better to have teeth straightened as soon as possible.

Good motivation is needed for young people to persevere with orthodontic treatment; they should really *want* to have their teeth straightened and be ready to follow the dentist's instructions. Sometimes they may feel self-conscious about wearing braces but you can help by encouraging them to look forward to the time when they will no longer need them and by praising them for being sensible.

Cosmetic treatment There have been great advances in what can be done to improve the appearance of teeth. While silver amalgam is the strongest material for filling the biting surfaces of back teeth, front cavities can be filled with resins mixed with minute particles of glass or ceramic. These are much more natural-looking than the white fillings of the past.

It is also possible to bond veneers to the teeth to cover chips or discoloration. This treatment is quite painless and can last for four or five years.

If, because of an accident, your son or daughter has the bad luck to break a tooth, a long-lasting porcelain crown can be fitted over the tooth, after the enamel has been drilled away.

Your dentist will be able to advise about the most appropriate treatment to make teeth look good. You need to check, however, if the treatment is available on the NHS or if you must pay for it privately.

Dental phobia

Being somewhat nervous about visiting the dentist is not uncommon but it is something that people usually come to terms with in order to have their teeth looked after. A deep-seated fear of the dentist, on the other hand, can mean that the dentist is avoided and teeth not properly cared for. Unfortunately dentists suffer from an image which owes more to the barbarities of nineteenth-century practice than to modern, pain-free dentistry, and this, in part, accounts for the irrational fear or phobia that some young people (and some adults) experience.

Sometimes all that a scared teenager needs is for you to sit down and listen to their fears, to reassure them and to point out the advantages of regular check-ups and treatment. But in cases where this approach is not successful, or when young people are persuaded to go to the dentist, only to refuse treatment when they get there, other steps must be taken.

What can parents do when adolescents are afraid of the dentist? It is important to understand that their feelings of fear and anxiety are real and physical, that they are experiencing the stress of 'fight or flight' symptoms (see page 177), keyed up to escape or to ward off danger, although neither is appropriate. Give them an opportunity to talk about their feelings (see pages 38–43), tell them you understand what they are feeling and reflect back something of it. For example, you could say, 'When you think about going to the dentist you feel quite panicky.'

Find out if they really want to have treatment even though they are afraid. Wanting to have treatment is a key factor in overcoming dental phobia. Young people who are strongly motivated can, with help, get over their anxiety and, in the end, it is a teenager's own responsibility to look after this aspect of their health. The following are good reasons for having regular check-ups and treatment and ones which may seem relevant to a young person:

- bad teeth spoil your appearance;
- bad teeth cause bad breath;
- crooked or protruding teeth also spoil your appearance.

Other reasons – like eventually needing dentures or bridgework – may seem less immediate, although without treatment they are real possibilities.

Practical steps If teenagers decide for themselves that they want to get over their dental phobia, there is a lot that can be done.

1 Persuade them to talk to their friends to find out the name of an understanding dentist. (Even talking about the dentist is a helpful first step in coming to terms with fears.)
2 Make an appointment for a check-up, or perhaps just a consultation to begin with. (Consultations, unlike check-ups, are not free for young people under the National Health Service.)
3 Make sure your dentist knows if your adolescent is very afraid. A sympathetic dentist will respond positively to this and help them to relax, explain what is happening, taking care not to hurt but also warning them if anything is likely to be at all uncomfortable.

Psychological techniques If the young person needs more than patience and gentleness, many dentists can use psychological techniques to calm their patients.

- *Behavioural techniques* The adolescent is allowed several visits to get used to the dentist and to the idea of being treated, taking small steps, one at a time. They come to know and trust the dentist and do not associate the dentist's chair with unpleasant experiences.

- *Hypnosis* Many dentists are trained in various methods of hypnosis, including neurolinguistic programming (NLP). They are able to induce a light trance in their patients and make suggestions which help them to get over their fears.

When you make your first contact with the dentist you can ask if he or she uses any of these techniques. Alternatively you can find out the name of a dentist who does, from one of the addresses on page 295.

Tranquillisers The vast majority of people can cope with dental treatment without needing to take tranquillisers, but they may be used if necessary. The dentist can give pills to be taken by the patient at home before treatment; it is also possible for the dentist to inject a tranquilliser directly into a vein.

General anaesthetic A last resort for a very few people is to be referred to a dental hospital for treatment to be carried out under a general anaesthetic.

Immunisations in adolescence[18]

To some extent the vaccination programme in your part of the country will affect the immunisations which are on offer for your own teenager. By and large there are two vaccinations which are taken up by adolescents: the BCG vaccine and rubella (for girls). There are also booster immunisations against tetanus and against polio to top up the vaccinations which most young people have already had during childhood.

BCG

This is the anti-TB vaccine. It is available, if needed, for all children in Britain and is provided through the school medical service. Children are first tested to see if they are susceptible to TB. A small scratch is made on the upper arm and the scratch is infected with tuberculin. If a blister develops, then the adolescent is judged to be immune to TB. The skin becomes rather inflamed and may feel itchy. The blister should be kept clean and dry.

Youngsters who do not develop a blister are given the BCG vaccine.

Rubella

Rubella, or German measles as it is commonly known, is very dangerous for unborn babies.

Babies whose mothers catch rubella while they are pregnant are in-danger of being born with seriously impaired sight or hearing, and with damage to the heart or brain. It is therefore very important that no young woman should be at risk of contracting rubella during pregnancy. Your daughter may have had rubella during childhood and so have developed a natural immunity. But because the symptoms can be slight, and other mild illnesses may be wrongly diagnosed as rubella, you may not be sure if your daughter has had it or not.

The only way to be certain is for her to have a blood test to see if she needs the vaccination. This may be done through the school medical service or by her doctor. It can also be done for girls who were immunised earlier in childhood to find out if they are still immune. Any girl who is not immune should be vaccinated before there is any risk that she might become pregnant. The vaccination can be carried out by the school medical service as part of its regular programme or, if she misses that, by the family doctor.

Young women who are not immune and who are actively planning to become pregnant should be vaccinated at least three months before the start of the planned pregnancy.

Sleep

The amount of sleep people need changes as they go through life. Babies spend a great deal of their time sleeping, especially in the early weeks and months. But as they grow older children spend less time asleep; they cut out daytime naps and they sleep for a shorter time at night until between about the ages of eleven and fourteen their sleep patterns become more like those of adults. Mostly this is a matter of staying up longer and surveys show that over the years teenagers' bedtimes become progressively later.[19] The basis of these changes is the hormonal changes of adolescence (see page 6), but the society we live in also has an influence on sleep patterns. For many thousands of years, bedtime and sunset were linked and people got up in the morning with the sunrise. In our society artificial light provides the possibility of extended evenings, for adults and for teenagers, and people adapt the rhythm of their lives accordingly.

As with adults, there is some variation in how much sleep individual adolescents need. To some extent this is because of inherited characteristics: needing much sleep or being able to manage on relatively little seems to run in families. However, sleep is a mysterious subject and a great deal still needs to be discovered about it. It can be a cause of conflict between parents and adolescents, either because sons or daughters want to stay up later than parents would like, or because they do not want to get up in the morning. What should parents do in these situations?

It is important to acknowledge that teenagers sleep less than younger children and so, as they enter and progress through their teens, it is to be expected that they should want to stay up later. People mostly take the amount of sleep they need, so that later bedtimes are only a problem if a youngster is tired when it is time to get up in the morning. If this is the case, then earlier nights are indicated and parents should point this out to teenagers and perhaps come to an agreement about later bedtimes being kept for weekends, when it is possible to sleep in.

Sometimes a teenager does not want to get up because he or she is reluctant to go to school and this may be apparent in other ways also: for example, if they frequently complain of symptoms such as stomach upsets and headaches, which lead to taking a day off school. Being unhappy at school is a possible reason to be considered for an adolescent not wanting to get up on school days (see page 235).

Sleepwalking

Sleepwalking is quite common in adolescence, more so than in childhood, but it declines in the late teens. The occasional episode of sleepwalking may occur as a result of some quite minor worry and is not a cause for anxiety on the part of parents – although it can be bizarre to find a son or daughter walking about the house, or the bedroom, eyes open yet quite obviously asleep and not paying attention to their surroundings. You should not awaken the sleepwalker, which could be very upsetting. Instead you should lead him or her gently and quietly back to bed. The next day the teenager will not remember anything about the episode. If the sleepwalking is repeated night after night, then it could be a sign of a deeper level of anxiety in the adolescent, which you should try to understand and do something about (see page 191).

Insomnia

A few nights of disturbed sleep may be unpleasant but they will not harm teenagers in the long run. They may be the result of unusual events or excitement that keep the brain whirling and inhibit sleep. Sometimes sleeplessness occurs because of hot weather, or if there is unaccustomed noise, or when someone is getting used to sleeping in a strange bed. These are rarely avoidable. But caffeine in coffee, tea and cola drinks can also contribute to sleeplessness and these can be avoided, especially in the evening.

But frequent, prolonged sleeplessness is a different matter; it is distressing in itself, it gives rise to tiredness and it may point to problems in the young person's school or personal life for which they need help. You should never give a sleepless teenager a sleeping pill which has been prescribed for another member of the family. This is a way of trying to escape from sleeplessness rather than supporting a teenager in tackling their difficulties, and carries the risk of dependency (see page 167). Instead you should try to find out what the problem is and offer what help you can (see page 21).

Adolescents and the National Health Service

Until they are sixteen, most adolescents have the same family doctor as their parents and for many this continues. But at the age of sixteen, adolescents have the legal right to choose their own doctor, if they wish, and to ask to be taken on as a patient.

Youngsters are entitled to free prescriptions and free dental treatment:

- if they are under sixteen; or over sixteen but under nineteen and still in full-time education;
- if they are pregnant, or have had a baby in the last twelve months;
- if they get income support or family credit.

Youngsters are entitled to free eye tests and NHS vouchers which can go towards paying for glasses, or for contact lenses:

- if they are under sixteen; or over sixteen but under nineteen and still in full-time education;
- if they get income support or family credit.

Registered opticians perform eye tests and supply glasses and contact lenses. Those under sixteen must obtain their glasses from a registered optician. After the age of sixteen glasses may also be obtained from a shop.[20]

The adolescent in hospital

Adolescents in hospital have their own special needs over and above whatever medical treatment is necessary. They are no longer children and so the atmosphere of either the children's ward or the adult ward may be less than ideal for them. They do not have people of their own age to talk to and share experiences with, and they may feel uncomfortable being treated in the same way as children or as adults. Children's wards may be too noisy and there may be little privacy, while adult wards may be experienced as very quiet. If an adolescent ward is unavailable, which is likely to be the case, and an adolescent feels that he or she would like to be transferred to a ward for children, or to a ward for adults, in preference to the one in which they were placed, parents should ask the ward sister or the consultant in charge of the patient if this can be arranged.

Adolescents who are ill need, where possible, to take some

responsibility for looking after themselves, as fits their developing independence. They should also be given information about themselves and about their condition, and they need someone they can trust to listen to their feelings and to accept them. These needs are recognised by the National Association for the Welfare of Children in Hospital, which says that adolescents in hospital (and, where appropriate, this applies to out-patients as well as in-patients) should be allowed to:

- express their confused feelings without fear or embarrassment;
- discuss honestly their medical or surgical problems and fears and have the opportunity to do so in private;
- enjoy recreational activities with their peers – and be noisy if they so wish;
- be alone;
- discuss health education issues of current concern and have access to the appropriate literature;
- participate in the planning and carrying out of their own care, as far as possible.[21]

When adolescents are in hospital, it is important that their social lives are disrupted as little as possible and so friends should be encouraged to visit and to write. There are also educational needs to consider and, especially in the case of a long stay (or a series of stays), arrangements should be made to continue education in hospital, or with a tutor at home during convalescence.

Parents should inform the pastoral staff at school that a youngster is in, or going into, hospital (see page 203). They can ask how, if necessary, hospital educational staff can liaise with the school about an education programme and what arrangements there are locally for a home tutor. The local education authority will also provide information.

Adolescents' Use of Alcohol, Tobacco and Other Drugs

Drugs are substances which alter the way the body functions. Here we examine the drugs which affect the nervous system and bring about changes in mood, behaviour and how people experience the world. Drugs can be roughly divided into three groups: depressants such as tranquillisers and alcohol, which slow down the nervous system; stimulants which speed it up and give a feeling of energy, including amphetamines and the caffeine which is drunk in tea and coffee; and hallucinogens, such as LSD, which alter people's perception of the world.

There are real dangers attached to the use of drugs which cannot be minimised. But parents should be aware that newspaper reports, and anti-drug campaigns directed towards young people, may both over-dramatise and mislead. The media can make drug-taking seem glamorous and rebellious to young people while, at the same time, raising great anxiety in the minds of parents. It is especially unfortunate that such publicity about illicit drugs takes attention away from two substances which are widely available, widely used by teenagers and capable of harming them substantially, even fatally, now or in later life – the use and abuse of alcohol and tobacco.

Drug use, the law and convention

Within different societies different conventions regulate the use of drugs. Laws and customs dictate who is to be permitted to consume which drugs, at what age and under what conditions. Some drugs – like the caffeine contained in tea and coffee – are readily available and their use permitted in society as a whole, including among young people. In the case of other drugs, there may be limitations on their purchase and use. Both alcohol and tobacco fall into this group and, in the UK and many other countries, may legally only be bought by those over the age of eighteen. At the same time, while these 'permitted' drugs can be acquired legally, there are some groups within society which forbid or discourage their use. For example, Muslims and members of the Methodist Church, traditionally, do not drink alcohol.

Other drugs are subject to much tighter control; for example, heroin, tranquillisers and amphetamines can only be obtained legally by means of a doctor's prescription.

If the law and other social conventions are observed there is little disapproval attached to the use of 'permitted' drugs and, to varying extents, they are familiar features of most adults' world. But 'conventional' drug use is not without danger. The consequences of cigarette smoking are well known (see page 159): each year it causes many deaths. Problems also arise from taking certain tranquillisers, to which it is all too easy for patients to become addicted. Other health hazards connected with drugs are those which involve other people as well as the drug user. These include the harmful effects of breathing in other people's tobacco smoke, the effects of alcohol, tobacco and certain 'illicit' drugs on the health of the unborn child, when used by the pregnant mother, and the crippling, lethal accidents brought about by drivers whose judgement is impaired by drink.

Understandably, parents tend to be more anxious at the thought of teenagers using illegal drugs than about the possibility of their using 'permitted' drugs while still under-age. Parents of today's adolescents have some experience of 'permitted' drugs like alcohol and tobacco, even if they do not use them themselves, while their knowledge of illegal drugs may be limited to the grim pictures painted of the effects of drug abuse by government health campaigns and in newspaper stories. It is true that, for a very small number of young people, using certain illegal drugs has disastrous consequences. But few young people use any illegal drugs regularly, or indeed at all, apart from some initial experimentation; and the drugs they most commonly experiment with are those which are least harmful (see page 168).

Tobacco and alcohol, on the other hand, are used widely by adolescents, sometimes before they enter their teens. The dangers associated with the use of alcohol and tobacco are very real.

Reasons for drug use

People use drugs for many different reasons. In the adult world, the use of certain drugs is associated with social events. It is customary to drink alcohol at parties and celebrations; champagne is seen by many as an essential component of a wedding. Less formally, the use of drugs may be a feature of the lifestyle and identity of some groups of people within society: visits to pubs and wine bars play an important part in the lives of many youngsters; the consumption of cocaine can be a conspicuous, mutual display of wealth for members of other groups. Individuals turn to tobacco, alcohol and other drugs for personal reasons as well as social ones because they seem to meet some particular need, perhaps to relieve stress, or out of boredom, or as a means of acting out feelings of rebellion.

When adolescents turn to alcohol, tobacco or other drugs, the same sorts of reasons operate as for adults, and many of the same problems arise. However, there are particular dangers in using drugs to which adolescents are vulnerable.

Clearly you want to protect your adolescents from the dangers which are inherent in the use of drugs. One of the most important things that parents can do to help their children is to pass on information. Young people need to know about the drugs which are commonly available – both legally and illegally – what the dangers are, and how to avoid them. The following section examines the various drugs which adolescents are likely to meet, the prevalence of drug-taking among young people and what parents can do to support and protect their children in a society where drugs are available.

Alcohol and young people

Today's adolescents are brought up in a society where more alcohol is drunk than was the case when their parents were the same age. In the UK, the consumption of alcohol went up by 60 per cent between 1960 and 1981 and in the USA by 72 per cent during the same period.[22] This may be linked to increased outlets for the sale of alcohol, including the supermarket, and the decrease in the price of alcohol compared with how much people earn. In the UK, for example, the price of a pint of beer decreased by half between 1950 and 1986 and of a bottle of spirits far more, because taxation has not kept in line with inflation. Also, the law on home brewing has been repealed and many people now brew their own wines and beer with kits which are readily available. In addition, it is now more acceptable for women to go into public houses and wine bars and to do so without a man as escort.

Alcohol, young people and the law[23]

After the age of five it is not an offence to give alcohol to children or adolescents, although this may be undesirable and dangerous.

At any age a young person can go into an off-licence, but they cannot buy alcoholic drinks until they are eighteen.

Up to the age of fourteen children are not allowed in the bar of licensed premises. They can only go into the parts of a pub where there is no direct sale of alcohol, such as a garden or a family room. They can also go into a dining room where alcohol is served only with meals.

After the age of fourteen they can go into any part of a pub but they may not legally buy or drink alcohol. It is an offence for anyone under eighteen to do so or for any adult to buy a drink on his or her behalf. It is also an offence to serve alcoholic drink to someone under eighteen.

At eighteen, when they are legally adults, young people can go into a pub and buy and drink alcohol.

It is an offence to be drunk and disorderly in a public place but over five thousand under-eighteens are convicted each year, most of them older boys.[24]

The laws relating to alcohol and young people are frequently broken. This is not to say that all youngsters drink, or drink illegally, and your own adolescent may be one of those who does not drink. A survey of young people in Scotland, England and Wales showed that by the age of seventeen one in ten were non-drinkers.[25] This leaves a substantial majority who do drink alcohol, to some extent, and among them is a group of adolescents who experience unpleasant and dangerous consequences as a result of drinking. Here are some of the other findings of the survey:

- In England and Wales 82 per cent of boys and 77 per cent of girls said they had had their first 'proper' drink by the time they were thirteen (meaning not just a taste from an adult's glass). In Scotland rather fewer young people have had their first 'proper' drink by this age.
- The number of adolescents who drink regularly increases with age.

In England and Wales, at the age of thirteen, 29 per cent of boys and 11 per cent of girls said they drank at least once a week.

By fifteen, 52 per cent of boys and 37 per cent of girls said they drank at least once a week.

By seventeen, 61 per cent of boys and 54 per cent of girls said they drank at least once a week.

In Scotland the percentage of young people who said they drank frequently was much lower.

- The adolescents in the survey kept a diary for a week, recording details of how much they had drunk each day. Many of them drank nothing, or only a little. But the amount drunk increased as they grew older. By the time they were fifteen half of the boys who drank at all, drank the equivalent of five pints of beer, or more, during the week. The girls drank less than the boys at every age. In England and Wales the boys drank twice as much as the girls, in Scotland three times as much.
- The youngest group in the survey said that they had their first experience of drink at home, with their parents. But by the time they were fifteen most of those who drank were usually doing so with their friends. For them, under-age drinking is part of the local youth culture; a significant activity for a group of friends. They drink at parties, in clubs and discos, often sharing bottles and cans with their friends. By the age of seventeen, the majority were drinking in pubs and a quarter of them were already doing so when they were fourteen, in spite of this being against the law.
- The survey showed that there were some adolescents, mostly younger boys, who said that they usually drank alone. This was true of one in twelve in England and Wales and one in twenty in Scotland.

Why young people drink

The reasons why young people drink are quite complex. In the first place, perhaps, they drink because drinking is an acceptable adult habit. They may be used to seeing parents or their friends drinking at home. It is often parents who give children their first sip of an alcoholic drink, or who may encourage them to have a drink at family celebrations. The customs of the wider community also play their part. One of the aims of adolescents, in their transition between childhood and adult life, is to adopt adult ways and, as drinking is part of adult life, many adolescents start to experiment with it. As they grow older, how much and how often they drink comes closer to the levels in young adult society, and young men in their late teens and early twenties are the group who drink most heavily. Even if parents do not themselves drink, there are many advertisements – often of a type which are very appealing to youngsters – which show drinking as a desirable aspect of adult life: it can seem mature, sophisticated and fun. On television, soap opera characters are often seen drinking. They, too, provide a model of drinking as a normal, often desirable, adult activity.

There are differences between the drinking habits of girls and boys. Girls drink less than boys and they tend to try a variety of drinks, while boys stick more to beer and cider.[26] Boys drink with other boys while girls go to the pub or a wine bar with their boyfriends, rather than with other girls.[27] As in other areas of adolescent life, gender roles make a difference.

There are also reasons for drinking which are more individual and less connected with socialising. Those who frequently drink alone fall into this category; there are some adolescents who drink out of boredom or to relieve anxiety or distress.

The effects of alcohol on young people

Adults who are heavy drinkers are at real risk of cirrhosis of the liver, of stomach and duodenal ulcers, and of brain damage. These are the results of a history of drinking. For adolescents – who do not suffer from illnesses which result from being addicted to alcohol – the dangers are different but just as real.

Perhaps the most important thing to bear in mind is that for many young people, because they are not used to drinking, the effects of small amounts of alcohol can be more pronounced than those experienced by an adult. This is in part because adolescents weigh less than adults and so alcohol is less diluted by body mass. Also they have no experience of knowing how much alcohol they can safely drink without running into trouble and may experiment by mixing their drinks. This may be especially true for girls who often choose a variety of drinks, whereas boys are more likely to stick to whichever drink they prefer.

The immediate effect of a small amount of alcohol is to stimulate the circulation and to produce a feeling of warmth. But after this initially stimulating reaction, alcohol quickly acts as a depressant. Larger doses of alcohol make the drinker feel cold. Even a small amount of alcohol is a depressant which works on the central nervous system and soon affects reaction times. This is particularly significant for young people who drive, or whose drinking companions offer them a ride. A driver's judgement can be affected even at levels of alcohol below those legally permitted when tested by the breathalyser: 80 mg per 100 ml of blood. The more that is drunk, of course, the greater the risks to driver and passengers. A shocking statistic is that *more fifteen- to nineteen-year-olds die in road accidents than from any other cause*, and frequently these accidents involve youngsters who have been drinking. Girls, even though on the whole they drink less than boys, can nevertheless be at risk if their boyfriends drink and drive.

After a drink a youngster starts to feel more carefree and relaxed. While this may be an enjoyable experience, the dangers of drinking increase with the amount that is drunk. As anxiety diminishes, adolescents can take risks which they would not find acceptable at other times. Their judgement and self-control desert them and they may make fools of themselves.

It is impossible to behave responsibly when drunk, and vandalism and hooliganism are often linked to teenage drinking. About one in ten of the boys questioned in the survey quoted on pages 151–2 said that they were involved in vandalism or had attracted the attention of the police after drinking too much. A quarter got into arguments or fights after drinking, or upset their parents or even felt that it would be better not to go home. There are also dangers arising from unwanted or unplanned sex.

The more that is drunk the worse the consequences; the adolescent becomes clumsy, dizzy and confused; they may be sick and suffer from headaches and hangovers. In England and Wales half the fifteen-year-old boys in the survey, and 39 per cent of the girls, remembered falling over after drinking. Perhaps the seventeen-year-olds had learned to hold their drink better because they did not report this. Nevertheless, many of these boys and some of the girls had been sick after drinking; some had had hangovers and had to stay at home the following day. It seems that for a small group of teenagers drinking too much is an established habit.

For youngsters who drink too much there is also the risk of alcoholic poisoning which can be fatal (see page 158).

Helping young people to drink safely

Your own experience of alcohol, and whether you find its use permissible or not, will affect how you feel about your son or daughter drinking. It may be that you yourself enjoy a drink or, on the contrary, that you have strong views against the use of alcohol. Your attitude towards drink, and towards young people drinking, is likely to influence your son or daughter. Research shows that parents who in fact approve of children having a drink sometimes are far more likely to have children who do so.[28] Whatever your own views on alcohol, it is advisable that your adolescent is well informed about its effects, understands the risks attached to drinking and knows how to avoid them.

■ In order to put off the age at which young people start drinking, do not offer them drink at home but wait until they themselves ask if they can try a drink.

■ At family celebrations, provide low-alcohol and non-alcoholic drinks.

■ Explain to adolescents the risks of drinking:
Drinking can lead to fights and arguments and trouble with the police.
It is not sophisticated to get drunk. People make fools of themselves when they are drunk.
Drinking too much results in sickness, hangovers and headaches.

■ Stress that *drinking and driving are dangerous*. Tell teenagers:
1 never to drink and drive;
2 never to take a lift from someone who has been drinking.
If necessary you can collect a teenager after a party or pay for a taxi, rather than risk a road accident.

■ Tell adolescents about safe drinking:
Different people are affected by drink in different ways. The amount that one person can drink without any apparent ill-effects could well be far too much for another. It depends on age, body weight, sex and experience of drinking.
Safe drinking means not trying to keep up with other drinkers, but keeping to a safe level.
Drinking on an empty stomach speeds up the effect of alcohol, so young people should eat before they drink, or while they are drinking.
Tell them to be watchful of being given outsize measures of drink, or

strange mixtures, at parties or in their friends' houses. Home measures are usually larger than pub measures.
Explain that different drinks have different strengths: very small quantities of spirits are as strong as larger amounts of beer, lager, and wine.

- Make sure they know the law about under-age drinking.
- Remember that the example of adults in the family can be important and this includes that of older brothers and sisters as well as parents.

Helping teenagers to have enough confidence to say 'no'

There are many occasions when a teenager may feel pressurised by other people to do something they really do not want to do. This can range from going to watch a football match, when they would rather be indoors, to being encouraged to drink, to smoking or using drugs against their own better judgement. They may find that a boyfriend, or girlfriend, is taking it for granted that they want to have sex, when in fact this is not the case. Some may find it difficult to reject the sexual attentions of an adult.

Teenagers can have a real problem saying 'no' even when they are perfectly sure that they do not want something. They may fear that if they say 'no' the other person will not like them any more or that it will end their relationship. They may worry about what the other person thinks about them. Will they go down in their estimation? Will they think that they are young and immature? Will it cause trouble?

Some secondary schools provide training for adolescents in interpersonal skills as part of the health education syllabus.[29] This can help them to be assertive and to trust themselves and their own decisions. Being assertive is a positive quality; it does not mean being aggressive, just not letting other people have their own way at one's own expense. Assertive people can let others know about their needs without manipulation or aggression; they can show warmth and appreciation and they are able to say 'no' when they want to.

Here are some tips which may help an adolescent to say 'no' when they want to:

- They need to be clear about what they want to say: 'I don't want to' or 'I don't want another drink.'

■ They may need to repeat this more than once. They should not let themselves be drawn into an argument about why they should or should not do something. If they do not want to, that is a good enough reason. There is no need to do this in an unpleasant way and they can, if appropriate, let the other person know that they are appreciative: 'Thanks for offering, but I really don't want to.'

They should appear confident when they say 'no', by looking the other person in the eye and by speaking clearly, not apologetically or jokingly. In this way the other person gets the message that they mean what they say.

What if your teenager gets drunk?

It could happen that your son or daughter makes a mistake about how much they can safely drink and on some occasion comes home having drunk too much. It is not a good idea to discuss the matter on the spot. An intoxicated teenager is unlikely to be feeling reasonable and may be aggressive; there is no point in saying anything which may make the situation worse. But, when they have recovered and you have an opportunity for a quiet talk, find out what happened and listen, without passing judgement, to their feelings about the incident. Ask them what they think they can do to avoid it happening again: choosing non-alcoholic or low-alcoholic drinks, for example; not trying to keep up with other drinkers; having the confidence to say 'no' rather than following the crowd. Show them that although you are concerned, you are not shocked and that you can trust them to behave responsibly and learn from their experience.

Teenagers who seem to be drinking too much

There is no need for a parent to be over-worried about an occasional episode of drinking; this can be put down to youthful experiment. But if a teenager seems to be drinking frequently, or too much, you need to find out why this is. Is it because drinking is a favourite activity of the group they go around with? Or are there any deeper problems, to do with school, family or friends, which they are trying to cope with by drinking? Could you or someone else in the family help them to find a more positive way of dealing with their difficulties?

Listen to what your adolescent has to say and explain how you feel about their drinking (see pages 187–90). If you are really worried and think that you cannot sort things out alone, there are some addresses on page 295 where you can seek help.

If your cultural background forbids the use of alcohol, it may be especially difficult to deal with a teenager who drinks. This may be the case, for example, for families who come from a Muslim background. Not only is there no experience of drink and its effects, but having an adolescent who drinks can be a source of shame for parents. There are now some special counselling agencies with staff drawn from the Asian communities who can offer help to those who need it (Alcohol Concern has details of these – see page 295 for address).

Alcoholic poisoning

Sometimes, perhaps out of a feeling of bravado, in order to experiment, or for some other reason, a young person may drink far too much and suffer from alcoholic poisoning. This leads to unconsciousness and, in some cases, death.

If a parent finds an adolescent who is unconscious, and there is an obvious smell of drink:

- Put them lying on their side so that if they are sick they will not choke or inhale vomit.
- Get immediate medical assistance: dial 999 and ask for an ambulance.
- Do not leave them alone while waiting for the ambulance.

When the crisis is over and the young person has recovered, choose an appropriate time for talking over what has happened and offering help and support.

Adolescent drinking and the school

Many schools provide lessons about alcohol and other drugs. If you think there is a drinking problem in the school which involves, or might involve, your own adolescent, ask to talk to a teacher about it and find out if anything could be done through the school about alcohol education. Or it might be that the Parent-Teacher Association could arrange a meeting for parents. Such a meeting would bring the problem out into the open and provide an opportunity for parents to discuss their concerns and find ways of helping their adolescents to live safely with alcohol.

There is a national body which provides schools with advice and visual material about alcohol and other drugs – Teachers' Advisory Council on Alcohol and Drug Education (see page 295 for addresses) – and which might be able to suggest other ways of helping.

You can also enquire from the local youth service if they have any constructive policy on alcohol. For example, in some places alcohol-free youth bars and clubs have been set up where young people can enjoy the ambience of a pub, or cocktail bar, without the attendant risks (see page 284).

Smoking and young people

Smoking causes:

- lung cancer;
- chronic bronchitis;
- emphysema;
- coronary heart disease;
- peripheral arterial disease;
- harmful effects in the unborn child.

Smoking is responsible for many deaths and much illness and misery every year. People who die from smoking-related illnesses die before their time and there is evidence that the younger a person starts smoking, the more likely it is that they will develop lung cancer.[30]

This information is gradually filtering through to the population. Today fewer people are smoking and many more established smokers are giving up the habit.[31] There is also evidence of a decline in smoking among young people. A survey conducted in England, Wales and Scotland showed that smoking among secondary school students declined between 1982 and 1986.[32] Research in the USA also shows a decline.[33]

Unfortunately women have been less affected by the health messages than men, both in the UK[34] and in the USA.[35]

And what is true for women is also true for girls: more girls are smoking on a regular basis than boys and, at the time of writing, the percentage of girls who smoke is not declining.

Smoking can start early – a few children report smoking for the first time as young as six years old! – but for the most part it is among older teenagers that the greatest number of smokers is to be found. For example, in the survey quoted above, 19 per cent of boys and 30 per cent of girls in England and Wales were smoking at about the age of fifteen. Sometimes children and young people smoke just to see what it is like. Usually it makes them feel sick or at best it has no effect at all, so they are unlikely to try smoking a second time. Unfortunately others continue smoking and there is a real danger that they will become addicted to the habit, continue smoking into adult life and eventually ruin their health.

Adolescent smokers and non-smokers

Why do some young people smoke, while others do not?

It is sometimes said that because smoking diseases occur in adult life, and are so far in the future, they do not have any relevance for teenagers. In one survey 98 per cent of youngsters in their mid-teens thought that smoking was harmful to health yet some of them still smoked.[36]

Research shows that some groups of young people are more likely to smoke than others and that both social and psychological factors are involved.

Adolescents who are regular smokers are more likely to come from families where the parents are less educated and less well-off than non-smokers. In this they echo the smoking patterns in adult society. Smoking has declined significantly in the middle and professional classes but less so among other groups. The links between smoking and ill-health have not yet got through convincingly to all sectors of the community.

Some youngsters smoke just because their friends do and secret smoking, on or near the school premises, can be a routine in which the risk of detection adds to the bravado. For teenagers who are in conflict with the school authorities, such activities bind a group of non-conformers together and boost fragile self-esteem. Smoking is a way in which they make claim to being grown up and independent. Boys may find smoking 'macho' and encourage one another to experiment, while girls may find the rituals of smoking adult and sophisticated.

There are also psychological differences between smokers and non-smokers. There is evidence that young people who smoke have less efficient ways of coping with life than those who do not. They tend to react to problems in an emotional way, including turning to cigarettes for comfort. Compared with other youngsters, they are less likely to try to find constructive ways of dealing with problems. Young people who smoke have a lower level of self-esteem; they tend to think less highly of themselves and their own ability to cope with life than non-smokers. They also seem to be youngsters who experience more crises and disturbing changes in their lives than other young people.[37]

Girls and smoking

Why more girls smoke than boys is something of a puzzle. When girl smokers are asked why they smoke, they give two main reasons. The first is that it calms their nerves. It is possible that girls feel under greater pressure than boys: on average, they become physically mature at a younger age than boys (see page 9) when they are less well equipped, psychologically, to cope with the problems that puberty can present. Or it may be that the demands of growing up are greater for girls than for boys and that they have less sense of being in control of their lives. It seems especially important that parents should help girls to feel good about themselves, for what they are, not just for how they look. It may also be necessary to help them to take an assertive approach to life (see page 156), to encourage them to find positive ways of expressing their feelings and coping with difficulties, rather than turning to cigarettes.

Girls also say that smoking stops them putting on weight. Perhaps this is a justification, in their eyes, for a dangerous and antisocial habit, but it is not one that stands up to examination. The way to control weight is to eat a healthy, varied diet (see page 101), not to use a lethal substance. It may be true, however, that some adolescents who stop smoking turn to eating to help them get over the habit and to fill the gap left by cigarettes. If this is so, they should be encouraged away from sweets and biscuits towards less-fattening snacks like raw carrots and celery and fresh fruit.

Another possible explanation for the fact that more girls smoke than boys is that there has been an increase in tobacco advertisements aimed directly at women. These suggest that the woman who smokes is sexy, sophisticated and in charge of her own life, although in many ways the opposite is closer to the truth. The effect of advertising on children can be seen from the fact that when cigarette advertisements were banned in Norway the decline in smoking was most marked among young people. Children as young as nine are aware of cigarette advertisements and receive positive messages from them.[38]

Discouraging adolescents from smoking

Although the tobacco industry is powerful, parents are also in a strong position to discourage adolescents from smoking and they should do so from early adolescence, if not before. Many children have the occasional cigarette before they reach their teens and there is evidence that those who smoke early are more likely to become regular smokers later.

What you can do to help Your own example and attitude towards smoking are both important. If you do not smoke yourself, this is a good model for your adolescent. Numerous surveys have shown that the children of smokers are at greater risk than the children of non-smokers. But it is also a good idea to communicate your reasons for not smoking. There are numerous occasions when you can discuss these – following misleading tobacco advertisements, for example, or after news items about smoking and the unpleasant atmosphere created by people smoking in public places, in restaurants, or on trains.

Even if you do smoke, your attitude towards smoking is still important. If you think of all the disadvantages connected with smoking, and explain to your son or daughter how you would like to give up, this can be a striking lesson in itself.

So, whether or not you are a smoker, make it clear that you do not want your adolescent to smoke. In a survey of 15,000 youngsters in the North of England, the majority of those who had never smoked felt that the significant people in their lives would not approve of them if they were to do so. Similar data were found for those who had tried a cigarette but had not gone on to become regular smokers.[39]

Adolescents need a strong message that smoking is both harmful and unpleasant, to counteract the advertisements and some of the pressures they may meet from friends. Here are some ideas which may be useful:

■ *Smoking is dangerous.*

Smoking is bad for young people's health *now* – they are more likely to get coughs and colds than those who don't. They will be less fit than non-smokers.

Smoking can have a serious and fatal effect on their health in the future.

Smoking can harm their children's health: children of mothers who smoke during pregnancy tend to have small babies, who are at greater risk than other new-born babies. Passive smoking – breathing their parents' smoke – is also associated with a greater risk of children developing chest infections.

■ *Smoking is unpleasant.*

Smoking is not elegant, sophisticated or sexy. Smoking is dirty. Smokers have breath that smells and their clothes, skin and hair, and rooms smell of stale tobacco.

Smokers have yellow teeth.

Nicotine-stained fingers are unattractive.

■ *Smoking is anti-social.*

The smell of smoke is unpleasant for other people. It hangs about curtains and furniture.

Ash-trays full of cigarette ends are disgusting.

■ *Smoking is expensive.*

Teenagers have better things to buy than cigarettes. Think of what could be bought with the money spent on cigarettes. For smokers who have a part-time job, their earnings literally go up in smoke.

■ *Smoking is a bad habit.*

Advertisements are misleading. Smoking is not tough, or sophisticated, or fun. The only people who benefit from cigarettes are those who make and sell them.

If your adolescent smokes

If you know or think that your son or daughter smokes, then there are various steps you can take, depending on their age. First of all talk to them about their smoking, listen to what they have to say and explain your own attitude towards it (see pages 187–90).

For the younger adolescent, ask them how they obtained their cigarettes and, if appropriate, complain to the tobacconist who sold them.

Find out what sort of health education there is at school about smoking and what measures are taken to discourage it – for example, what policy is there about staff smoking on school premises? Could the Parent-Teacher Association take concerted action against smoking? Or make an approach to local shops to explain the school policy about smoking and ask them to co-operate by not selling cigarettes to schoolchildren (see below).

For adolescents over the age of sixteen, who may be in full-time or part-time work, tell them that you would prefer them not to smoke at home. This is especially important where they have younger brothers or sisters who may come to think that smoking is just part of growing up.

Adolescents, tobacco and the law

It is against the law to sell cigarettes or tobacco to anyone under the age of sixteen and the penalty for doing so is a fine of up to £400. However, many shopkeepers ignore the law and sell cigarettes to youngsters. Some of them even open packets of cigarettes and sell the contents in ones and twos to schoolchildren.

Older adolescents are more likely to be served than younger ones and girls are more likely to be served than boys. This is possibly because girls look more grown up for their age than boys and the shopkeeper may find it hard to be sure if a girl is under-age. Regrettably, more than half the eleven-year-old smokers in one survey said that they had been successful in buying cigarettes.

If you know that children are buying cigarettes in your area, or in shops near your child's school, then it is worth complaining to the shopkeeper concerned. If they ignore your complaint, contact the police or the Trading Standards Department at the town hall.

Never ask your adolescent to buy cigarettes for you or for anyone else.

Illegal drugs and solvents

Although there are proven dangers attached to their use, tobacco and alcohol are widely and legally available for adults. Tobacco and alcohol, the drugs most used by adolescents, are supplied to them illegally by publicans and shopkeepers. Other drugs, the 'illegal' drugs, are legally restricted for adults and adolescents alike. Their supply and use require a doctor's prescription, otherwise they are outside the law. The subject of illegal drugs is emotive. Parents are well aware, from press and television coverage, of the havoc that drugs can create in people's lives and the tragedies which can result from their use. They also know that some young people take drugs and that there may be youngsters, at their own adolescent's school, who use and possibly share drugs. However, they themselves may have little or no experience of people who use illegal drugs and little knowledge about the different sorts of illegal drugs – in many cases adolescents know more than their parents. *Parents need to understand about illegal drugs so that they can pass on accurate information to their adolescents.* They also need to be fully informed about drug-taking so that their reaction to the problem, should they ever have cause to think that their own adolescent or their friends are using drugs, is realistic and does not exaggerate the possible consequences.

Illegal drugs include a wide variety of substances which have an equally wide variety of effects, some of them more dangerous than others:

Amphetamines Dexedrine is the most usual.
APPEARANCE White or brown powder; pills or capsules.
SLANG NAMES Speed, uppers, sulph.
HOW TAKEN Sniffed, injected or taken by mouth.
EFFECTS Amphetamines are stimulants. They speed up breathing and heart rate and make people lively, wakeful and talkative. Users can quickly develop a tolerance and need increased doses to achieve the same effect. Side-effects for heavy users can include sleep problems, irritability, anxiety and feelings of persecution. Withdrawing from them can cause depression. There may also be dangers associated with injecting, including infection (see page 95).

Barbiturates These include Nembutal, Tuinal and Seconal.
APPEARANCE Pills and capsules.
SLANG NAMES Downers, barbs.
HOW TAKEN By mouth or injection.
EFFECTS Barbiturates are depressants. They make people feel relaxed

and can produce a feeling of drunkenness which can lead to accidents. They may cause unconsciousness. Overdoses can be fatal, especially when taken with alcohol. Injecting is particularly dangerous, quite apart from the risks of infection and physical injury. Withdrawal from barbiturates can be unpleasant and needs medical supervision.

Tranquillisers Librium, Valium, Ativan.
APPEARANCE Pills and capsules.
SLANG NAMES Tranx, downers.
HOW TAKEN By mouth.
EFFECTS Initially tranquillisers reduce anxiety, but prolonged use can actually give rise to anxiety and withdrawal symptoms can be very unpleasant. The judgement and skill of people who are taking tranquillisers may be impaired, affecting both their driving and use of machinery.

Cannabis APPEARANCE Cannabis comes either as a dried herb or as pieces of hard brown resin.
SLANG NAMES Pot, dope, hash, grass.
HOW TAKEN Cannabis is either smoked, eaten or drunk, or, occasionally, inhaled.
EFFECTS The effects are variable but it usually produces a relaxed, rather drunken feeling with some changes in perception of music and colour. People on cannabis may be less careful when driving. There is no physical dependency but people can come to rely on cannabis as a psychological crutch and a way of avoiding problems. Prolonged smoking may have the same unhealthy effects as tobacco.

Cocaine APPEARANCE A white crystalline powder.
SLANG NAMES Coke.
HOW TAKEN Cocaine is usually sniffed (or the slang word is snorted).
EFFECTS It is a stimulant which produces similar effects to amphetamines. The effects are short-lived and there is a greater likelihood of dependency than with amphetamines.

Heroin APPEARANCE White, pink, grey or speckled brown powder.
SLANG NAMES Smack, scag.

HOW TAKEN Heated on a spoon or a piece of foil and inhaled; sniffed or injected.
EFFECTS The first doses can cause nausea and vomiting. Heroin makes the user feel relaxed and detached from reality and they may seem drowsy or a little drunk. Dependency can develop rapidly with regular use. There are also the dangers attached to injecting (see page 95).

LSD (Lysergic Acid Diethylamide) APPEARANCE Various forms including tiny tablets and microdots on blotting paper, wrapped up in clingfilm, or impregnated stamps.
SLANG NAME Acid.
HOW TAKEN By mouth.
EFFECTS It can make everything seem more intense and alter consciousness of time. A bad 'trip' can produce anxiety and panic. Driving is dangerous during an LSD trip and in the recovery stage.

'Magic mushrooms' These are certain species of mushrooms which grow in the wild. It is illegal to produce or possess preparations made from them.
HOW TAKEN By mouth.
EFFECTS The effects can be similar to those produced by LSD. The main dangers are from eating other poisonous mushrooms by mistake and from accidents as a result of intoxication.

Glue and solvent sniffing For the sake of convenience, the misuse of glue and solvents is included in this section, although their supply and use is not legally restricted. Many different vapour-producing substances can be sniffed, including glues and other products.
EFFECTS Sniffing produces a feeling of drunkenness; much depends on the mood of the individual, or group of individuals, involved. The main dangers are: *death*, either by suffocation when sniffing is carried out with the head in a plastic bag, or when the adolescent becomes unconscious, is sick and vomit is inhaled; *accident*, when sniffing is done in dangerous surroundings such as near railway lines or on high buildings.

Note: There are many different slang names around the country for drugs and for the activities associated with them, and only the more usual ones are given above. There are also new developments and varieties of drugs which come on to the illegal market and which relate closely to the categories described above, for example crack which is related to heroin.

Drug dependency

Drug dependency – or addiction – can come about with the 'permitted' drugs like alcohol and tobacco just as easily as with drugs which are used illegally, like heroin.

Someone who is drug-dependent has a craving for whatever drug they are addicted to. For some people who are dependent, the craving may be so strong that they will go to virtually any lengths to obtain the required drug. In addition to becoming psychologically addictive, in that people find it hard to get along without the escape they provide, some drugs carry a risk of physical dependency, which means that the body has become tolerant of the drug through regular use and a larger amount is needed to obtain whatever pleasant effect is produced. Physical dependency means that unpleasant withdrawal symptoms are experienced if the drug is not used regularly.

The law and drugs

The Misuse of Drugs Act 1971 makes the unlawful manufacture, supply and possession of drugs illegal. All the drugs listed above come under this law, with the exception of 'magic mushrooms' in their natural state, and glue and solvents. If the mushrooms are prepared, cooked or dried, then they too come under the law. With regard to glue- and solvent-sniffing, this is not a criminal offence although, in Scotland, anyone found doing so can be referred to the Reporter to a Children's Panel (an officer in the childcare system) and may then be taken into care. In England, Wales and Northern Ireland the police may intervene if they find children or adolescents sniffing glue and solvents and advise parents and children about the dangers involved. They are also empowered to arrest young people caught in the act of glue-sniffing, on the grounds that such behaviour may lead to a breach of the peace. As a result those concerned may be 'bound over' to keep the peace, but this does not constitute a criminal record.

It is not an offence, in itself, to sell solvents and other substances to children and adolescents. In Scotland it is an offence to sell such things knowing that they are going to be misused and in the rest of the UK it is an offence to sell them if the shopkeeper has 'reasonable' cause to believe that they are being bought for sniffing.

Illegal possession, supply or manufacture of all the other drugs listed above are criminal offences which can result in fines or detention.

The severity of the penalty depends on the type of drug, and the quantity, involved and whether the offence is that of drug possession, supply or manufacture. But if a youngster is found to be in possession of even a small quantity of one of the less dangerous drugs, and consequently receives a lenient penalty, he or she has nevertheless been convicted of a crime and now has a criminal record (see page 278).

It is also an offence for parents knowingly to permit an illegal drug to be used in their home.

If a parent finds what they suspect to be an illegal drug, the law requires them to hand it over to the police, or destroy it to prevent it from being used. However, there is no obligation for parents to go to the police and most would not want to take such a step. Calling in the police could have the effect of starting criminal proceedings against the adolescent concerned. If a parent feels that help from outside the family is needed, there are various organisations which can be approached (see page 295).

The extent of illicit drug use

It is not known how many adults use drugs illegally. The only indications of the extent of drug misuse among adults come from the following information: the figures for notified addicts; the quantity of drugs which are seized by police and customs each year; the number of judicial proceedings involving drug offences. All these have increased over the last decade although the higher statistics may to some extent be due to changes in policy rather than to an increase in drug use.

Various surveys give some indication of the extent of illegal drug use among adolescents and, from these, perhaps the most useful information for parents is the following:

Most young people have no experience at all of illegal drug or solvent use. The proportions of those who have ever tried either illegal drugs or solvents are different in different places. For example, a survey in Inner London, carried out in 1987, found that 20.5 per cent of all youngsters had experimented at some time with drugs or solvents, with no marked difference between the percentage of boys and the percentage of girls.[40] A Lothian survey[41] carried out in 1979–80 found that 15 per cent of boys and 11 per cent of girls had experimented at some time, while in a survey in Portsmouth and Havant in 1986–87 the proportions were 14 per cent of boys and 9 per cent of girls.[42]

The proportion who go on to use drugs on a regular basis, rather than merely experimenting with them, is known to be much smaller, as is the fact that the majority of users use the 'safer' substances and not hard drugs. Nevertheless there is a small group who do use the more dangerous drugs on a regular basis and who are therefore at greater risk.

Why do some adolescents use drugs?

To a large extent the answer to this question is because drugs are part of our society. Many adults use drugs, legally or otherwise, for a variety of purposes: in order to feel better, to kill pain, to help them to lose weight, to calm themselves down or to perk themselves up. Some of these drugs are self-prescribed, others are prescribed by doctors. Whatever the reason, there is evidence that drugs are over-used in adult society. This is particularly true of the abuse of alcohol, which can end in lost jobs and broken relationships, and also of tranquillisers, which are over-prescribed as easy answers to difficult problems, and which can quickly lead to painful addiction.

Some adolescents who turn to drugs use them as a psychological crutch in much the same way that adults do. They are following the example set by adult society. A finding of many research reports which points to this fact is that teenagers who use alcohol and, more especially, tobacco are more likely than others to use illegal drugs as well.[43] For them drugs provide 'simple' ways of coping with the difficulties of life, including low self-esteem and uncertain identity.

Other youngsters are motivated by a sense of risk; they are curious about the effects of drugs and go along with suggestions from friends to try out substances. Or they may be in rebellion against over-strict parents or trying to claim attention from parents who do not seem to care.

Preventing adolescents from turning to drugs

Although an occasional experiment may cause no harm, most parents will want to do all they can to safeguard their children from the dangers of drugs. The following could help:

- Set an example to adolescents which shows that you take drugs seriously, that you take medicines only when they are necessary and that you do not think of drink or cigarettes as easy answers to problems.
- Be careful with prescribed medicines and throw away any which are not needed.
- Be ready to trust your adolescent and to give him or her increased independence as they grow up, into and through their teens.
- Give them the attention they need; listen to their problems and help them to find positive ways through them.

■ Welcome signs of assertiveness in them; encourage them to say 'no' rather than accept things they do not really want. This may include saying 'no' to you on occasion (see page 156).

■ Take time to talk about drugs, when a natural opportunity arises, but do not be alarmist about them. If they, or their close friends, have ever experimented with drugs, without apparently coming to any harm, they will find an exaggerated attitude unconvincing and will not feel able to trust what you have to say.

■ Find out if the school covers drugs in its health education programme, or if the Parent-Teacher Association is interested in putting on talks to inform parents (see page 201).

■ Do what you can to encourage your adolescent to find interesting and enjoyable activities, either with the family or with friends. The local authority youth service may be able to advise (see page 284).

Signs of drug-taking

Parents may not be at all aware that their adolescents are taking drugs as there are no sure signs. Much of the behaviour that accompanies drug-taking, such as mood swings and high spirits, can be fairly normal for adolescents in any case. But if you notice several of the following signs, then it would not be unreasonable to suspect that drugs are involved:[44]

■ Inexplicable changes in mood, from happy and alert to sullen and moody.
■ Unusual shows of temper and irritability.
■ Lack of appetite.
■ Unusual drowsiness.
■ Spending an unusual amount of time away from home.
■ Losing interest in usual activities and friends.
■ Schoolwork falling off.
■ Being especially secretive about friends and activities.
■ Truanting from school.
■ Lack of care about appearance.
■ Heavy use of perfume, aftershave and burning incense (to disguise the smell of drugs).
■ Unusual smells about the house.
■ Loss of money and belongings from the house.
■ Wearing dark glasses to hide the eyes.
■ Finding unusual powders or tablets, scorched foil, needles, plastic bags with glue or solvents.

What if your child uses drugs?

For parents whose adolescents are in the small group of repeated drug-takers (8 per cent in the London research quoted earlier,[45] but fewer in other surveys), finding out can be a shock. In many cases, however, there is no cause for great alarm. The 'sociable' use of cannabis, the most common of the illegal drugs, is not a very dangerous habit. It is, however, a criminal offence and not to be encouraged.

Solvent abuse, which is also common especially among younger teenagers, presents greater dangers. The Institute for the Study of Drug Dependence points out that many of these could be avoided if adults, parents and teachers were prepared to inform youngsters about what is dangerous and what is less so.[46] Many adults may be reluctant to pass on such information for fear of seeming to encourage glue-sniffing. This is the advice the Institute offers:

- It is less dangerous to sniff glue than to sniff gases and cleaning fluids.
- It is dangerous to experiment with unknown products and very dangerous to use combinations, for example, glue and pills or glue and alcohol.
- It is dangerous to risk suffocation by sniffing with the head in a plastic bag.
- It is dangerous to sniff alone and in secret where no one will notice if things go wrong.
- Dangerous places like roads and high buildings should be avoided, as should enclosed places.

If you believe that your adolescent is experimenting with drugs, or they tell you that this is so, make sure that your own feelings are under control before you take any further steps. It is possible that you will feel very anxious about what has happened and angry that your son or daughter should be behaving irresponsibly. You may also feel angry with any of their friends who have taken part in using drugs with them. You may feel inclined to blame yourself, or someone else in the family, for what has occurred. All of these feelings are to be expected but you need to be aware of them in order not to let them get in the way of the main task, which is to support your adolescent. It is important not to react in a way which will make them more likely to carry on taking drugs, secretly, out of a sense of rebellion, but to give them an opportunity to talk over any problems which may be worrying them.

First of all, remind yourself that the use of drugs is not necessarily the start of a slippery slope to addiction and a life of crime. For many teenagers it seems to be a passing phase. Give yourself time to calm down, and then talk to your adolescent about what has happened. Do not over-dramatise the event, certainly do not voice fears based on sensational media reports. Listen to what your son or daughter has to say without interrupting and let them know that you understand their point of view. It is probably more useful for you to spend more time listening than talking (see page 38). They need to know that you still accept them and listening is one way of showing this. Ask them if there is any problem troubling them and if there is anything that you can do about it. Do not blame them or their friends but tell them, without exaggerating, the reasons why you would prefer them not to use whichever drug is involved. Let them know about any dangers which are particularly to be avoided with the drug in question.

If you feel that you need help from outside the family, there are people you can turn to in confidence, whose addresses and telephone numbers are given on page 295.

In case of an emergency

If your adolescent should overdose, and is obviously drowsy or unconscious, lie them on their side, so that they do not inhale vomit, give them fresh air and telephone a doctor or the local hospital immediately.

Keep any pills, powders or suspicious substances or objects and give them to the doctor so that they can be identified.

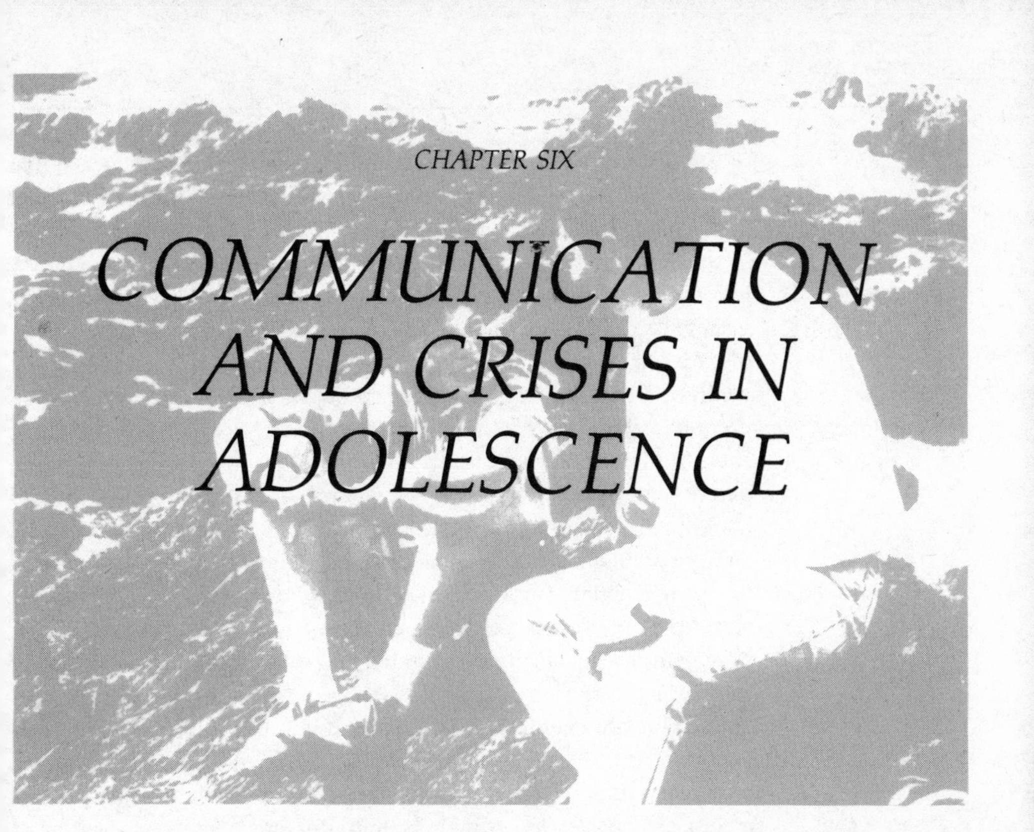

CHAPTER SIX

COMMUNICATION AND CRISES IN ADOLESCENCE

ALTHOUGH PARENTING teenagers is not always easy, parents have their own resources and their own particular ways of overcoming problems. For the most part they do not need any outside help in order to cope with the ups and downs of family life: those occasions when feelings run high with anger or the other times when both parents and adolescents are feeling miserable. They have lived together for a number of years and built up trust and understanding; none of this comes to an end when a child becomes a teenager. During the teenage years most parents and children continue to get on well together and to communicate about events and feelings which are important to them.[1]

This chapter aims to be of help at those times when family life seems to be more than ordinarily difficult and the usual ways of coping do not seem to work. It is about events that can arouse strong feelings in parents and children alike. The subjects covered include death, divorce, conflict between different members of the family and what parents can do to maintain an atmosphere in which mutual respect and good communication prevail. Next comes a section on stress and on what to do if it seems that a young person's behaviour or their emotions are causing serious problems either to themselves or to other people in the household. It ends with the stress that parents themselves experience and how to manage it rather than let it get the upper hand.

How do you feel?

In a family with adolescents, feelings are often close to the surface: a youngster is delighted because he is going to a party; a sixteen-year-old anxiously awaits an exam result; the whole family grieves at the death of a grandparent; brothers and sisters quarrel over who should do the washing-up; parents worry and are angry when an adolescent stays out late; a teenager slams the door rather than listen to criticism; parents are full of pride at signs of independence in their sons and daughters. Feelings are present to a greater or lesser extent in all family communications; they need to be expressed and they also need to be listened to and acknowledged. Unless they are given due attention they can stop parents and teenagers from expressing what they want to say clearly or from hearing what someone else is trying to communicate (see page 40).

Feelings are experienced as physical sensations, whether as a reaction to events, to memories or to thoughts. If you hear sad news, you may feel a lump in your throat as the muscles tighten; when you are anxious, you get an uneasy feeling in your stomach, your heart pounds and your hands get damp with sweat. Feelings are not only experienced, they are also communicated to other people. They can be expressed in words, for example, 'I feel so happy', or without words, that is non-verbally, by facial expressions, gestures, tone of voice, sighs, laughs, touch and in many other ways. Although teenagers sometimes hide their emotions, parents probably have a good idea how they are feeling most of the time.

Responding to feelings

When you become aware of someone's feelings, happy or otherwise, there are three possible responses:

1 You can *ignore the feelings altogether.*

An adolescent comes home from the youth club 'in a bad mood'. His father has had a bad day himself and so decides to ignore his sighs, frowns and silence and carries on with his work as though he has not noticed.

2 You can *openly deny someone's feelings.*

An adolescent looks depressed and her mother, who doesn't want her offspring to be unhappy, says 'Cheer up, it may never happen!'

Both of these approaches leave the adolescent feeling misunderstood.

3 If an adolescent is really worried or upset about something (no matter how trivial or how serious it seems to you) a third sort of response is needed: *accept and acknowledge the feelings.*

> A youngster comes home from school frowning and throws her books down on the table. The mother says, in an accepting tone of voice, 'You look as though something has really got you down today.'

By acknowledging feelings in this way the mother lets her daughter know that she is understood and accepted.

Acknowledging young people's feelings, letting them know that you understand, helps them to feel secure and confident and encourages them to communicate about themselves.

Noticing how they are feeling, and telling them that you notice by saying 'You're feeling a bit worried' or 'You're upset about it' or 'You're really pleased about that homework', communicates your understanding and this in itself is reassuring. When strong feelings are involved it is especially important that youngsters should be able to express them to someone who will accept them without criticism and who is prepared to spend time listening to their experience. Often it will fall to parents to provide this sort of support but other people inside and outside the family can also help.

Losing Someone Close

Separation and loss of loved ones arouse strong feelings, feelings which are experienced by many adolescents. A friend leaves the district, a pet dies, a romantic relationship breaks up, there is a death in the family, parents may divorce or separate. All of these circumstances involve sadness and readjustment for adolescents and patience and understanding from parents. In some situations, such as a family death or a divorce, parents are themselves involved and have feelings and wishes which may or may not be similar to those of the adolescent. This complicates matters and makes it less easy for the parent to provide the support which adolescents need. But if parents can remain aware of this difficulty they can none the less be of help, supporting their adolescent so that he or she comes through loss, with pain, but without damage.

Death

It is becoming commonplace to say that in today's society people are uncomfortable talking about death and dying, while talking about sex is comparatively easy. In part this may be because for many people death is unfamiliar. Although we see people die in countless films and on television news reports, this is often the result of a distant catastrophe or of a violent act and may not be experienced as at all immediate by those watching. Moreover, in real life, death is much less visible and immediate today than it was in the past: people live longer and often die in hospital rather than at home. In consequence, there is less occasion in the present day to talk about death, to explain it, than there would have been a century ago when major illnesses more frequently claimed the lives of adults and of children. Death may also be a topic which adults are reluctant to discuss because they themselves do not know what to say about it and they may want to shield both themselves and their children from a painful issue. While people with a religious background have a framework within which death can be discussed, others may not yet have evolved a way of thinking about it, and its place in their lives and experience, so that they can communicate about it at all easily.

Telling an adolescent about death

A taboo about death can colour parents' responses to their adolescents when a member of the family dies. Yet death is as much a part of human experience as birth, work, and falling in love, and needs reclaiming as something about which we can communicate without embarrassment. Without communication, grieving can be a very lonely business.[2] If someone in the family is seriously ill and likely to die, it is better to inform an adolescent rather than keeping them in the dark. They may otherwise be worried and suspicious yet unable to ask direct questions, sensing that the adults concerned are unwilling to tell them the truth. It is also necessary to prepare young people for the fact that a close relative is likely to die so that they have an opportunity to say goodbye in their own way. Not to tell them suggests that they are not to be trusted with information which affects them closely. In addition, if they are totally surprised by a death for which they could have been to some extent prepared, they are left feeling angry, shocked and misled.

When a death has occurred, information should be given as simply and directly as possible. In order to avoid troubling fantasies and uncertainties, the young person concerned should be told what was the cause of death and when it happened. Adolescents should also, if they wish, be given the opportunity of seeing the body and attending the funeral. This can help them to come to terms with the reality of what has happened, an important part of the process of grief.

Grieving Not all loss is equally serious; grief can be more or less intense and can be experienced over several years or be over in months, depending on the closeness of the relationship involved. There are three phases of grief which follow each other in sequence.[3] This sequence holds true for all sorts of loss, whether of a pet, or of a friend who moves away, or when a close relative – a parent, brother or sister, or a grandparent – dies.

Early grief In the first phase, various reactions are possible.

Bereaved people may react with shock and disbelief; they may feel for a short time quite numb and distanced from their feelings. Or they may seem to treat the death almost casually, as though cutting themselves off from its reality. It should not be seen as heartlessness if at first they want to carry on with their own lives and amusements as though nothing had happened. Nor should lack of open grief be seen as a sign that they have 'got over' a bereavement. More open grieving may follow later and adults in the household should be ready to respond to this when it happens.

Just like an adult, adolescents may sometimes have a strong experience of the dead person's presence, for example, sitting in their usual chair or the sound of their step coming down the stairs. These experiences are quite normal: a way of denying, for the moment, what has happened. They should be acknowledged and if a parent has similar experiences, it can be helpful to the adolescent to say so.

The bereaved person may also experience anxiety; the death of someone close can make the world seem much less safe. Anxiety states are physical reactions to alarming events. The heartbeat quickens, adrenalin and proadrenalin flow into the bloodstream, blood pressure rises, muscles tense, the mouth can go dry and the stomach start to churn. The person who has these reactions is keyed up for danger, they are physically ready to escape either by running away or by fighting off an attacker. They have energy at the ready, waiting to be used, and their blood is chemically prepared to clot more quickly, in case they are wounded. They are poised for 'fight or flight'.

In modern life the occasions when people need these defences are rare but they are called up when danger is sensed, whether physical or otherwise. Feelings of anxiety are stressful and exhausting when there is nowhere to run to and nothing to fight. When an adolescent is anxious, they need to have their feelings listened to and acknowledged. They also need the security of physical contact – of hugs, cuddles and a reassuring arm round their shoulder.

Acute grief The second phase is characterised by strong feelings as numbness and denial disappear.

The bereaved may experience waves of yearning for the person who can never come back, followed by fresh realisations that their yearning is to no avail. There is a repeated process of holding on to an unreal hope, letting go, and returning to the reality of loss. These feelings of yearning and sad acceptance can be accompanied by guilt about past 'failures' towards the dead person and by anger with them for going away.

A young person can be so preoccupied with their grief in this early stage that they become quite disorganised and find it hard to concentrate and get on with the rest of their life. They may need help completing homework or just getting off to school.

Some youngsters have episodes of total bleakness and despair; others are irritable and have unaccustomed outbursts of bad temper. These all need to be met with patience and sympathy.

Coming to terms with bereavement In the final phase, there is a coming to terms with what has happened. This may take a longer or shorter time depending on the seriousness of the loss. Eventually the young person is able to accept the reality of their situation. They also realise that they have been able to survive their loss. Although they still miss the person who has died, especially at times like birthdays and anniversaries, coping with the loss is no longer paramount in their lives and they get on with what life has to offer.

Helping a bereaved adolescent

The best way you can help an adolescent to cope with their grief is to accept their feelings and to let them know that you accept them. This is not always easy. In many situations of loss, feelings of parents are strongly involved too. These may be similar to those of their child in some ways, but different in others, just as their relationship with the dead person was uniquely their own. It is painful to be with someone who is suffering, and especially so when the person concerned is young and dear to you, but trying to cheer a youngster up, or trying to ignore their feelings, is to deny their grief. If you let them know that you can accept how they are feeling, allowing them to cry, giving them physical comfort, sharing your own sadness and tears, you are also letting them know that they are not alone (see pages 174–5).

For yourself, having a good friend in whom you can confide your own feelings can give you the strength to be of use to other members of the family. If you feel there is no one you can talk to, you may find that the organisations listed on pages 295–6 can help. A teenager may also want to turn to someone outside the immediate family.

Let the school know Parents should inform the school if there has been a death in the family or if someone very close to a young person has died. The best person to tell is a member of the school pastoral staff, such as a year tutor or head of house (see page 203). The staff should then understand if there is any falling off in schoolwork, and give help and encouragement to catch up.

At home Do not avoid talking about the person who has died. Just let their name come up naturally in conversation as it occurs to you: 'Granny would have liked this ...'; 'Do you remember when Daddy ...'; and follow any leads your adolescent gives. Censoring dead people out of conversation is like denying that they lived and were important to you. Grief is painful, but if it is lived through and not denied it does not destroy people. After a death, be prepared for an adolescent to be more dependent on you for a while; some may at first want to spend more time with you than they have for some years.

Divorce and separation

It is becoming increasingly common for marriages to end in divorce: one in three couples divorce in the United States and almost as many in Britain. There are also separations which do not feature in official statistics. Because of divorce, many teenagers live apart from one of their parents; most commonly they live with their mother and see their father from time to time.[4]

The experience of divorce or separation differs from family to family. One partner may want to end a marriage more strongly than the other; the parent who remains in charge of the children may be distressed, relieved, guilty, sad, or frankly pleased that the marriage is over. The material circumstances surrounding a divorce also differ. For some families there is a marked falling off in income; it may be necessary for a mother who was not previously employed to get paid work or, where she is already working, to work longer hours. A family may need to move house or even to move out of the district, which entails changing schools for children and adolescents. Because of the differing circumstances which surround divorce it is impossible to say how it affects any one adolescent. So if you are a divorced parent, you will need to measure what follows against your own experience, not forgetting your unique relationship with your son or daughter and his or her individuality.

Telling an adolescent about divorce or separation

At least one partner in a marriage has reached the point of divorce because it seems to make sense: life will be better without this particular close relationship. The second partner may not feel the same; for him or for her it may seem that the relationship was satisfactory or at least that it could have become so. Because of a fundamental difference such as this, quite apart from other problems, the couple can find communicating difficult. Yet it is essential, for the sake of the children, that they should communicate effectively with one another. They need not struggle to do this alone; parents can get help to be as constructive as possible about their divorce from organisations which are experienced in marriage breakdowns (see page 296 for addresses). A counsellor from such an organisation can help communication between the divorcing partners. By listening carefully to what each person has to say, and helping each partner to listen to the other, the counsellor can assist parents to identify common ground and to find ways of meeting common interests upon which both parties can agree. Common interests include arrangements about maintenance and about access to children. In a case where there is joint custody, a person outside the immediate situation may also be able to help parents to come to an agreement about issues such as their shared responsibility for the young person's education.

Whether or not parents seek help from a counselling agency, it is advisable that they work out in advance what they are going to tell the children about their separation, who will tell them, and when they will do so. An advantage of both being present when the news is broken, and talking about their decision jointly, is that the adolescent is not left with any uncertainty about the divorce going ahead. Also, both parents can show that they are in agreement about how contact will be maintained with the parent who is leaving. It is important for the adolescent to know what has happened in as simple terms as possible: 'We have not been happy together and we think it would be better to end our marriage'; and what is going to happen: the timetable of the divorce and the arrangements for the adolescent to have access to the absent parent.

Adolescents' feelings about divorce

Most adolescents probably know full well when their parents are not happy together. Nevertheless, the news that they are to separate can still come as a shock and, although they probably have friends whose parents are divorced, it may take time for them to adjust to the situation.

In some cases, of course, they may be relieved to hear about the divorce. But other teenagers, even though they understand the reasons why their parents are parting, will still be saddened or alarmed at the thought of 'losing' their mother or father and their grief can go through the stages already described (see pages 177–8), from denial that it is really happening, through cycles of wishing for it to be otherwise, followed by acceptance. Teenagers, unlike younger children, are quite realistic and rarely seem to believe that they are to blame for their parents' separation.[5]

If an adolescent is very distressed and you think that schoolwork is likely to suffer, get in touch with a member of the school pastoral staff (see page 203) and explain about the separation.

As well as a clear statement about what is happening, adolescents need to be able to express their feelings to someone they trust, to you, to your former partner (their mother or father), or to someone less closely involved in the immediate situation. Friends and relatives can provide good emotional support at a time when parents are so involved that they find patient listening difficult.[6] Parents themselves may experience an adolescent's outpourings as pressure against the divorce or as blame that it has happened. Try to arrange things so that there is someone who can provide a listening ear, a relative or friend who will offer support around the time of the divorce and after.

Keeping in touch

After a divorce adolescents may want to keep in touch with grandparents and relatives on both sides of the family. Such decisions and wishes should, if possible, be respected and, according to their age, young people may be able to make their own arrangements for doing so. The same is true of access to an absent parent. Adolescents should themselves have some say as to how much contact they have. Arrangements for access should be made as soon as possible after a separation. Once a pattern is established it should continue but it may be difficult to maintain contact if it does not take place from the outset.[7]

The outings and activities which younger children often have with a parent who no longer lives with them may not be appropriate for a teenager, so it may be necessary to find other ways of maintaining contact.[8] Just being able to visit the absent parent and make themselves at home may be what adolescents need: perhaps a place in their parent's new home that is theirs, a room if that is available, or some drawers for their belongings.

For some parents the contact between their son or daughter and an ex-partner is not easy. But if the adolescent wants it, this should be accepted and bitterness and anger left unexpressed, even though the association may be painful for the parent. Disclosing such feelings can leave the adolescent with conflicting loyalties. Parents whose feelings are so strong that they have difficulty in keeping them to themselves should find another adult to confide in, whether a close friend or a counsellor who is quite separate from the situation.

New partners Parents as well as children need satisfying relationships, and for lone parents there arises the possibility of a new life partner, a new friendship and sexual relationship. Introducing a friend who is a potential partner into the family needs to be done with consideration for the adolescent. It can be difficult for an adolescent, who may still be struggling with accepting his or her own sexuality, to have to accept that a parent leads a sexual life. Introductions should be gradual to avoid the need for sudden adjustments. Young people also need to be given information about what is happening, at least in so far as it is likely to affect their own lives. 'We like one another and want to try living together,' for example; or 'I've asked Tony to stay overnight.' It is embarrassing for a teenager to have to meet a comparative stranger on the way to the bathroom without advance warning.

Step-parents Introducing a new adult into the family on a permanent basis, as a step-parent, needs to be done tactfully and gradually. It should not be a surprise. An explanation of the course of events is necessary so that the adolescent knows where he or she stands and has time to consider a situation which may change many aspects of his or her life. This may include whether there will be any house-moving or change of school and whether there will be step-brothers and -sisters.

If the adolescent seems to take time to warm towards their step-parent, loyalties towards their real father or mother should be taken into account and respected. They may also need to be reassured that they themselves are still loved by their mother or father and have not been pushed aside for the new partner, which may entail making time for parent and adolescent to spend alone together. On the positive side the new partner brings fresh resources to the family. The adolescent is then relieved of being the main support and confidant for a lone parent. As one of the main features of adolescence is for the close ties between parents and children to be gently loosened, this is all to the good.

Getting on together When a new partner is introduced into the family the needs of adults and children must all be taken into account. A household which had its own way of going about things, its own history and customs, its own view of what is acceptable behaviour on the part of adults and children, is being opened up. The newcomer will inevitably change the balance of the family and introduce new elements into how it functions. These can be changes for the better but it is wise to be aware of the various pros and cons of the new situation before embarking on it.

It is important for the two adults to sit down and sort out where the problems are likely to arise and how to tackle them, or avoid them, before starting out.[9] Practical differences in lifestyle, which may already be apparent, have to be acknowledged and solutions found that both partners can agree to. It is also necessary for both adults in the new household to reach agreement on what they see as appropriate behaviour for young people, such as the time they come home in the evening and doing homework systematically. Just as with biological parents, it is best for the couple to have a united front even though some adults may decide that it is the 'real' parent who takes the lead over difficulties with their own adolescent.

The adolescent's need for privacy should be respected by a newcomer to the family and this may need to be discussed in advance. Perhaps a ground rule would be for the step-parent to respect the adolescent's need for privacy in the same way that they would that of an adult: for example, not going into his or her room without permission, not looking at homework until asked and not making personal comments of the sort which would be unacceptable to an adult. Step-parents and step-children should take time to get to know one another; they should not expect too much to start with, but allow their relationship to grow naturally.

If problems arise which seem to need some outside help there are the names of appropriate agencies on page 296.

Conflict Between Parents and Adolescents

Situations are bound to arise when there is conflict between parents and adolescents. Sometimes they are critical of you while on other occasions you may feel anxious or angry about some aspect of their behaviour. Different families have different styles of communicating about conflict. In some there can be a lot of yelling without any harm being done; others are quieter and for them raised voices would indicate some sort of crisis. Whatever the style, there are ways of handling conflict which are more constructive than others and achieve a better outcome for everyone concerned.

Some people are anxious about bringing concerns into the open; they bottle up their feelings, causing stress to themselves and running the risk of resentment coming through in other, less direct ways, or about trivial matters. Eventually, when they can put up with things no longer, they explode and more damage is done than if the problem had been tackled earlier. When this happens in a family the person under attack understandably feels aggrieved and says, in effect, 'Why didn't you tell me before? I didn't know I was causing problems.' This can be the start of sorting out what has gone wrong but it can also make communications more difficult than might otherwise have been the case. Conflict between parents and adolescents does not have to lead to quarrels and upsets; it can be a starting-point from which you come to understand one another better, take more account of each other's point of view and find constructive solutions to problems.

When adolescents criticise you

Just as parents need to confront adolescents from time to time, so adolescents occasionally feel the need to tell their mother or father that they are not happy with some aspect of parental behaviour. They have reached an age when they realise that parents are not perfect and this new realism is one way in which they become independent. They may blurt out their criticism in the heat of the moment or they may tell you in a more rational way about whatever is bothering them. For example, teenagers may feel that their parents are not treating them in a way that is suitable for their age: 'You worry too much about me, I can look after myself, now' ... 'Why did you tell Grandma about that? It's my business, I don't like being talked about, I'm not a kid' ... 'You've been going through my drawers ...'

For parents there may be something to be gained from criticism, even if the way it is expressed is hurtful. And if adolescents can talk to you in a rational way about something which affects them adversely, you have reason to be proud of their maturity, although this may not be your feeling at the time! Here are some ways of being constructive:

1 Cool things down In the face of criticism, be aware of your own feelings. You may feel angry or hurt, so much so that you cannot at that moment respond without causing the whole situation to escalate.

A teenager is upset because they think, mistakenly, that their mother has treated a sibling better than they have been treated. They are angry and jealous and shout out insults. The mother's immediate reaction is of anger at being spoken to so 'rudely' and for no apparent reason. If she allows her own feelings to become involved in the situation it could blow up into something so stormy that neither side would really hear what the other had to say.

In cases like this, get some breathing space, even a few minutes, to cool down so that you are able to think constructively about what has been said, decide how you are going to respond to the criticism and what, if anything, you should do about it. If you feel anxious or angry, a conscious effort to calm down is useful. Some people follow the old custom of literally counting up to ten, but just telling yourself to keep calm and taking a few deep breaths can also help.

If your adolescent is very upset you need to decide whether your conversation should happen 'here and now'. Would a cooling-off period help? Explain that you are taking what they have to say seriously but that you are both upset and that you would like a few minutes to think. You could say something like: 'I can see that you are angry and when you said that I felt angry too. I want to hear more about what you said but I need to calm down first.'

2 Listen and let them know you understand Let your adolescent say what he or she wants to say without interrupting: hear them out. This is very important. Even if you think they are mistaken about some detail, do not interrupt but *listen carefully*. In this way you will understand more fully and your son or daughter will feel satisfied that you have listened. Next, let them know that you understand by *summarising* what they have said and how they feel: 'You are feeling angry because she can go on the school-trip, and you weren't allowed to go last term.'

This is also a way of checking that you understand properly, because if you have misunderstood he or she will soon put you right.

Any solution, explanation or apology you want to give may not be properly heard until your adolescent knows that you do understand his or her point of view and that you are not avoiding it or denying it; in short, you are taking their experience seriously. They may need to repeat what is on their mind more than once, because their feelings are still strong and they need to be sure that you have understood.

3 Apologise If you are in the wrong, apologise. Everyone makes mistakes, it is part of everyday life. It could be that you had misunderstood, or forgotten something, or perhaps you had not realised what effect your actions would have. So acknowledge that there is cause for complaint, say that you are sorry and, if appropriate, what steps you are going to take to put things right.

4 Put right misunderstandings In some cases all that is necessary is to put right any misunderstanding that underlies the criticism.

5 Find ways for both of you to win If the situation cannot be resolved by a simple explanation or apology, then the most useful attitude in any conflict is to want the best outcome for everybody (see page 189).

How to discuss problems with your adolescent

There are three sorts of problems that can arise between parents and adolescents:

- when sons or daughters do something that offends parents' taste but has no serious consequences;
- when they do things that are inconsiderate and cause trouble for other people in the family;
- when their behaviour is worrying because it could lead to serious problems.

Behaviour that irritates you

In everyday life with a teenager there may be situations that do not please you but that are not really important enough to make a fuss about. Young people can be genuinely careless and forgetful and, in some matters, they have standards and tastes which are quite different from your own. For example, their bedrooms can be in a permanent mess and their clothes, and how they do their hair, may seem totally outlandish.

It is not worth wasting your energy over differences between you that are not causing problems. Your teenage children are making choices to suit themselves, not you, and this is a part of becoming independent. If they are happy to sleep in an untidy room, that is their business; there are no serious results and it affects no one but themselves. The same is true of strange fashions and hairstyles.

Behaviour that inconveniences you

Sometimes adolescents are thoughtless and cause problems for you and other members of the family. The business of growing up and the various pressures on young people can lead them to forget that other people need consideration. They constantly overlook some household job which they had agreed to do. They are untidy about the house and leave behind a trail of shoes and homework. They play loud music late at night and do not clean the bath after use. They spend long hours on the telephone at your expense and stop other calls from getting through for the rest of the family.

In some instances parents may decide to turn a blind eye to this sort of behaviour, too. A young person may usually be kind and helpful so that one episode of thoughtlessness does not seem worth mentioning. Parents may also be aware of any particular stresses that their adolescent children are under, ranging from the approach of examinations to trouble with a boyfriend or girlfriend, and feel that there is good reason to be patient and put up with whatever is causing a problem. There are occasions, however, when it is necessary to confront young people about their actions and to tell them how their behaviour affects you.

Behaviour that worries you

Other behaviour is more of a worry. For example, it could be that your son or daughter has come home very late without letting you know in advance; or you suspect that they have been smoking or drinking, under-age, or sniffing glue. Although all these eventualities can be alarming for parents, isolated incidents are often not serious. They could result from thoughtlessness or be one-off experiments. While parents will not wish to ignore them, they should not be overdramatised at the risk of encouraging rebellion.

Sometimes, however, a young person's behaviour seems to be leading directly to serious problems, either imminently or in the long term. For example, they may have decided not to attend school or you may have noticed that they have lost a lot of weight and are refusing to eat, or you may think that they are drinking too much.

With any worrying behaviour you need first to communicate with your adolescent about it in a manner that respects their developing independence. Some suggestions about doing this are given below. Sometimes parents may, in addition, decide to seek outside help about behaviour which is seriously threatening their adolescent's well-being (see page 190).

Communicating about conflict

What follows is advice for when you need to talk to your adolescent either about behaviour that is worrying you because you think it could have serious consequences, or when you want to confront them about something that is causing you unnecessary trouble. There are similarities in the approach recommended here and that suggested earlier for reacting when your adolescent criticises you (pages 184–6). Both are ways of sorting out small problems at an early stage, as well as dealing with serious issues. They encourage open and constructive communication.

Be calm when you want to tackle a problem

In the heat of the moment it is not easy to be calm and for some people it is more difficult than for others. There is no harm in letting your adolescent see that you are feeling angry or worried about something. But the moment when your feelings are at their height may not be the right one for listening to what he or she has to say or for deciding on a constructive course of action. Anger or anxiety on your part can arouse equally strong feelings in your adolescent who may then be too preoccupied fending off your feelings to listen to what you have to say. So, in a crisis, remind yourself to be calm and in control before you say anything. The old trick of counting to ten actually works.

If either of you is very angry or distressed, you have to decide if this is the best time and place to deal with a problem. And the more serious the problem, the more important it is to avoid dealing with it while feelings are running high.

Check misunderstandings

Sometimes problems arise because of misunderstandings. The first step is therefore to check (politely, not between clenched teeth) that there is no misunderstanding on your part or that of your offspring. For example, a pleasant 'Are those my socks you've just taken from the drier?' gives you the opportunity to apologise if the mistake is on your part (they were not your socks), and the adolescent a chance to apologise if the mistake is theirs. This may be all that is needed; just mentioning something could be enough to clarify the situation. If there are no misunderstandings, and if you think that it is important to take things further, the next step is to help your son or daughter to understand your point of view better.

Explain how you are affected

Tell adolescents how their actions affect you, putting the emphasis on you and on the problems they give rise to: 'Because you didn't bring your coffee mugs downstairs and let them collect in your room, I had to hunt round the house to find them.'

As well as talking about the material consequences you can also say how you feel: 'When you come in late without telling me I feel anxious because of what might have happened to you.' Or: 'When you leave your clothes all over the house instead of putting them away I feel angry, because if I want the house tidy I have to put them away myself.'

Not blaming

Notice that by talking about the effects of young people's behaviour on *you*, you are not commenting adversely about their character or even about their behaviour, or comparing one youngster unfavourably with another. In short, you are not levelling 'blame' in the hope of brow-beating them into conformity. Statements like 'You are so lazy and untidy', 'Staying out late is really inconsiderate' or 'We never had this trouble with your sister' can put adolescents on the defensive and make them unwilling to see your point of view. The strongest message that comes across is that you do not approve of them; the idea that their actions can have consequences for the people they live with fails to get through. Another disadvantage is that hearing themselves being put down can sap their self-esteem at a time when they need to develop confidence and a sense of responsibility.

Not blaming is vital for keeping communications open, but it may not come naturally. Many of us are accustomed to situations where blame and criticism are used in order to control, or attempt to control, other people. Perhaps you can remember times when, as a young person, you were at the receiving end of criticism and how you felt about it.

Listen patiently Listen to whatever your son or daughter says, encourage them to talk, do not interrupt, and when they have finished show them that you have understood by repeating the main things they have said back to them (see page 42).

If there is a problem, try and solve it together Involve your adolescent in finding ways round the problem that you can both agree to. This may mean setting new rules between you about such things as a suitable time to come home in the evening or at the weekend. Teenagers appreciate the opportunity to make decisions, alongside their parents, about things which affect them.

■ Adolescents whose parents consistently tell them what to do without consulting them or, at the other extreme, let them do whatever they like, without question, feel rejected and unwanted by their parents. But when parents involve teenagers in making decisions and explain their reasons for setting boundaries, adolescents are more likely to have confidence in themselves, to have a high level of self-esteem and to be able to make up their own minds, without being over-influenced by other people.

■ Involving your adolescent in decisions, with both of you making a contribution, helps them to exercise some independence and, at the same time, to retain a sense of security. It gives them a model, guided by you, of how to deal with problems in a constructive way; it shows that you care about them and about their welfare, that you love and respect them.[10]

If the problem seems to need outside help In most cases there is no need to seek outside help, either because difficulties can be solved at home or because they are not big enough to cause serious concern.

If behaviour *is* causing serious concern, then it is necessary to find extra resources from outside the family. Key questions to ask yourself are: Is this behaviour severely endangering the young person, either now or for the future? Is there a marked change from the behaviour you were used to?

There is advice and information about many of the problems which can occur for adolescents throughout this book. The index lists them under subject: for example, anorexia, drug or alcohol abuse, school refusal. The appropriate sections give details of further reading, if you need it, and the addresses of organisations you may wish to contact. If one organisation cannot help, try another. Give your son or daughter all the support you can, both practical and emotional. In the end you may need to come to terms with the fact that it is their problem and that only they can solve it. Becoming an adult means, among other things, living one's own life and making one's own mistakes.

Quarrelling between brothers and sisters

Quarrelling between brothers and sisters can be hard to live with. The scientific literature on adolescent sibling rivalry is very sparse but fortunately what there is suggests that most brothers and sisters get on well together. There can, however, be conflict and competitiveness, especially between boys.[11]

When your children quarrel you may decide that the conflict is their problem, not yours, and that they need to sort it out between them. But if you feel that there is a misunderstanding that needs to be put right, or if you are asked to give an opinion, what should you do? It is not advisable to rush into snap judgements, no matter how clear it may seem to you that one person is in the right and the other in the wrong. In situations like this, blaming one or the other child will not help, in fact quite the reverse. Tell them that you can see that there is a problem and that you are willing to help them find a way out. What is needed is a joint effort to reach a solution from which neither loses face and both emerge as winners. This means that each has to listen to the other's point of view and be prepared to discuss alternative ways of getting what they want which are acceptable to both.

Brothers and sisters may not always be ready or willing to try this sort of approach. Quarrels can arise from feelings which run deep and of which they are not totally aware. In such cases parents should not feel guilty. Young people have their own individual temperaments and are also, largely, responsible for their actions.

Emotional Disturbances

A few adolescents experience emotional disturbances which limit their capacity to function well at home, at school and with their friends. Adolescents are notorious for their mood swings; young people can be 'over the moon' one day and 'down in the dumps' the next. It is quite normal for adolescents to be sad, to have outbursts of temper and to feel anxious. When you consider the physical and hormonal changes that are taking place (see pages 6–8), together with the changing expectations placed on youngsters by parents, teachers and friends as they progress through their teens, it is not surprising if they find life stressful at times. There are disappointments and challenges which, by and large, they take in their stride but for an unlucky few the stresses are too severe and get the upper hand.

Stress

To some extent stress is a part of life and one that we all experience. There are people for whom life would seem very dull without a certain level of challenge and uncertainty, but too much of this is distressing and can interfere with how people function. Perhaps the most painful sort of stress occurs when a young person feels highly threatened but at the same time powerless or inadequate and continues to experience these feelings over an extended period of time. Inescapable bullying is a typical example of a situation which can give rise to stress (see page 244). But stress does not arise only from physical threats; examinations, a hostile teacher, the loss of someone close, losing the approval of parents, are all potentially stressful. For a few youngsters, adapting to the physical and sexual changes of adolescence is itself a source of stress.

Signs of stress and emotional disturbance

- Youngsters may start to behave in a way that is potentially harmful, like taking drugs (see page 169), drinking (see page 157) or shop-lifting (see pages 273–6). (*Note*: These sorts of behaviour do not in themselves indicate that a young person is suffering stress or emotional disturbance; young people who are quite happy may experiment with all of them.)
- Adolescents may become physically ill as a result of tension and

anxiety, with frequent headaches, stomach upsets and skin rashe
Some become worried about their health without any serious physic
cause. They may develop a tic such as a frequent grimace or
repetitive movement to brush hair away from their face.

- They may feel low and depressed, with little energy, a poo
appetite, difficulty in sleeping. He or she may not want to have soci
contact with other people and may be frequently irritable.
- They may seem to be obsessive about something, perhaps abou
cleanliness, feeling a compulsion to wash and to keep changing the
clothes; or they may be preoccupied by thoughts – for example,
illness – which they cannot dismiss.
- They may have phobias of different sorts. For example, they ma
go berserk if they see a spider, or refuse to be in the same room as
cat. Sometimes they are afraid of the dark.

For the most part adolescents who are disturbed or under stre
need someone to listen to them, either one of the family or a frien
a teacher or youth leader perhaps. They may also need encourageme
and practical support. Do not let them get overwhelmed by th
amount of schoolwork or preparation for examinations that needs t
be done. Help them to break work down into small steps, which ca
be tackled one at a time and crossed off the list when they a
completed. Encourage them to take time off for themselves, to rela
with friends and with the family. Work can be done more easily whe
they are fresh. Parents need to assure their sons and daughters
their support when they run into trouble – even when they do n
approve of what has happened. When they are in serious difficulti
teenagers need to know that their parents are standing beside the
and will remain beside them, whatever happens.

Whether a young person needs professional help for an emotion
disturbance depends on the answers to the following questions:

- Are the problems severe?
- Do you think that they interfere with his or her social life, schoo
work or relationships in a marked way? For example, a phobia abo
bats may have little effect on everyday life if an adolescent lives
town, and only cause occasional panic on holiday or at the zoo; b
refusing to go out alone stands in the way of social development.
- Are the problems very upsetting for the adolescent? For you ar
for the rest of the family?

If the answer to any of these questions is yes, then you should loo
for help from outside the family. Addresses are given on pages 295–

Suicide

In many countries the suicide rate is increasing among adolescents and young adults.[12] Many suicide attempts are not the result of a momentary impulse but are a final attempt to find a way out of overwhelming difficulties when all seems hopeless.

Not all young people who kill themselves give warning in advance but some do. It is vitally important to take any threat of suicide seriously, to encourage the young person to talk and to get advice from outside the family (see page 190).

When Parents Experience Stress

Parents as well as adolescents experience stress from time to time; they too have to face challenges and difficulties, which sometimes seem to come from all directions. Adolescent sons and daughters can themselves be a cause for stress because at times they are careless, exasperating and worrying. It is easy to be preoccupied by them, wondering how their lives will turn out; whether they are serious enough about schoolwork; whether they are drifting, or hurtling even, into trouble; saddened by their disappointments or infuriated by their untidiness. And at one and the same time, stress can present itself from other quarters such as work, relationships, elderly parents, money and housing. It can even arise out of events that are supposed to be pleasant like Christmas or other festivals, visits from relatives or preparations for a holiday.

At a personal level some parents realise that they are entering middle age and that the possibilities they may have hoped for earlier in life are no longer available. Until parents come to terms with such disappointments, they too can be an underlying stress.

For parents, as for adolescents, a certain amount of stress makes life interesting, but too much is unpleasant and threatening. It affects how people feel so that they can become agitated, depressed and restless. It also has repercussions on thought processes so that someone who is very distressed can be deluded into thinking that there is nothing that can be done to improve a difficult situation, that they are totally powerless and that the future is very dismal indeed. This can even occur when there are positive and, to an outsider, obvious steps to be taken to deal with problems.

When someone reaches a point where they feel they are having difficulty in coping with life, their actions and responses, under stress can cause situations that are already difficult to become worse. Unless stress can be kept to manageable proportions, it can affect the way parents react to adolescents, to other members of the family, to colleagues and to people who play an important part in their children's lives: to their teachers or their friends, for example. Under severe stress it becomes easy to over-react to what at other times would seem minor problems. One common answer is to do everything possible to escape from difficult situations; perhaps ignoring letters which should be answered or avoiding people with whom there is conflict, rather than attempting to sort out differences. Another response is to lose control, to say things which are regretted later or even to resort to violence.

And too much stress not only leads people to feel unhappy and powerless and to react in inappropriate ways; prolonged stress can also contribute to physical conditions such as high blood pressure and be a factor in heart disease and ulcers.

People are different in the amount of stress they can handle without becoming over-stressed. In part this may be on account of their own individual temperament but it can also be because some are well supported by family and friends, others less so. But for everyone finding ways of coping with stress and crises when they arise and of preventing life from becoming too stressful are important.

Here are some ways of managing stress which can help parents and therefore, indirectly, their adolescents and other members of the family. Underlying many of these is the idea that parents must take time to look after themselves and their own interests as well as being available for their sons and daughters.

■ Mothers and fathers need friends, someone to confide in whom they can trust and who can listen patiently, when necessary. Talking about problems can help to put them into perspective, can relieve feelings and can stop a parent from feeling isolated. Sometimes life partners can support one another in this way, but at other times, when a difficulty affects both partners, or when a parent is bringing up an adolescent alone, it can be useful to go to other friends or relatives. It is important, therefore, to know whom you can turn to and this means maintaining friendships and family links with people who can offer support and whom you can support in turn, even though life is busy and taken up with work and looking after the family. In some cases it may also be useful to turn to a professional helper – a counsellor or sympathetic doctor for example.

- Parents need to be able to take time for themselves, to relax and to enjoy life, away from everyday pressures. This may mean guarding precious time to sleep late on Sunday morning or on Saturday afternoon perhaps; or maintaining old interests or developing new ones. Sometimes it is necessary to set boundaries as to what the rest of the family can expect of a parent.
- Holidays and days off are important.
- If parents find physical relaxation difficult then they may be able to find somewhere, such as a yoga class, where relaxation techniques are taught.
- Feelings of guilt about family crises are not always realistic and can make stress worse. Parents should try to remember that they are not entirely responsible for their adolescents' behaviour. Young people themselves have some responsibility and society itself plays some part.
- It is not possible to control an adolescent's behaviour. Parents can have an effect on what teenagers do but in the end teenagers make their own choices. When parents are worried about them, they should talk to them, calmly, and try to find ways out of problems together (see page 189).
- Sometimes when there seems far too much to do, and far too little time available, it can be helpful to sit down for a few minutes, to write down all that needs doing and number them in order of importance. It may be necessary to break a task down into all its smaller parts. Identify what must be done first and decide to make a start on that. Put at the end of the list whatever is less essential and jettison what is not really necessary.
- Ask other people for help when it is needed.
- Avoid setting unattainable standards and goals. If parents fall into the trap of being perfectionists, only content with the very best from themselves, their adolescents and others, they are doomed to disappointment and anxiety.

CHAPTER SEVEN

ADOLESCENTS AT SCHOOL

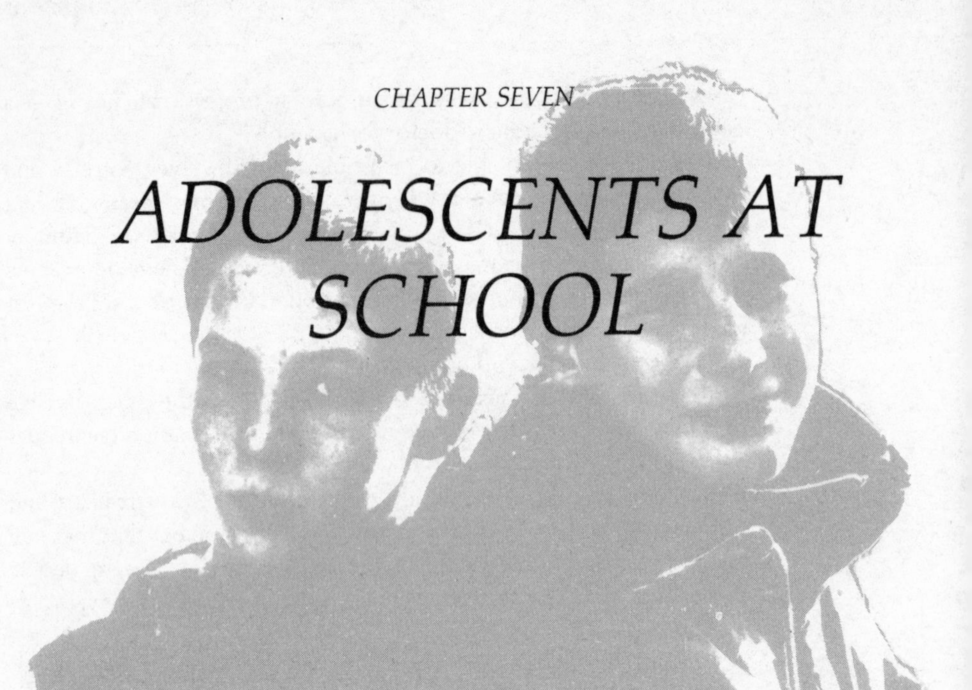

GOING TO SCHOOL TAKES up a large part of your adolescent's waking life. It is where he or she learns, makes friends and prepares for the future. For youngsters to make the most of their secondary school careers, the responsibilities rest jointly with the individual student, their parents and the educational system, including the schools they attend.

The part of parents in education

Parents are in the best position to have an overview of their children's school career at the time when they transfer from primary to secondary school and throughout their years there. It is true that primary schools forward the records of pupils when they change schools, providing some continuity between the two. But the knowledge that parents have of their son or daughter's happiness and progress at school quite apart from events at home which may be affecting schoolwork will enable them to decide whether to liaise with the school about any problems that arise.

Parents can also support adolescents in the ups and downs of school life, helping with homework, being ready to listen and encouraging them to make their own decisions about school subjects and about future plans. The participation of parents need not be limited to looking after the direct interests of their own child, however. With recent legislation there is now a real opportunity for parents to be partners in their children's education. Together with other parents, and the school staff, they are in a position to contribute to school policy and to influence the sort of service provided for adolescents and for the local community. Not all parents wish to involve themselves in this way, or have the time to do so. But should you want to take action over a general or a particular school issue, ways of doing so are suggested at many points in this chapter.

There is also information about how schools are organised; about choosing a secondary school and settling in; about homework, examinations, options and reports; about children who have special needs; about problems that arise at school and what steps you can take to put them right.

The Secondary School

In the United Kingdom children change schools at the age of nine, eleven or thirteen, according to the policy of the local authority. Starting secondary school plays an important part in the development of an adolescent's identity. The primary school or middle school quickly comes to be seen as a place belonging to the past, to the world of childhood compared to the broader horizons of the 'big school'. In the primary school, one teacher looks after the varied educational needs of a class and is responsible for each child's progress and well-being. By the time they reach secondary school, young people are developing intellectually and socially. They are ready to explore various fields of knowledge in greater depth and to develop new skills and gain fresh understanding. At this stage they need the expertise of specialist teachers, for example, in the sciences, in languages and in drama. They also need access to sophisticated resources like an adequate supply of computers, a language laboratory, scientific laboratories, a well-equipped gymnasium, art studios and craft workshops that are well stocked with tools and materials.

One of the functions of the school is to prepare pupils for public examinations; another is to advise them about further education and training possibilities and about work. At the same time staff look after the day-to-day progress and welfare of pupils. So a secondary school is a complex organisation, different in many ways from the relatively simple world of the primary school. In order to get the most out of a secondary school it is useful to understand how it is organised. Not all secondary schools are run on exactly the same lines and the titles used for staff can differ from one school to another. Here are some details about the structure of secondary schools and the different sorts of staff who will be involved in your child's secondary education:

Independent schools

Independent schools are fee-paying schools which may be owned by a charitable trust or by an individual. There are many sorts of independent school: some are day schools and others are boarding; some are provided by a local ethnic group to meet the needs of its own parents and children. Independent schools include traditional public schools as well as experimental schools, and the laws which apply to them are not the same as for state schools. For example, the staff in independent schools do not need to be qualified in the same way and there is no obligation for independent schools to follow the national curriculum. However, all secondary schools have to reach certain minimum standards in order to be registered by the educational authorities and many of them far surpass these. Further information about independent schools can be obtained from the addresses on page 296.

It is possible in some cases for parents to obtain state assistance with fees and information about this is available from the DES addresses on page 296.

State schools

Within the state system of free secondary education there are the following different categories of school:

Schools maintained by the LEA

County schools These are financed entirely by the LEA (the Education and Library Board in Northern Ireland), which employs the teachers.

Voluntary-aided schools or denominational schools Among the schools whose running costs are met largely by the LEA, there are some schools which are owned and managed by religious groups. These include the Roman Catholic Church, the Church of England and the Jewish Community. In these schools the governors employ the teachers.

Schools maintained by central government

Grant-maintained schools These are funded directly by the government with money recovered from the LEA. In these schools, the governors have powers over and above those of governors in LEA schools. For example it is they, and not the LEA, who are the owners of the school and who employ the staff. Parents may vote for the school to *opt out* of LEA control and to become *grant maintained* by means of a secret postal ballot. It is then the responsibility of the Secretary of State for Education to decide whether their vote is to be accepted or otherwise.[1]

In Northern Ireland the present policy is to allow grant-maintained status only to schools with an integrated intake of Protestant and Catholic pupils.

City technical colleges These are independent colleges which provide free education and concentrate on science and technology, or in some cases on music and the arts. They receive funding for both capital and running costs from the government and from private sources such as industry.

As well as these differences in the management and financing of state secondary schools, two other characteristics are important:

Age-range:

- In most LEAs children transfer from primary to secondary school at the age of eleven and can stay on at school until they are nineteen, if appropriate.
- In a few schools students finish at sixteen but may then transfer to a sixth-form college or to a college of further education.
- There may be a system of middle schools (or of junior high schools) catering for children between the ages of eight and thirteen. At this point they transfer to secondary school or to senior high school.

Selection: In some LEAs there are two types of secondary school: *comprehensive schools*, which take youngsters of all abilities, and selective *grammar schools* which only admit those who have reached a certain level of attainment. This may be ascertained by testing and on the basis of teachers' reports. It is no longer permitted for any grammar school to charge fees for entry.[2]

Information about the sorts of state school be found in your area can be obtained from the local education authority, whose address is in the telephone book under your local council.

The Organisation of Schools

School governors

School governors are the group of people who, together with the head teacher and staff, have responsibility for the general running of the school. It is the governors who, whether they choose to exercise their powers or not, can make decisions which have a real impact on the life of a school and, through it, on the local community.

Parent governors

In their annual report (see page 201) the governors should tell you who they are and who they represent. The composition of the governing body differs according to whether the school is a voluntary school or a county school, or if it is maintained by central government. By and large governors include representatives of the local community, of the LEA, of the teaching staff and, if he or she wishes, the head teacher. Among the governors are a number of parent governors elected by other parents; for most secondary schools the number would be at least five. As a parent, you could be asked by other parents to stand for election as a governor.

Governors' responsibilities

Effective governors should know their school well and this involves being ready to visit the school, during the daytime and for special events, and getting to know staff, parents and students. Part of their work is to see that the wishes and views of parents and of the local community are taken into account, as well as those of professional teachers.

The powers of governors differ somewhat in the different types of schools, but in all schools governors have responsibilities for the school *curriculum* (see pages 205–7). The curriculum is made up of the school's educational aims and all the experiences it offers young people in order to achieve these aims. The curriculum in the broadest sense is about the atmosphere of the school, the policies which are worked out about school meal-times, about out-of-school activities, about ways of seeing that all pupils have equal opportunities, about everything in fact which has an impact on school life as well as about lessons. A major part of the curriculum is laid down by the government through the national curriculum (see pages 206–7) and governors must ensure that this is implemented and decide, with the staff, how it is done. Governors must also decide on subjects which are not part of the national curriculum and how these can be combined with obligatory subjects in a satisfactory way. An important duty of governors is to make decisions about sex education in schools (see page 43), about whether it is taught and how it is taught. It is recommended by the Department of Education and Science that these decisions should be made in consultation with parents.[3] Governors also have the power to decide whether or not a parent may withdraw an adolescent from sex education (see page 46).

Governors have responsibility for the school budget and for interviewing and selecting staff.

In certain cases parents may appeal to governors against the action of the head teacher, for example, if their son or daughter has been suspended for disciplinary reasons (see page 247) or for reasons to do with special education procedures (see pages 241–2).

Governors' reports

Every year governors must produce a report for parents covering specific subjects, including examination results, how allowances have been spent, and information about the school's relationship with the local community. They must also hold an annual general meeting for parents to discuss the report. At this meeting parents may pass resolutions asking the governors to consider subjects they feel strongly about. In such cases, the number present at the meeting must at least equal 20 per cent of the number of students on the school register.

Parent-Teacher Associations

A Parent-Teacher Association (PTA) is not part of the school management structure but where one exists it can provide a forum for communication between management and parents, especially between parents and the parent governors.

The PTA tries to bring together the people who are most concerned about the education and welfare of students. They may also be known by other titles such as a Home-School Association, a name which suggests a wider community than Parent-Teacher and which could include, for example, school welfare staff and supervisors.

A good PTA can help staff and parents to get to know and trust one another through jointly attending meetings and other events. In addition it provides a means of informing parents about school policy and gives staff and parents an opportunity to explore educational matters together. For example, a meeting could be devoted to the practice of preparing students for new tests and examinations, so that parents can find out more about this. Sometimes outside speakers are brought in to provide up-to-date material and ideas, and to lead discussions, on such subjects as religious or sex education. As well as educational activities, PTAs can organise social evenings and fund-raising events.

Through the PTA parents get to know other parents and this is an invaluable way for them to know how to make informed choices when it comes to electing parent governors.

The PTA meeting is not a place to air individual problems, such as how one particular adolescent has been treated by a member of staff. There are other ways of dealing with this sort of issue (see pages 245–7). PTAs are concerned with more general matters, for example, exploring how to smooth the transition from primary to secondary school and what part, if any, the association could play in this. They can also become involved in aspects of local educational reorganisation or in a move for a school to opt out of local government control.

If the need arises, a PTA can bring its concerns to the notice of the school governors, to the local education authority and, indeed, to central government.

If there is no PTA at your adolescent's school the National Confederation of Parent-Teacher Associations can give advice about how to start one (see page 296 for address).

Secondary school staff

The head teacher

The head teacher is in charge of the overall management of the school. This includes responsibilities as varied as the physical running of the school, the allocation of classrooms and equipment, school cleaning and so on. Head teachers must see that examinations are organised, and timetables arranged. They must give time and thought to developing the school curriculum, in conjunction with governors and staff, and be responsible for teachers and standards of teaching. It is the head's duty to oversee the admission of new pupils and to see that there is a good relationship between staff and pupils and between staff and parents. The head teacher has to liaise with outside bodies such as the local education authority and the Department of Education and Science as well as being in communication with the school governors, either as a member of the governing body or otherwise.

While the head teacher is responsible for all aspects of the school, he or she delegates to other members of the staff. Deputy heads and senior masters and mistresses have a large part to play.

Deputy heads and senior masters and mistresses

There may be one or more deputy heads and, coming under these in the school hierarchy, one or more senior masters or mistresses. Each will have responsibility for certain tasks like devising the timetable, organising examinations, in-service training for staff, relationships with parents, pastoral care (see below) and communicating with outside agencies such as social services and the police.

Pastoral staff These are senior staff who have special responsibility for the progress and welfare of pupils. A secondary school may be very large and any pupil is likely to be taught by several different teachers each week. It is important that pupils are kept an eye on by someone who knows something about their history at the school and about any special problems which they may have at home (a death in the family, for example) and which may have an effect on school behaviour and progress. The pastoral staff can be turned to by pupils and by parents if there are any difficulties which need to be sorted out.

There are different systems for arranging youngsters into small enough groups for them to be known as individuals.

- *Year groups* In this system there will be one teacher appointed as 'head of year' or 'year tutor'. This teacher is responsible for all the pupils who are admitted in any one year. In some cases the year tutor takes charge of the full first-year intake to the school and remains with that group throughout its school life. In others the pupils have a different year tutor each year. Within the year group, there may be smaller tutor groups, with a tutor who will stay with that group throughout.
- *Upper schools, middle schools and lower schools* Some schools are divided into three age-bands, a lower, a middle and an upper school, each with its own 'head' who is responsible for individual pupils' progress. Again there are likely to be smaller tutor groups within the larger whole.
- *School houses* In these a pupil is allocated to a named 'house' at the beginning of his or her school career. These are not physical buildings (as were their predecessors in boarding schools) but groups of youngsters of different ages. Houses can be subdivided into tutor groups. Each house has its own housemaster or -mistress who is responsible for knowing the individuals in the house. Houses can also be the basis for organising out-of-school activities such as games.

Sometimes there may be a mixture of two of these systems, so that pupils are in year groups for pastoral care and houses for mixed-age activities.

Pastoral care systems are set up so that individual pupils can be looked after in what could be an overwhelmingly large system, but it should be said that this caring aspect may not always be experienced as such by pupils. Tutor groups are also used for organisational matters like filling in the register and handing out letters for parents, and they may be the settings for telling off the whole group or one unlucky adolescent. Nevertheless pastoral care staff are the teachers who come to know most about students as individuals and youngsters should turn to them first if there are any problems which cannot be sorted out in lesson-time.

Specialist pastoral staff

Pupils can also obtain advice from specialist staff like the careers officer who should be able to advise about entry requirements for various jobs or for higher education.

The school may or may not have a school counsellor. This person is in a position to help young people about problems that crop up at school or outside. The relationship with the counsellor is a confidential one. It may be suggested by a member of staff that a pupil consults the counsellor but the initiative can also come from the young person concerned.

Heads of departments

These are teachers who are in charge of a certain school subject, or group of subjects, taught by several different staff. There may be a head of history and a head of geography or – if these departments are grouped together, as sometimes happens – a head of social studies.

Subject teachers

Subject teachers are responsible to their heads of departments for teaching their subject according to the school curriculum. Sometimes staff may combine teaching a subject with pastoral responsibilities.

Organisation of classes

At the time of writing, in primary schools children of all abilities are usually taught together in the same class with other children of the same age. In some secondary schools, however, children are, from the beginning, divided into different classes according to their supposed ability. This may be done on the basis of reports from primary schools or as a result of school tests. In other schools they may be taught in mixed groups until they are about fourteen when they are regrouped according to their achievement at school so far. Streaming, banding, setting and mixed-ability grouping are all terms used by schools to describe how children are organised according to ability.

Mixed-ability grouping

The name speaks for itself. If you choose a school for your adolescent where there is mixed-ability grouping, he or she will be put into a class with youngsters of every level of ability. Either pupils are allotted to classes at random or the school makes sure that each class has the same proportion of boys and girls who at present seem to be above average, average or below average.

The arguments in favour of mixed-ability grouping are that in this system less able pupils are not segregated to form a group which is possibly demoralised and troublesome. They are more highly motivated to work and may make unexpected progress. More able children are encouraged to work according to their ability, doing more advanced work. Proponents of mixed-ability grouping also point to the mistakes which may be made about a pupil's ability in the streaming system and the difficulties that can arise in reallocating them later.

Streaming

This is the opposite of mixed-ability grouping. In this system children of the same year are grouped strictly according to 'ability'. So if two hundred pupils start at secondary school together there will be seven streams, beginning with the highest and working down to the stream which contains adolescents of the lowest ability, in the judgement of their teachers. Sometimes there is an attempt to prevent pupils and parents from knowing which stream an adolescent is in by identifying each class in a way which does not give any information as to where they stand in the hierarchy. The stream may be called by the initial of their class teacher, for example.

People who are in favour of streaming believe that it is easier to teach the whole class by this method, that bright children are not held up and that slow children go at their own pace.

Banding

This is a modified form of streaming. In streaming there is a gradation of classes, each at a different level; with banding there are three broad bands, high, average and low, with two or more classes in each group.

Setting

Pupils are sometimes put into 'sets' or 'divisions' for different subjects. Whether they are taught mostly in a streamed class or in a mixed-ability class, they are put into sets for certain subjects, like maths or French, where they are taught with others at the same level *in that subject*. This recognises that a boy or girl may perform above average in some subjects and less well in others.

The school curriculum

The curriculum can be thought of as the service which the local education authority, school governors and staff offer through the school. It aims to provide a certain sort of educational experience for your adolescent and to make a range of options open to him or her. The curriculum encompasses many aspects of school life. A school may seek to promote easy relationships, based on respect, between staff and pupils. It may, or may not, have worked out a policy on equal opportunities, on leisure-time, on meal services and on out-of-school activities. All of these contribute to the ethos of the school, its own particular sort of educational environment. In addition there are the various timetabled subjects like English and physics, which constitute the more formal aspects of the school curriculum. When you consider the range of subjects which it is possible to learn at school, it immediately becomes obvious that it is not possible for an adolescent to follow all of them. At certain points choices have to be made. Nor is it possible for a school to offer all the subjects which can be taken in public examinations; there are just too many.

The national curriculum

State schools no longer have a free hand about what subjects are to be taught. The law (Education Reform Act 1988) lays down that in every secondary school it is obligatory to have religious education as part of the curriculum although parents have the right to withdraw adolescents from this subject if they wish (see page 210).

England and Wales

In addition, up to the age of sixteen, students must learn the following subjects:

English, mathematics, science (these are the 'core' subjects), and technology, history, geography, art, music, physical education and a modern language.

In Wales students must also learn Welsh.

Scotland

The subjects covered by the Scottish curriculum guidelines are:

English, mathematics, environmental sciences, expressive arts and religious and moral education.

Northern Ireland

The following areas of study are obligatory:

English, mathematics, science and technology, the environment and society, creative and expressive studies, language studies (including Irish in some schools).

There are targets set for all secondary schools in these subjects and students' attainments are assessed at fourteen and sixteen.

Schools have to decide for themselves how much time is allocated to the national curriculum and how much time can be given to other subjects which are not included in it. It has been estimated that the national curriculum takes up about 70 per cent of the timetable, leaving the school with about a day and a half to fill according to its own wishes.[4]

It is up to the school to decide how subjects are taught, for example, whether they teach the subjects as separate entities or combine them in order to study topics which cover more than one subject (see page 209). The school must also decide what other subjects are to be taught, or made available in greater depth, in the time which remains after the national curriculum has been covered. For example, students could learn a second language, or take a subject to a more advanced stage than is required by the national curriculum, in the hope of obtaining a high grade in a public examination.

The national curriculum can be suspended or modified for children with special needs (see page 241).

Choosing a Secondary School

Parents' rights

In law parents have the right to choose which school their child should go to (Education Act 1980 and Education Reform Act 1988). There are, however, limitations to this right:

- Sometimes a school has more applications from parents than it has places available. When this happens, places are offered according to a priority system. For example, youngsters who have brothers or sisters at the school could be given priority over others.
- Some voluntary-aided schools may reserve a proportion of places for students who share the school's religious background. In such cases, even if there are unfilled places, the governors are allowed to turn down applicants from other backgrounds.
- Selective schools, such as grammar schools, can refuse to accept people who do not reach a certain standard of attainment.
- By definition, single-sex schools are for members of that sex only.

Right of appeal when choice is not granted

If your son or daughter is not offered a place at the school you have chosen, you have the right to appeal against the decision to a special committee. This does not mean that you will necessarily get the place you want. The committee will review your application in the light of how your child stands in their priority system and, more importantly, according to whether they actually have a place available.

Practicalities in choosing a school

While the right to the school of your choice exists in law, for some parents who live in a small town, or in the country, in practice only one school is available (although in some cases the LEA can help with travel expenses to a school which is further afield).

For other parents, who live in urban areas, choice is no problem. They have very clear ideas about which school their adolescent should go to, as well as easy access to a range of schools. These ideas could be based on the experience of an older brother or sister, or on a preference for a single-sex school, a co-educational school, or a school belonging to a particular religion. Not least, an adolescent might have a strong preference for one school rather than another. These feelings on the part of an adolescent should be treated with respect; the person most concerned in what school is chosen should be involved in decisions about it.

But the choice is not always clear-cut and, if you have more than one option, the business of choosing a secondary school can be an anxious one. Your child is going to spend five or more years at the new school and what happens during that time can influence their lives as adults, including the career they take up. But if your child has no marked preference and you cannot make up your mind between two schools or, perhaps more difficult, if you find that the school of your preference is over-subscribed, what should you take into account when it comes to making the choice?

There is no easy answer to the question 'What is a good school?' There are many ways in which a satisfactory school for one child would be less satisfactory for another, so a more relevant question might be, 'What sort of school would be a good school for my child?' Another question to consider is, 'What sort of school is acceptable to me as a parent?' Schools differ in many respects and can have a way of life, an ethos, which suits the values of some parents but not others. We live in a pluralist society where people have different backgrounds and different ideals. For example, some may put a very high value on academic progress and want, more than anything else, their child to emerge at the end of their school career with a large number of the highest-grade exam passes. Others may feel that an extremely academic emphasis is not what they require, especially if it is at the expense of other experiences. Sometimes, after consideration, parents can reach the conclusion that some of the values they hold are at odds with one another; for instance, a school cannot encourage children to compete as individuals and to be very co-operative at one and the same time.

Although we all have our own values, they are not always to the forefront of our minds and we may not have thought much about what goes to make a good school until we are faced with choosing one. You may find it easier to make a choice if, before you start to gather information about schools, you think about what you want for your child from secondary education. In that way you will have a better idea of what to look out for in any particular school. Below are some of the areas that need consideration. You may find it useful to discuss what is most important with your partner or with a friend.

Considerations in choosing a school

Schoolwork

Would you like your adolescent to go to:

- a school that puts a high emphasis on academic achievement?
- a school that values all-round education, including academic, artistic, health and personal education?
- a school where any particular gift your child has will be encouraged, such as music, art, sports or athletics?
- a school where any special needs will be catered for; for example, if your child has general learning difficulties, or has specific difficulties in reading or spelling; or has physical disabilities or an illness such as asthma; or has visual or hearing impairment? (A school which has not had experience of certain special needs in the past may be willing to accept a youngster who has such needs and make special provision for him or her.)
- a school which, especially in the first few years, makes links between different subjects, perhaps combining several, with staff working as a team to explore for a short time a topic such as 'Food in our society'?
- a school which has a single-subject approach?

Parents and school

- Is it important to choose a school where parents are encouraged to take an active part in the life of the school, perhaps through a Parent-Teacher Association?
- Would you be just as happy to be in the background, encouraging your adolescent to do homework, to be punctual, to keep other school rules and only liaising with the school if specially required to do so?
- How important is it that staff are ready to listen to any queries or

problems which parents may have, and prepared to treat them with respect and co-operation?

Discipline

■ Do you want a school where the emphasis is on school rules maintained by a system of rewards and punishments (for example, house points and detentions) or would you prefer a school where students are encouraged to think about the consequences of their behaviour and take responsibility for it?

■ Do you want the school to be considerate of students as individuals and to take special circumstances into account in their treatment of them?

■ How important is having, or not having, a school uniform?

Religious and ethnic considerations

■ Do you want a school that makes an effort to relate to the larger multicultural society? For example, circulating information to parents translated into languages used locally; including representations of people from different ethnic groups in visual displays; employing teaching staff from different ethnic groups.

■ How important is it to choose a school which belongs to a particular religious group?

■ You may wish to send your child to a denominational school (see page 198), but if there is not a suitable one available, have you any requirements about religious education and worship?

The law specifies that there should be religious education and worship in state schools and that this should be wholly or mainly in a Christian framework. However, parents are permitted to withdraw children from religious assemblies and from religious education classes. Schools are also allowed to apply for permission to hold separate assemblies for youngsters who come from other religious backgrounds or, alternatively, to adopt a 'multi-faith' approach. It may be possible to arrange education in faiths other than Christian, within school-time.

Equal opportunities for girls and boys

■ How high on your list of priorities is single-sex education or co-education?

■ Do you want your son to have the chance to specialise, if he wishes, in subjects like art and music as well as the traditional 'masculine' subjects like chemistry and motor-vehicle maintenance?

■ Do you want a school where your daughter will be encouraged, as a girl, to be active in all parts of the curriculum; for example, in sport (see pages 122–3) or in science and technology and those subjects which lead to well-paid work and many different opportunities?

If you choose a single-sex school these high-status subjects which are not traditionally studied by girls must, in law, be available for them, just as they must be in a co-educational school. In all schools a full range of technology options should be on the timetable, for both boys and girls, without pressure for girls to opt for subjects like home economics and boys for woodwork and metalwork. Encouraging boys and girls to feel equally at home in subjects which are not traditional for them needs special effort and imagination. In maths and science, material needs to be chosen which does not seem to be directed more towards members of one sex than the other. Girls can feel excluded by examples drawn from the workings of a motor car and boys if examples are drawn from cooking! The school may choose to separate boys and girls into different groups in science or maths, because while girls can do well in these subjects they may feel inadequate compared with boys. It does seem that separating them for a time helps to build up their confidence.[5]

A school which makes a positive feature of equal opportunities for both sexes is likely to keep records of girls' performance in examinations and of how many of them go forward to further training or education in maths, science and technology (see page 231).

Is there anything else not mentioned above which you think is important and you would like to find at the school your adolescent goes to?

Some of the items on the list may seem to you to be quite insignificant, while others have overriding importance. When you have thought them over you will have a clearer idea of the sort of school you require.

Finding out about schools

When you have given some thought to the type of secondary school you want for your teenager, it is time to start collecting information about schools in your locality. The main sources of information are other parents, pupils, and the information supplied by the school at interviews, open evenings, governors' reports, school magazines and brochures. It is also very useful to visit the school during school hours to see what it is like for yourself.

Ask parents

Other parents who currently have a child at the school are a very good source of information. The following questions are all worth asking:

- Is their child reasonably happy at the school and is he or she making reasonable progress?

- Do they feel that a special effort is made to make the whole curriculum accessible to both boys and girls?
- What opportunities are there during the year to talk to members of staff about a child's progress, or to discuss difficulties?
- If there have been any problems, how were they handled?
- Do they have the impression that at least some members of staff know their adolescent as an individual?
- What sort of a body is the PTA? Is it a fund-raising organisation only, or are there chances for discussion and to make proposals about different aspects of school life?
- How accessible are any parents on the board of governors (see page 200)?
- How are their adolescent's option choices managed (see page 230), how much homework is set, and are they satisfied about the way careers advice is given?
- Do they have the impression that there is an over-large staff turnover or that classes are often covered by supply teachers because regular staff are absent or vacancies are not filled? Either of these, although unavoidable at times, can be a sign of poor staff morale as well as causing problems for pupils.

Ask the students

Students who are currently at the school can also be asked about their experience.

- Do they think that bullying is a problem?
- For the most part, are classes fairly well behaved so that people can get on with work without distraction?
- How do teachers usually deal with misbehaviour?
- If there is a system of rewards and punishments, is it considered a fair one?
- Do they feel that there is at least one member of staff who knows them quite well and takes an interest in their progress?
- Do they feel that all pupils are respected, whether they are among the more academically advanced or not?

Read governors' reports, school magazines and brochures

The brochure for the parents of new students provides facts and statistics about the school and its organisation. It can tell you about the size of the school and the age-range, whether youngsters can stay on until nineteen or if they must leave or go elsewhere after their sixteenth birthday; and, where appropriate, the number of students who stay on after sixteen. The brochure should also tell you to what extent students are streamed or set, according to ability (see page

204), and what provision, if any, there is for those with special needs (see page 241). You should be able to find out whether subjects are seen as distinct entities or whether they are grouped in subject families. There should also be information about how students choose their options and what combinations of subjects are possible for them to take for public examinations.

The governors' report will carry a statement of last year's examination results. Rather than make judgements about a school on the results of one year's examinations, it is probably better to look at these in relation to the results from earlier years. Judging a school by its results, or comparing these with the results of another school, does not necessarily provide a fair picture, however. For example, results can be affected by the local catchment area, and are likely to be better than those of other schools if only academically inclined pupils are admitted in the first place.

Relevant questions to ask yourself include:

- Does the pass rate seem to have stayed at about the same level over the past few years?
- Are students sitting exams in more or in fewer subjects?
- Are they passing with higher grades than in previous years, or are they doing worse?

The answers to these questions may need to be weighed against any changes in the school population over the preceding years.

School magazines, the governors' report and parents' brochures can also be a good source of information about the life of the school in general. When you read them, look out for what they do not tell you, as well as what they do, especially about the following:

- Is there any indication that the school is developing a policy of encouraging girls to take a full part in school life, for example?
- Are the achievements recorded in these publications mainly to do with academic work and sports success?
- Are other sorts of activity also represented?
- If the school has an intake from different ethnic groups, is this reflected in the content of brochures and magazines?

Open evenings and visits

Sometimes parents who are perfectly self-assured in other situations can feel inadequate when they enter a school building and need to talk to teachers – perhaps even to the head teacher. It could be that visiting a school brings back memories of one's own schooldays and shortcomings! There is also the feeling that you do not want to say or do anything which might reflect badly on your own adolescent. These feelings are understandable but it is better not to let them influence your relationship with the school too much. Whether you are going to an open evening or just paying a visit to the school, make the most of the opportunity to find out what you need to know, whether by asking questions or by observation.

Some schools require an interview with prospective pupils and parents before admission. In this situation much of the time may be spent in asking your child questions but there should be a point at which you are asked if there is anything you want to know about the school. It can be helpful to have decided in advance what you want to ask; perhaps you need to know more about an item in the brochure, or would like to ask about something not mentioned in it.

You may be particularly interested in a school's record in a particular subject or group of subjects. If it seems to you that the pass rate is low, or that there are comparatively few entries, ask the head teacher or the head of department why this is. It might be that an unforeseeable and lengthy absence on the part of one or more teachers has played its part. Be wary, however, if a teacher tries to explain a poor record by blaming the students. 'They just don't seem to knuckle down to the hard work involved' would not be an acceptable explanation. You need to know what steps the school is taking to encourage the students to work harder.

Open evenings can also be used for this general fact-finding and to learn something about the atmosphere of a school. It can be very impressive to be shown around by neatly dressed and courteous older students and you may get the impression that the school is putting its best face forward. Nevertheless you can look out for things which will help you to decide if this is the right school for your adolescent. Notice how pupils and staff talk to one another. Does this suggest to you that the school is more formal or less formal in its relationships with students? What do they call one another? Are boys called by their surnames? Are staff addressed as Miss or Ma'am or Sir? Or are they called Miss Smith or Mr Jones? Do they seem to be friendly and relaxed with one another? How would this atmosphere suit your own son or daughter?

Ask the students questions about the school – what they most appreciate about it and whether there is anything they would like to see changed. Encourage them to talk about their own experience at the school. This can all help to fill in the picture.

Open evenings, interviews and brochures can also give you an idea as to whether or not the school is efficiently managed. For example, if there is a timetable of events for an open evening is it, by and large, kept to? Does the head teacher speak to the assembled parents at, more or less, the advertised time? Do other members of staff share the platform with the head teacher and explain their responsibilities? If you have been given a time for an appointment, is it kept to? Are there helpful signs indicating how to get to different parts of the building? When you read the brochure, is it reasonably easy to find the information you need? Are there any typing errors?

If you can visit the school during school hours and see it in everyday operation this can be most useful and it is reasonable to ask to do so. Notice the general atmosphere of the school and ask yourself the following questions:

■ Does it seem to be bright and cheerful, with evidence that staff care about the impression it makes?
■ Are there well-presented displays of work in public areas and in classrooms?
■ How are the noticeboards kept: is the material old and dog-eared or in good condition?
■ Are there notices about school activities which suggest that the students themselves participate in organisation and responsibility? For example, do they produce posters for school plays and discos?
■ Is the school library well stocked, and is it in use during your visit?
■ Is there a separate, well-resourced careers room?
■ Would you be happy to eat your lunch every day in the dining room (see pages 112–13)?
■ Are the toilets clean, with lockable doors and replenished sanitary towel dispensers for girls (see page 46)?
■ Is most of the space in the school playground during break or at lunch-time taken over by older boys playing football, or does it seem to be used by all the pupils? Are students allowed to spend some of their lunch-time in doors?
■ What do you notice about students' behaviour? Between lessons, are there stampedes along corridors and up and down staircases or do boys and girls make their way from one class to another without too much noise or horseplay?
■ In the classrooms and workshops does there seem to be an atmosphere of work – not necessarily of stillness and silence, but of youngsters getting on with a task?
■ How many students are using art rooms and technology rooms, such as home economics rooms, computer rooms and laboratories, at any one time? Do they seem to have enough room to work properly

and is the teacher/pupil ratio low enough for each pupil to have individual attention? In most secondary schools there should not be more than thirty pupils to a teacher, but in these classes, for reasons of safety as well as for efficient teaching, there should be far fewer.

When you have made your choice

You may find that you have to settle for a school which you are not altogether happy about, or a school which is not your first choice. Once you have made the decision, however, and have been given a place for your child, it is only fair to the school – and to your child – to give the school a chance to prove itself. It is best to support school rules, for example about school uniform, even if you do not agree with them, rather than confuse your adolescent. If he or she asks for your opinion, give it honestly but say that you accepted a place at the school knowing what the rules were.

If there is something that you feel very strongly should be changed, you will need the support and agreement of other parents in order to have any effect. Bringing about change takes great tact and hard work. The Parent-Teacher Association, if there is one, will enable you to find out if your feelings are shared by others (see page 201). Together with other parents, you could talk to a parent governor about your concern (see page 200) or you could raise it at the annual general meeting of parents (see page 201) if it relates to the governors' report. At the end of the chapter there is more detailed advice about dealing with school problems of a general nature.

Settling into the Secondary School

There are many things that schools can do to help your adolescent settle in and there are other things that you can do yourself.

What schools can do

Secondary schools can ease the process by inviting prospective pupils to visit during the term before the transfer takes place. Members of secondary school staff can also visit the primary school to talk to pupils on their own familiar ground and to answer questions. These contacts can be reassuring. Primary school teachers can also help by encouraging discussion of what will be expected at the new school and by reminding children of pupils from the year above them, who have successfully made the transfer to different schools.

Some secondary schools, as well as bringing out a brochure for parents, issue a special one to welcome new pupils. These explain in simple and informal terms such things as the way the lunch hour is organised, or how lockers are allocated. It is a good idea for parents to read this as well!

Preparations for school

Preparing to start a new school can be a time of anxiety for an adolescent even if it is mixed with excitement. It helps both parents and adolescents to feel more secure about the coming change if practical matters have been thought about and dealt with in advance.

Equipment

It may be necessary to buy school uniform and sports kit that were not required at primary school. The school will almost certainly ask you to mark all of these with your child's name, otherwise it is very difficult to recognise and reclaim lost clothing. Pupils also need to be provided with writing materials, a pen (the school may have requirements over what sort of pen is to be used), pencils, a sharpener, a rubber and a ruler. Fine-point coloured felt-tips are useful for diagrams and maps, and a compass, protractor and set square are needed for mathematics. A calculator will also be needed, whether now or later, because learning to use one efficiently and accurately is necessary both in the maths class and in everyday life. A pencil case is needed to keep all this equipment accessible and in good condition.

A school bag is another necessity. It should be roomy, because it will need to accommodate sports clothes as well as books; strong, because it will get heavy use; and light, because it may need to be carried from class to class throughout the day as well as backwards and forwards from school. Your adolescent may have views about what is acceptable, by current standards, and as he or she will carry it around throughout the school day, these should be taken into account.

Help towards expenses

Starting at a new school can be expensive, with new equipment to buy, perhaps a longer journey to pay for, and any increase in pocket money you may feel is appropriate at this time. If you have a low income you may be entitled to a very small grant towards clothing. Although LEAs are not obliged to provide meals without charge for everyone, if you are receiving income support your adolescent is entitled to a free school meal in the middle of the day. There is also free travel for all youngsters who live beyond a certain distance from school. The education department, whose address is obtainable from the local town hall, will be able to supply more details about these possibilities.

The journey to school

If the new school involves a complicated or unfamiliar journey your adolescent may want you to go along as well, either on the first morning or on a trial run before term begins, checking where to get on and off buses or trains and noting what money is required. If he or she is going to travel by bicycle, check that it is in good repair (see page 265), complete with lights and a padlock, so that it can be locked during school-time.

Do what you can to see that your adolescent is on time for school. Being late is often stressful and the whole journey can be taken up with worry: 'Am I going to get there in time? ... What will happen? ... Will I get into trouble?' Youngsters who are always late get a bad reputation; they miss registration, school announcements and parts of lessons. Because the journey to the new school may be different and longer than before, some adolescents need more support than when they were at primary school in order to be in time. Until they have settled into the new routine they may want you to wake them up and get their breakfast and help to collect their school things together, which they did not need before. Being punctual is a responsibility they can take care of for themselves after the first few days.

Feelings about a new school

Going to secondary school is a change from the familiar to the unknown, with different teachers, different classmates and a different routine, so it is a time for being especially ready to listen to how your son or daughter is feeling. At primary school, children knew where they stood and, as senior pupils, were treated with some respect. Now they are the youngest members of a school where the oldest students are themselves young adults. To start with, they may not know what is expected of them. In addition, starting secondary school for many teenagers coincides with physical and sexual developments and this can further challenge their sense of identity.

It is important to listen carefully to what your adolescent says about the new school, and to how they say it. They may say that everything is fine, but in a way that suggests the opposite. They need you to accept their worries and to let them know that you understand (see page 38). Do not try to brush worries aside as unimportant because you feel that they are minor. Encourage them to say what they want to say and give them enough time to say it, without interruption. Let them know that you see things from their point of view. When you have heard them out you can then give whatever realistic encouragement you can, from your own experience, and, if necesssary, take practical steps to overcome any problems.

Homework

At school youngsters are given new skills and information and are led into a more advanced understanding of different school subjects. Because schools have a rather short day and rather long holidays, there is not enough school-time for adolescents to consolidate what has been learned. For this reason homework is set so that, outside class-time, they can put their new knowledge into practice, review new learning and commit work to memory. Homework also gives them the opportunity to work independently and to learn how to organise their own timetable.

Homework can be something of a bugbear for adolescents and parents alike. Parents are encouraged to supervise homework by checking homework diaries and exercise books. This is, effectively, transferring responsibility for schoolwork from teachers to parents and in some families homework can be a source of conflict. Some schools make arrangements for adolescents to stay at school to complete their homework. In doing so they are mirroring the boarding school 'prep' system which has a long and successful history. It also overcomes the problems of youngsters who, for one reason or another, do not have suitable conditions for study at home.

Where there is the option to do supervised individual work at school it may need to be supplemented with visits to local libraries, to obtain reference material. There is a lot to recommend an extended school day. It means that adolescents have the evenings free for leisure with family and friends, and for whatever help they give in the home. A longer school day also matches parents' working hours better and relieves those who work full time of worries about leaving younger adolescents unattended when they come home from school.

The length of the school day is for the governors to decide in the light of their overall priorities for allocating the school budget. Some Parent-Teacher Associations have devised ways of providing 'homework' supervision at school for pupils and parents who want it.

If homework supervision is not available at school or if your adolescent prefers not to use it, what can you do to help?

Time and space

It is helpful to establish a homework routine from the time your child starts secondary school; it may be much more difficult to do so later. Different families plan their evenings in different ways and you will have your own ideas about what fits in best for you. Most youngsters benefit from a short break, including some refreshment, before settling down to do their homework, after which the evening is free. It is much easier to study in a suitable place, rather than stretched out on the floor or curled up in an armchair in the living room, with the television and family conversation in the background.

Do what you can to encourage concentration. Is it possible to turn a corner of a bedroom or some other room into a quiet study area? There should be a desk or table with enough room to spread books and a good source of light. Fend off possible distractions. For example, it is not a good idea for the desk to face pictures of pop groups or football teams which can easily be a diversion. Music in the background can be helpful because it masks the sounds made by the rest of the family, but it should not be too exciting! Ask others not to interrupt homework. Every time concentration is broken it can require a real effort to get back to work again.

If space is limited and there is no possibility of a special corner being reserved for homework, organise a special box or drawer for homework equipment and books where they may always be found.

Helping with homework

Although part of the rationale for homework is that it helps adolescents to learn to study independently, you may find that your son or daughter often turns to you for help. Do not do all the work yourself, let them stand on their own feet, but be ready to lend a hand if necessary. A good encyclopaedia is very useful for many subjects and, if you have one, you can help your adolescent to use it. In some secondary school subjects you may feel that you do not understand or remember enough to be of any help. Should this be the case, youngsters can often help one another and a quick phone call to a friend may be all that is needed. If you *can* give help, resist explaining everything you know about the subject. Providing simple information or, in maths for example, giving a demonstration is probably most useful. An adolescent will not continue to ask for help if it entails prolonging homework and being given more information than he or she needs to know. Other help you can give is to listen and test work that has been learned by heart.

For some parents, teaching their own adolescent proves difficult because of the emotions it arouses. If you try your hardest to explain something, it is very frustrating to find that someone else just cannot understand. It is vital not to push adolescents further than they are ready to go, so do not press a point if your adolescent is obviously becoming anxious or restless. Stay calm and do not blame them for not understanding. Take the responsibility on yourself for not being able to explain well enough and apologise for it: 'I'm sorry, I just don't seem to be able to put it across. You must be feeling you want to get on and finish what you can yourself.'

Amount of homework

Parents worry because their adolescent seems to be doing too much or too little homework. You can find out from the pastoral staff at school how long homework should take. If your own child is doing less than this, it could be that he or she is not doing work that is set, or is not doing it adequately, or that teachers are not setting it on a regular basis.

If homework is being avoided, then you need to talk with your adolescent about it and find out why. Neglecting homework is a sign that something is wrong and it can lead to further problems. Perhaps he or she just needs your encouragement to settle down and do it regularly. But it could also stem from a problem at home or at school which needs to be sorted out (see page 245). If you think that the situation arises because teachers are not setting homework regularly, it is a good idea to check this with other parents, if you are in touch with them, before taking the matter further (see page 246).

Some youngsters seem to spend too long over their books and do not leave themselves any time for leisure and friendships. Again you need to find out why this is so. It could be because they are not properly organised, or find it difficult to concentrate so that homework drags on all evening. Helping them to find a regular time and space, and fending off distractions, is particularly necessary in these cases. Other youngsters are over-anxious and try to do too much or sometimes they struggle with work that is too difficult for them. An inexperienced teacher may be setting too heavy a load.

As always when something seems to be going wrong you need to talk to your adolescent about it and to listen to what they have to say (see pages 38–43). You can then take whatever action seems to be appropriate, which may mean asking a member of the school pastoral staff for help.

Accepting adolescents' achievements

Some adolescents let you know about their successes and failures as they occur. With others you do not find out how they are doing until a parents' evening or when you get their school report. Work that is well done should, of course, be praised and encouraged and so should hard work and efforts at improvement. Poor results may need looking into (see page 239) but they should not be a cause for nagging or blame. Do not compare your adolescent with other pupils, or enquire how others have got on. It is equally important not to reserve praise only for those times when they do especially well. This may lead them to believe that they can only gain your approval when they are outstandingly successful. Irrespective of results, adolescents need to be reassured that you accept them whether they do well or otherwise; if they know that you accept them, they will find it easier to accept themselves and to retain their self-esteem.

Examinations and Tests

Examinations and tests give pupils, teachers and parents information about progress, about which areas need more work and where strengths and weaknesses lie, and are a useful guide to future subject choices. Public examination results are also used by colleges, universities and employers as a quick and easy basis for sifting out suitable applicants.

The Education Reform Act 1988 stipulates that pupils should be tested at the ages of seven, eleven, fourteen and sixteen. The first two tests are carried out in the primary school and the latter two in the secondary school. But these are not the only examinations or tests which adolescents have to face in the course of their school career. There may be short tests quite frequently to give pupils the chance to revise subject matter and so that teachers can find out what further teaching is needed before moving on. There is also a range of public examinations, some of which are familiar to parents but others of which are fairly new.

Most examinations, at least until the sixth form, no longer consist of sitting down to a written paper of exercises and essays. Other forms of testing have been developed that are far more revealing about young people's ability than the old-style examinations which put such an emphasis on memory and being able to think and write quickly, under pressure. You will find that your adolescent is being examined by the following methods as well:

■ *Course work assessment* A certain percentage of marks is allocated on the strength of how well a pupil does in course work. All written work, including long projects in some cases, may be taken into account or a selection of work may be presented for assessment. It is important that course work is neat and well presented and handed in on time. Written projects should be of the suggested length, pages need to be numbered, there should be an index of contents and illustrations where relevant. In some subjects practical work and oral work are also assessed.

■ *Multiple-choice questions* In multiple-choice questions the candidate must indicate the right answer from a list of four possible answers to a question. For example:

The most important way to help relieve world food shortages is by:
A trying to kill insects with sprays
B controlling the size of cities
C giving more education about balanced diets
D developing adequate birth control schemes (right answer)

One way of doing multiple-choice questions is to look at the question and try to give an answer before looking at those suggested, then to eliminate the obviously false answers in order to decide on the right one.

■ *Traditional written examination papers* The tasks set and some of the subject matter will probably be different from what you remember from your own schooldays. In history, for example, the candidate is sometimes asked to show *empathy*, which is to demonstrate that he or she can understand different people in the past and take their point of view. If you want to know more about new methods of examining students, then individual subject teachers can give you information.

Examinations and anxiety

Examinations are often a source of anxiety both for adolescents and for parents; even internal tests and exams can be a cause of stress. Much can depend on the outcome of an examination. It can affect career plans and self-esteem.

Anxiety about exams can affect young people in different ways. For some it can put them on their mettle and help them to perform well. Others may find that anxiety stands in the way of doing themselves justice. What can parents do to help?

First of all, listen to the way your son or daughter talks about forthcoming exams. Some youngsters panic and get into a self-defeating mood, feeling convinced that there is nothing they can do to pass. If they feel like this they are unlikely to take the steps necessary to prepare themselves for the examination. At whatever age, if your son or daughter is very negative about a forthcoming exam then they or you should talk to a member of the school pastoral staff about it. As well as teaching examination subjects, schools can also teach study skills and examination techniques. Staff are in a good position to help youngsters who feel anxious to do as well as they can. Throughout their school lives young people need to develop the feeling that they are in control of their own development; that how they plan and carry out their work matters and that there is always something positive they can do. In the approach to an exam, a year tutor can help youngsters to take responsibility for planning their study time. They can help them to break up a subject into its component parts and suggest ways of organising revision so that all subjects, and all parts of subjects, are covered.

Mock exams should be seen as a rehearsal for the main exams and as a learning point. They can show where weaknesses lie and show what areas need to be covered in greater depth. If a young person gets grades that are much lower than expected, he or she should discuss their results with the teacher concerned and try to find out what went wrong. It could be that their examination technique was at fault or that they had not revised efficiently. Advice about both of these follows.

Revision

In the weeks leading up to the examination adolescents need support and encouragement but nagging about work is counter-productive. If you can, encourage them to balance work with relaxation. Some young people are better at working in longish blocks of time while others find that shorter spells of study, with short breaks, suit them better. It is a matter for the individual to learn how best to pace him or herself.

Here are some tips about revision which may be taught and practised as study skills at school, but which you can pass on at home if necessary.

Reading

It is probably not a good idea to read a textbook, or a chapter in a book, straight through from beginning to end and hope to remember the contents. A well-tried method is known as SQ3R, which stands for Survey – Question – Read – Recall – Review.

Survey The first step is to survey the material being studied. If it is a book, look at the contents of chapters, the index and any preface. Scan the introduction and the conclusion. If it is a single chapter, skim through the introduction, the conclusion and any headings and sub-headings. Look out for summaries and glance through them. By using this approach the student gets an idea of the material that is covered and how it is structured.

Question When you are in a position to know what information is covered by the book, or by individual chapters, you should be able to put into words the questions it can answer. If you read it in order to answer questions then you are reading with a purpose, not just in order to do homework or revision but to find something out. Chapter headings and various sub-headings should suggest some questions; for example, a sub-heading like 'Respiratory Pathway' might suggest 'What is meant by respiratory pathway?' After skimming through a chapter it should be possible to frame four or five main questions that need answering.

Read Now is the time to read carefully through a chapter, or important section, looking out for answers to the questions. At a second reading you can note down the main points the author makes, or underline them in the text (if the book belongs to you).

Recall When you have finished reading and note-taking, try to recall the answers you have found to your questions, including the main points which the writer has made. Test yourself either by repeating these aloud or by jotting down notes. Doing this helps you to remember.

Review The final step is to review the material to see if you have recalled it accurately, checking any notes you have made and noticing anything you may have missed out.

Note-taking When you make notes, try to structure them as this makes points easier to remember. For example, a subject may have four main areas and each area may contain three sub-divisions. Sometimes it helps to draw a diagram to show this structure. Underlining, using capitals for headings and asterisks in the margin for key points, can also help to sort out material and make it easier to learn.

Mnemonics Making up mnemonics (not too many) can help you to remember important facts and structures (see page 25). Here is an example from biology. The characteristics of living things are: Growth, Excretion, Respiration, Movement, Sensitivity, Nutrition, Reproduction and Cells. This can be remembered by the mnemonic GERMS NR Cs, based on the initial letters and pronounced 'Germs in our seas'.[7]

Help from friends

Some youngsters find it helpful to revise with friends, working individually on a subject and then testing one another. Others find this kind of co-operation distracting.

Previous examination papers

Looking over examination papers set in previous years gives youngsters familiarity with the way questions are worded and the different sorts of information which examiners are looking for. They can use them to test their memory by producing outline answers to different questions. They should beware, however, of being alarmed by old papers, which might be based on a slightly different syllabus to that used at present in their school.

Illness at examination time

Youngsters who suffer from recurring conditions like hay fever or painful periods are particularly unfortunate when these coincide with examinations.

Hay fever

The pollen count is often high at exam- and revision-time; anti-histamine treatment helps but it can make the patient drowsy, the opposite of what is needed when taking an examination. If your son or daughter is sensitive to pollen, they should see the family doctor in the January before a summer exam and ask for a course of treatment. Sometimes this treatment needs to be repeated for several years to be effective, so get advice before your son or daughter reaches public exam age.

Painful periods

If your daughter suffers from painful periods she needs help in any case (see page 14). It is possible to use drugs to suppress periods during examination-time but there are differing opinions about how helpful this is. Again she may want to see the family doctor.

If your adolescent is ill at the time when he or she takes an examination you should *immediately* inform the school and ask them to notify the examination board. It is possible that the board will take this into account, but only if they know about it in advance of awarding the grade. They are most unlikely to change a grade after it has been awarded.

Sitting an examination

Make sure that your adolescent takes the right equipment, including an extra pen and, where needed, an extra pencil.

Some youngsters perform badly in exams because they do not read the paper carefully. It is very important to read and follow the instructions about how many questions should be answered and from which sections. They should work out how much time they have to answer each question, allowing about ten minutes to check over the whole paper at the end. The next step is to read the questions carefully and to choose those which seem to be the easiest. They should always try to do all the questions required because even if they feel they know little about a subject, that little may be enough to gain some useful marks. They should be sure to answer exactly what is asked. For example, if a question says 'Account for the USA's entry into the Second World War' it is asking *why* the USA entered when it did. An answer that describes the part subsequently played by the USA may be accurate but it will not gain marks.

Checking the paper over at the end is important because it gives a chance to spot and correct careless mistakes and to insert brief information. All of these can gain useful marks.

Appeals and resits

What should a pupil do if one result – or more – in a public examination is disappointingly low?

Appeals

If the result goes against all expectations, then it is possible for you as a parent to appeal to the examination board, through the school, on your adolescent's behalf. The result of this procedure is that you will receive a report on how he or she performed. It is extremely unlikely that a result will be upgraded.

Resits

Whether your adolescent should resit a public examination in order to get a higher grade depends on how important the subject is for his or her future plans. The same considerations apply here as for choosing options (see page 230). Will having a low grade in a particular subject narrow down possibilities for work or further study in an unacceptable way? This is the only justification for retaking exams, since these may otherwise compete for time with new courses in the sixth form or at a college of further education. Careers teachers and local authority careers officers can offer advice about this.

Reports

Twice or three times in the school year parents receive a report from the school about their adolescent's progress. The report format differs from school to school. Some schools use a single sheet with room for a one-line comment and a mark, or marks, for each subject; others, and especially for the end-of-year report, give a quarter-page per subject. There is also information about punctuality and attendance, together with a short overview from your son or daughter's year tutor or group tutor. The head teacher may sign the report and, in smaller schools or in special cases, add a short comment.

Report grades

Often there are two sorts of grades given for each subject, one for effort and the other for attainment, with different letters of the alphabet, or numbers, to designate high grades or low grades. The grade system being used should be explained in the report.

Effort grades cover whether homework is completed and handed in on time and whether a youngster pays attention and makes a contribution in class.

Attainment grades may tell you how your child stands in his or her particular class: average, above average or below average. Higher up the school the grades given may relate more closely to grades in public examinations and may reflect a teacher's current expectations for a student in a specific subject.

Another sort of attainment grading is known as *profiling*. This takes into account all the information, understanding and skills which pupils can acquire in a subject from the time they start school until they are sixteen. These are sorted into different levels, from 1 at the lowest end to 10 at the most advanced. At the age of seven, for example, a child might have reached levels 1, 2 or 3 in, say, mathematics, depending on what they had learned during the time they had been at school. Most eleven-year-olds will have reached levels 3, 4 or 5; fourteen-year-olds would be at levels 5, 6 or 7, and sixteen-year-olds at levels 7, 8, 9 or 10.

If the meaning of marks or grades does not seem clear, ask for it to be explained.

The teacher's comment which supplements the mark gives you more information to go on. The more specific the remark, the more helpful it is. Unfortunately some teachers still make use of comments like 'could do better'. Remarks like these may raise a feeling of guilt in pupils and some anxiety in parents, but they make no suggestions about how to improve matters: whether homework needs more attention or, for instance, a youngster should spend more time learning vocabulary.

Grades and comments in reports should, for the most part, confirm what you already know about your adolescent's progress at school from other sources: from what he or she tells you and from what you learn at open evenings.

Reports are useful

- when they alert you to recent improvements or problems;
- when they provide a written record so that you can compare grades and comments between one report and another or from one year to the next;
- as a basis – among others – for your son or daughter to make decisions about study and career options.

Talk to your adolescent about the report and get their opinion on it, especially about anything unexpected. Sometimes they may find that a grade is higher or lower than they had expected and in either case this can encourage them to work harder, in the light of plans for the future. It could be that a problem needs attention and that you can help, whether at home or through the school. Congratulate them for progress, for effort and for maintaining grades, not just for high grades.

Sometimes there is a space for you to write a comment of your own, to be returned to the school. If you are worried about something, and you think the school could help, the space provided is probably not large enough to allow you to explain the problem in detail. Write a covering letter, asking if you can see your adolescent's pastoral tutor or the relevant subject teacher (see pages 203–4).

Records of achievement

These are a new form of report put together by the pupil and by the teacher who come to a joint agreement about what should be written. Records of achievement take up more staff time than ordinary reports but they have the advantage of involving pupils in the process of their own education and encouraging them to take responsibility for building on strengths and overcoming weaknesses.

Records of achievement cover both academic and personal achievements and also set goals for the future, whether about aspects of school life, like punctuality, or about progress in individual subjects. They are very specific in how they describe achievement and in the goals they set.

The record of achievement at the end of schooling serves as a useful account of the various activities and responsibilities which youngsters have undertaken during their school years, their own personal qualities and their academic attainments. It is a record which they can keep and which gives employers more information than a public examination grade.

Choosing Options

It is important for you to be aware of points in your son or daughter's school career when options are being chosen, and of the implications of choosing certain subjects rather than others. Although all national curriculum subjects (see page 206) must be taken until students are sixteen, there may be an opportunity to study some in more depth than others. The main time for choosing options is at the end of the third year when choices are made for GCSE subjects. Study options after GCSE are also important but they can be limited by what has been chosen earlier and the standards achieved in attainment tests and in examinations at the age of sixteen.

Optional subjects

At the end of the third year, that is, at about the age of fourteen, your son or daughter has the opportunity to choose what optional courses they are going to follow in the next two years. It is an important time because at this point decisions have to be made that have a real effect on the future.

Youngsters do not always choose wisely. They may decide not to do a subject just to avoid a certain teacher who may, as it happens, already be planning to leave. Or they may like the sound of a new subject – motor-vehicle maintenance, for example – fit their other options around it and then find that it is not what they had hoped.

In some schools – particularly in smaller schools where there are fewer staff – it is just not possible to arrange the timetable so that everyone can have a complete choice of options. Students are almost certainly able to choose their most preferred option but they may also have to make do with some second-bests.

Despite the fact that the national curriculum is designed to ensure that pupils take a wide range of subjects until they reach the age of sixteen, some pupils may 'opt out' of certain subjects psychologically and so not obtain useful standards; in other cases they may even leave school before taking examinations.

The guiding principle for your adolescent should be to keep as many career options open as possible, by getting reasonable grades in the most widely required subjects. It can be difficult and time-consuming, although not impossible, to make up lost ground later.

Adolescents should note:

- English language at GCSE, with a reasonable grade, is often called for by employers, as well as being an essential requirement for further and higher educational courses.

■ Many jobs, or training schemes, require science, technology and maths to a reasonable standard at the age of sixteen.
■ It is impossible to train for teaching without acceptable grades in maths and English at sixteen.
■ For many subjects, including art and languages, an acceptable grade at sixteen is usually required if these are to be studied for higher-level exams at eighteen.
■ The following jobs all require, or prefer, science and maths qualifications:

Agriculture, air traffic control, work with animals, archaeology, architecture, astronomy, aviation, bacteriology, beauty therapy, biochemistry, biology, building, cartography, catering, chemistry, chiropody, dentistry, design, dietetics, engineering, environmental health, factory inspectorate, fish farming, floristry, food science, forensic science, forestry, geology, hairdressing, home economics, horticulture, laboratory work, landscape architecture, marine biology, medical laboratory sciences, medicine, meteorology, microbiology, midwifery, nursing, nutrition, oceanography, occupational therapy, optical work, patent work, pharmacology, pharmacy, photography, printing, psychology, physics, physiotherapy, radiography, remedial gymnastics, speech therapy, surveying, teaching, technician, trichology, veterinary science, zoology.[8]

Girls particularly may need help and encouragement to make sure that they do not close down the routes to interesting jobs which require maths, science and technology.

Options after sixteen

Parents are obliged to send their children to school until the Easter or the summer holiday after their sixteenth birthday. Although attendance is compulsory up to this point, students do not have to leave school at sixteen. The local education authority is obliged to provide free education for those who want it until the age of nineteen.

At the time of writing, after the examinations taken at the age of sixteen, the national curriculum no longer applies and pupils can go on to subjects of their own choice. There are a variety of examinations and courses available, either at school, at sixth-form colleges or at colleges of further education.

There is also the possibility of going straight into a job or into a training scheme.

Again, careful decisions need to be made and help will be available from a school's careers teacher or from the local careers office. The basic choice is whether to stay on at school or go to college and which subjects to study, or whether to get a job or take part in a paid training scheme.

Continuing education

If your son or daughter chooses to continue with education they must decide if they want to do so at their present school or at a sixth-form college or college of further education. They should take the following factors into account:

- What courses do I need to follow for the sort of work I would like to do?
- Are there any examinations I should take?
- Is my school able to offer the course and the facilities I need?
- Can a local college of further education or a sixth-form college offer the course and the facilities I need?
- What other advantages and disadvantages are there for me in staying at my present school?

The advantages of staying on at school include knowing staff and fellow students and being known by them; wanting to be in the school sixth form with any privileges that has to offer; and avoiding change. The advantages of moving include the chance to make a fresh start; being with friends who are also moving on; being in a college geared to the needs of older students.

Training

If, at sixteen, your son or daughter wants to go into a job or a paid training scheme, the following questions need to be asked:

- What skills will be learned and will these be helpful in getting other work later?
- In paid training schemes, what are the chances of being offered a permanent job at the end of the training period?
- Are there opportunities for going to college, part time, for extra training and qualifications?
- What sort of supervision is there, especially in a job where there are safety hazards?

Options at eighteen and nineteen

If your son or daughter has stayed at school until the age of eighteen or nineteen, again they have the option either of continuing their education or of getting paid employment. By this time they will be able to find out for themselves about different courses and types of employment, although careers teachers and officers will be able to help. There are addresses from which you can get further information on page 297.

It is not necessary to go straight into higher education even for those who want to do so. Some may decide to take time off from education to earn some money and to get some experience of work or to travel. Others who decide that they do not want to go to college or university may, after some years away from education, change their minds.

It is never too late for people to return to education and although there can be practical difficulties, there are also benefits in being a mature student. Universities and polytechnics may be willing to waive their entry requirements for students over the age of twenty-one. People who come back to education have the reputation of being more highly motivated than younger students and they bring a wider experience of life to their studies.

Absence from School

In the United Kingdom parents must see that their children receive full-time education 'in school, or otherwise'. This is a legal obligation under the Education Act 1944. Notice that the obligation is that children should receive a full-time education – not that they should attend school. Families who can afford it may employ people to educate their children full time at home. Other parents may decide to educate their children themselves. Sometimes these decisions are challenged by the local education authority on the grounds that the education they provide is not satisfactory. In such cases, the parents sometimes win and sometimes lose. It is, of course, much more difficult to educate an adolescent according to their 'age, aptitude and ability', in the words of the law, than it is to provide the education needed by a younger child. And school provides more than formal education: it offers the chance to mix with other youngsters, to play, to form friendships, to exchange opinions and experience. For most families the local school is an acceptable way of meeting their legal obligation.

Once children are registered at a school their parents are obliged to see that they attend school regularly. There are some reasons which, in law, a parent is allowed to offer as an excuse for frequent absence, including sickness and religious festivals. The insistence on regular attendance is understandable; absences are interruptions that can put children behind with their work, whether these are prolonged owing to illness or frequent short absences due to the need for hospital check-ups or treatment. Short-term absences can cause particular problems because teachers may not be as aware of them as they are of students who are absent for longer periods and, therefore, not realise that the pupil's understanding of a subject is patchy. Youngsters themselves may not appreciate the need to catch up as they would if they had been away for a longer time.

Parents can help prevent adolescents being held back by absence from school. Older adolescents will know how to find out from staff and friends what they have missed and how to make it up, but younger adolescents may need some assistance from you. When you write explaining the reasons for absence, tell the year tutor (see page 203) or appropriate member of staff if missing school is likely to occur frequently. Ask if subject teachers can be informed and request help – and allowances to be made – for missed work.

About a quarter of youngsters are absent from school at any one time and absence is more prevalent among adolescents than younger children. Mostly pupils seem to stay away with their parents' consent and provide a reasonable excuse, but there is a small percentage of youngsters – and surveys differ about its size – who stay away from school without 'justifiable' reason, at least in the eyes of the education authorities.[9]

Truancy, school phobia and school refusal

These are all expressions used to describe the behaviour of youngsters who, for reasons of their own, stay away from school. It is not easy to sort people into categories and pupils who are described as 'truants' by some people might be seen as 'school refusers' or 'school phobics' by others. A problem about such labels is that they place responsibility for absence on boys and girls and on their parents, without suggesting that events at school may have led to absenteeism. So truancy is seen as bad conduct, delinquency even, while other youngsters who opt out of school are labelled in a way that suggests that they are mentally disturbed.

Truancy

This is the label usually given to youngsters who stay away from school without their parents' knowledge or consent. Often they spend their time out and about in the neighbourhood, perhaps with other truants. One concern about this group, apart from the fact that they miss lessons and homework, is that they make a nuisance of themselves and get into trouble. Truanting is most frequent in the secondary school.[10]

School phobia and refusal

Both terms are used of pupils who refuse to go to school in spite of their parents' efforts to get them there. School fills them with anxiety and they feel they just cannot face up to going. If parents or others try to talk them into it, they may promise to go but refuse at the last moment. Their anxiety may produce physical symptoms like headaches, nausea, a racing pulse and so on, which disappear when pressure to go to school is removed. Although the symptoms are emotional in origin they are none the less real and distressing. Sometimes there is a slow build-up to a complete refusal to go to school, which starts with occasional absences or reluctance to attend because of minor ailments. In other cases the onset can be sudden. Like truancy, 'school refusal' is also thought to be more common among adolescents than younger children.[11]

Why do adolescents play truant and refuse schooling?

For 'truants' and other youngsters who refuse to go to school, the reasons for their absence can often be found in their experience of school. Poor progress, being bullied by other pupils, disliking or being afraid of a teacher and fearing tests or examinations can all lead to staying away. Sometimes other factors enter and complicate the picture or can themselves be at the root of the problem. Refusal can start, for example, when there is some sort of upheaval at home and the adolescent feels anxious about leaving home and family to go to school. It is also possible that for some children refusing to go to school is a retreat to an earlier stage of development at a time when the demands of secondary school, and of adolescence itself, are threatening their security. Another explanation for absenteeism is that in some families school is not valued highly, either by parents or by adolescents, and absence is permitted for a variety of reasons.

What should parents do when adolescents stay away from school?

It is most important that if you become suspicious that your son or daughter is not attending school you try to sort it out immediately. If you do not do so, the original problem can be compounded with all the consequences of staying away from school. With each day's absence there can be a growing reluctance to return because of the need to give explanations to friends and teachers and the knowledge that more and more work is being missed. At this stage you and your adolescent still have some control over the situation: you can take the initiative even now. If things go further you may find that the school welfare officer, the law, social services, the child guidance clinic and psychiatric health services become involved. This is not to suggest that intervention by these agencies is unhelpful, indeed their services may sometimes be necessary and useful, but when they enter the picture the whole situation can become more complicated for parents and adolescents.

You may have reason to believe that your adolescent has been staying away from school without your knowledge, perhaps taking days off or just 'bunking off' after registration. Or you may notice that he or she is reluctant to go to school; perhaps there is a pattern of (perfectly genuine) headaches or stomach upsets on one particular day of the week, or absences on account of head colds seem longer than necessary. If you have worries on any of these counts then you or your partner should try to find out what, if anything, is amiss.

Your main objective is to find out if anything about school is worrying your child so that you can do whatever you can to put matters right and to get him or her back to school on a regular basis. Often children are themselves worried about being absent[12] and may welcome your concern. You will need to create an atmosphere in which he or she is able to confide in you, so choose your time carefully – not, for example, when they are on their way out of the house to meet friends or when you are likely to be interrupted. Follow the framework suggested earlier (see page 187) for confronting them when something seems to be going wrong. First of all, check whether what you suspect is correct. A possible approach might be: 'I've noticed that you seem to get a lot of tummy aches these days that stop you from going to school. I've been wondering if anything is happening at school that's worrying you?'

Listen carefully to what he or she has to say (see page 38) and then decide what steps you need to take. Some of the things that can go wrong at school are discussed below, with possible remedies suggested (see page 239). Arrange an appointment to see a relevant member of staff – one who has pastoral responsibilities (see page 203) – and explain the situation. Ask what can be done about it and offer co-operation from your side. Action like this may be all that is needed to ease a youngster back into school before a history of absence builds up.

If adolescents cannot be persuaded to return to school, or if they are frequently absent without a satisfactory explanation, the school welfare officer or educational social worker (employed by the education authority to liaise between LEA, school and family) may call to find out why they have been away.

They will try to clear up any problems and will also point out the legal penalties of staying away from school. If there is a history of non-attendance this can result in the parent being fined or, after subsequent appearances in court, imprisoned. The magistrate can place a supervision order on an adolescent, so that they are obliged to see a probation officer regularly. It is also possible for an adolescent to be taken into the care of the local authority if judged to be beyond the control of his or her parents.

For some youngsters, however, negative feelings about school are very strong and not easily overcome. In these cases, what can parents do?

First of all, it should be remembered that the law requires children to be educated, not that they should go to school, and so for some parents the idea of taking over the child's education might seem to be a possibility. Educating an adolescent at home is not, however, a task which any parent would undertake lightly and there are mutual support groups for those who have taken this path (Education Otherwise, see page 296 for address). Not only does it require commitment, time and resources, but it may not be recognised as satisfactory by the LEA (see page 233). For example, parents are unlikely to have command of all the subjects laid down by the national curriculum; also an adolescent educated at home misses opportunities to mix and get on with other youngsters. A local education authority may claim that home education is inadequate and bring a court case on these or other grounds.

If you have made approaches to the school and these have been to no avail, then you will need to bring in other resources. What other alternatives exist for parents whose adolescents refuse to attend school? One possibility is to consult your family doctor, making clear that you are concerned about your child's refusal to attend school, not about the symptoms he or she sometimes exhibits at the prospect of going to school and which the GP may already have treated. Ask if the doctor will refer your adolescent to the *school psychological service* or the *child guidance clinic*. Once the school psychological service is involved in assessing your adolescent, then the local authority will not bring legal action against parents for non-attendance.

If you feel that the school staff understand the situation and are sympathetic, you can ask them to make this referral without involving your doctor; they may in fact suggest it themselves.

The child guidance clinic and the school psychological service are staffed by teams of professional workers, including a social worker, a psychologist, a psychiatrist, a psychotherapist and specialist teachers such as remedial teachers. They use a variety of approaches, according to local policy and to the individual nature of each case. These can include *psychotherapy*, in which school refusal is viewed as a symptom of underlying problems in the adolescent, or in the family as a whole. The adolescent, or the whole family, is encouraged to talk out their problems in regular sessions with a therapist. It is hoped in this way to change how the individual, or the family, functions and so get the adolescent back to school again.

A different approach is through *behaviour modification techniques.* With these, the aim is to recommence education rather than deal with any supposed underlying reasons for missing school. There may be a gradual reintroduction to school, taking one small step at a time, together with support from school staff and members of the school psychological service. Another behavioural technique, practised by some local authorities, is to insist that attendance restarts immediately, and a school welfare officer or an educational psychologist may be enlisted to accompany a child to school. The parents' obligations under the law, and the consequences of breaking the law, are made clear to both parents and adolescents. At the same time there is back-up from school staff who try to remedy school-based problems. An educational psychologist may also help the adolescent to cope with difficulties, like teasing at school or how to answer questions about why they have been away, and keep in touch with them to see how they get on. There is some evidence that this second approach can get youngsters back to school quickly and without psychological ill-effects. The method runs into criticism, however, because of the force – psychological or physical – which it uses to ensure attendance.

In the case of some adolescents, it may be decided that special education methods are needed, either in the school they already attend or in a special school or unit (see page 241); alternatively the local authority may provide a tutor to teach them at home. (This also happens when youngsters are away for prolonged periods due to sickness.) This service is not widely available, however, and one survey has suggested that whatever other benefits may result from the procedure, it is not a successful way of overcoming school refusal.[13]

If it is believed that a youngster is very disturbed there may be recourse to drug therapy or to a psychiatric unit. Remember, though, that the administration of drugs requires the consent of parents and, if they are capable of understanding the treatment, of the adolescent as well (see page 249). Sometimes a combination of these methods is used.

Clearly it is better, if at all possible, to see that school attendance problems are nipped in the bud rather than given time and opportunity to develop.

Difficulties at School

If an adolescent is not making progress

What should you do if your adolescent does not seem to be doing well at school, whether in one particular subject, or in overall performance?

There are three possible reasons to consider when a youngster is not making good progress:

- Is poor motivation the problem?
- Is the teaching as good as it should be?
- Does an adolescent have any general or specific learning problems that the school is not catering for?

These three conditions are not mutually exclusive, they may in fact be connected with one another; for example, losing interest in a subject, poor teaching and learning problems can go hand in hand.

Poor motivation

Sometimes adolescents do not do well at school because they are discouraged for one reason or another. Perhaps they are unable to keep up with other students because of learning difficulties (see page 241), or have special problems with reading or spelling (see page 243), or they are preoccupied or unhappy about other aspects of school life, such as bullying (see page 244) or getting on badly with a particular teacher. If you think there are problems which are affecting your adolescent's performance, talk about them together and see if, between you, you can find a way out of the difficulties.

Poor teaching

It is difficult for a parent to know if the standard of teaching an adolescent receives in secondary school is good enough. In the primary school fewer teachers are directly involved in a child's education and it is easier to keep informed about a class teacher because evidence comes from many sources. You can see work in different subjects, all taught by the same person, set out on parents' evenings. It is also easier to meet the teacher informally when you go to the school on social and other occasions.

When adolescents are at secondary school, on the other hand, many people are involved in teaching them and there may be staff changes which you do not know about from time to time. Public examination results are not always informative because the staff who teach at this level may not be those who teach your son or daughter. There is also the problem that parents cannot be expected to know a great deal about subjects taught at secondary school, and so feel hesitant to criticise the staff who teach them. There are, however, sources of information which may help you to decide if you have any cause for concern about the standard of teaching in any subject.

Take seriously what your adolescent has to say if he or she complains about a teacher. There is much research to indicate that pupils are aware of their teacher's performance.[14] They may not give you the whole picture, for example they may not make allowances for an inexperienced teacher, but they know whether lessons are well prepared and presented, if teachers explain things clearly and ask good questions, if they are fair and can keep order. Workbooks also give some indication about teaching standards. Is homework set and marked regularly and are books returned promptly to the pupils? It is encouraging for youngsters when they get work back without delay, so that they know how well they have done and can see what their mistakes are. A lot can be learned about standards of teaching from the teacher's written comments. The more specific these are, the more useful they are. For example, 'You do not explain what is meant by the nitrogen cycle' or 'You have only given one reason, what about . . .?' is a great deal more helpful than the curt comment 'Too brief' at the end of an essay.

A teacher should take any opportunity to praise work and to say if there is an improvement. This is encouraging and gives a pupil something to build on.

In the case of younger adolescents, it does not matter if some spelling or grammatical mistakes are left uncorrected. Too much red ink is discouraging and a youngster who makes many mistakes might not find it helpful to have all of them pointed out at once. A teacher should have a system for drawing attention to common errors like misspelling *their* and *there* or using *was* instead of *were* and, until these are overcome, it is not worth drawing attention to mistakes in more difficult words which are not often used. Getting basic mistakes put right improves work generally and if, in spite of correction, they recur in written work the pupil would obviously benefit from individual help.

In the light of what you find out, you may decide that there is good reason to be worried about a particular teacher and that you want to do what you can to improve matters. If you have a complaint about teaching, the person to go to in the first instance is the head teacher. On page 245 there are general suggestions about how to do this. If you are worried because your son or daughter does not get on with a particular teacher, a member of the pastoral staff would be more suitable.

Learning difficulties and special educational needs

The term 'learning difficulty' has a legal definition as well as its more commonplace meaning. Under the Education Act 1981, adolescents are said to have 'learning difficulties' if, for whatever reason, they find learning significantly more difficult than most youngsters of the same age or if they have a disability that prevents them from making use of educational facilities of a kind generally provided in schools. (This includes young people with sensory impairments such as limited vision or impaired hearing or any other physical disability.) The law says that the local authority has a duty to provide for an adolescent's special educational needs. It can do this by providing a place in an ordinary secondary school, together with special facilities to meet the learning difficulties, or in a special school, residential or otherwise; or by providing a tutor to teach the child at home. The policy is to integrate pupils with special educational needs into mainstream schools so that their education will be as 'normal' as possible and so that other youngsters, by sharing the same educational community, may learn important lessons about people with disabilities.

But although the law promotes integration, it is not always possible for parents and children to obtain it at a local level. The following conditions have to be met in providing special education in the ordinary secondary school:

- the parents' views have to be taken into account;
- the pupil must receive the special education he or she needs;
- integration must be an 'efficient' use of resources;
- integration must be compatible with 'efficient education' for other children.

Before a local authority will provide special education a formal assessment procedure has to be undertaken, ending with a *Statement* that a child has special educational needs. This entitles the child or young person to special facilities. At the same time, however, the right to education at a school of the parents' choice (Education Act 1980) may be lost. If adolescents who attend ordinary schools are 'statemented', it may mean that they are moved from their present school to a special school or that the right to move to a different ordinary school is lost.

Statementing

Both parents and the school are allowed to start the process that leads to an official statement that a pupil is in need of educational facilities over and above those which are already supplied by the school. If it is found that a young person has learning difficulties that are severe or complex, a Statement can be made to provide such facilities in one way or another.

If a local authority decides to assess a pupil with a possible view to 'statementing', the parents are entitled to full information about it. Parents are given twenty-nine days to put their point of view before the assessment begins. If you wish your child to remain in mainstream schooling it is as well to get independent advice at this stage; without experience of the process you may find it difficult to get what you want without expert help. Parents whose first language is not English are at a special disadvantage. (See pages 295–6 for addresses of TACADE and of Special Education experts.)

The local authority must make a draft Statement which parents are entitled to see, and make representations about, before any final Statement is made.

After a Statement, parents are entitled to appeal against it to the Secretary of State for Education.

If the local authority decides not to make a Statement in cases where parents think that it would be appropriate, parents have the right to appeal against this decision also.

An adolescent who has a Statement must be reassessed between the ages of twelve-and-a-half and fourteen-and-a-half. All Statements must be reviewed every twelve months.

Less severe learning difficulties

There may be a remedial department in the school, staffed by teachers who are specially trained and experienced in teaching youngsters who are having difficulty with learning. Pupils may be withdrawn from some ordinary classes so that they can get individual attention here or they may be taught alongside others with learning difficulties in a special remedial class. In some schools staff would aim for this to be a short-term remedy only.

Reading and spelling difficulties

Some children and adolescents have great difficulty with two skills which are of paramount importance in education: the abilities to read and to spell correctly. Not to be able to read and spell with ease is an extreme handicap at school and a source of embarrassment and disadvantage in adult life. By adolescence some children who have had difficulties learning to read initially have made progress, but spelling problems can still cause frustration and they may read with less confidence and less fluency than is required to keep up with homework.

When a youngster has such difficulties there can be a variety of reasons. Some poor readers have general learning disabilities. They are slow to understand and are behind other children of their age, in many ways. Others are handicapped by hearing and vision problems, which may or may not have been detected. Still others were often absent from school at the time when their classmates were acquiring reading skills, and have never made up early losses. For some, emotional disturbances lie behind their inabilities at school and still others may have been unlucky enough to have had teachers who have not given them due attention.

Dyslexia or specific learning disability

When all of the above possibilities have been ruled out, there still remain young people who lag far behind others in literacy skills; who do well in school subjects other than reading and spelling, who have no history of emotional disturbance and have good hearing and vision. When there is no other explanation it is thought that this lack of progress could be because of some specific learning disability to do with reading and spelling skills; these disabilities are also known as dyslexia.

Research about what underlies specific learning difficulties is under way, but as yet it seems that there is no single explanation. Possible sources of difficulty include not being able to organise or 'decode' visual information; not being able to differentiate the syllables which go to make up a word; having difficulty with remembering; and having difficulties with language in general, not just with written language.

Because the underlying cause may be any of these, there is obviously no one clear-cut way of helping every child who seems to have specific learning difficulties.

Helping adolescents with literacy problems

All children are entitled to education that meets their needs, including those with literacy problems. Adolescents who find reading and spelling difficult are handicapped at school and are likely to leave with poor qualifications. As well as this obvious handicap a history of failure leaves its emotional mark. Adolescents who are struggling to keep up and those who seem to have given up both need extra help and encouragement, whatever the underlying cause of their difficulties.

The first line of help should be the school and parents should get an interview with a member of the school pastoral staff (see page 203) and explain why they are worried and ask what can be done to help, whether in school or at home. They should make clear that they want to try to find out *why* their adolescent has problems so that relevant steps may be taken. It is possible that the school remedial department can offer special help with the difficult task of diagnosing what is wrong and suggest what help is needed to put things right.

If such help is not forthcoming and the parents believe that their adolescent has specific learning difficulties they can ask to be referred, by the school, to the child psychology service for diagnosis. It is possible that for some youngsters a Statement of special need could be made (see page 241).

If necessary local dyslexia associations (see page 297) can give advice to parents who wish to know more about how adolescents can get help. For example, they may be able to suggest psychologists to whom an adolescent could be referred by the family doctor. The psychologist will take a history of the young person's physical and emotional health and carry out various tests to ascertain the adolescent's ability and to find out what the problems might be. He or she will also suggest some course of action, suited to the particular individual, which should be communicated to the school. It is possible, in some cases, that a psychologist will suggest that a young person is encouraged to use a word processor and may recommend that some allowance is made when they sit examinations; for example, they might be given extra time to check written work.

Whatever remedial work is suggested, whether systematic rote spelling, or reading exercises, it will involve patience and hard work. Teenagers need all the encouragement they can get in these circumstances; if parents have not experienced similar difficulties themselves, they may at times be tempted to think that a youngster is just not trying or is being lazy when progress is slow. In fact, the parent can come to experience the frustrations that their sons and daughters are undergoing and sometimes need all the patience at their disposal. They should not blame teenagers who are struggling and becoming dispirited. Parents should listen to their anxieties and weariness and let them know that they are understood and accepted for themselves, whatever their progress or otherwise. They should also encourage their adolescents to be pleased with themselves for persevering and for completing work. And, although schoolwork is important, there are other aspects of life adolescents can enjoy with their friends, and with the family, when school can be forgotten about. It is worth while for parents to help adolescents to experience life in a positive way, alongside the disappointments they meet in the course of their school career.

Bullying

Bullying can lie at the root of much misery in schools and research shows that it is widespread.[15] Bullying takes many forms; it can consist of physical attacks and threats, vicious teasing, insults about parents, stealing belongings, extorting money and spoiling homework. For youngsters from ethnic minorities, bullying can be specifically racist and for girls there can be harassment through name-calling, such as 'slag' to suggest promiscuity and 'drag' and 'lezzie' for girls who are not promiscuous.[16]

The distress that bullying causes can result in great unhappiness, with children staying away from school rather than face the bully. If your adolescent tells you that he or she is the victim of bullying, then it is wise to take their complaints seriously. Sometimes parents simply advise their adolescents to take no notice. This may be easier said than done and, in any case, may not stop the bully. Continued bullying which is having an effect on a young person's attitude towards school, and making them miserable, calls for action. While you can ask school pastoral staff for help about a particular case, bullying is also an issue which should be tackled throughout the school. This means implementing strategies for building respect between pupils, staff and school care workers, such as dinner attendants. It means working on a curriculum which extends lessons about personal relationships from the classroom out into the playground, the school canteen and the journey home. It also means the open discussion of bullying, what leads to it and how to deal with it, in the classroom.

Developing a 'whole school policy' which works, because everyone feels secure and of value, needs the active co-operation of staff and of the governors. It may be necessary for you and other parents to bring bullying to the attention of both and to encourage them to take positive steps against it.

When things go wrong

If your adolescent's school encourages easy communications and you play your part in this, many minor difficulties can be sorted out before they develop into major ones. A word with teachers at open evenings, or a note explaining small problems like lost PE kit or missed homework or necessary absence are ways in which you can help to prevent problems building up.

Similarly a good Parent-Teacher Association can help parents to develop an informal relationship with staff and with governors, and make it possible to talk about general concerns without anyone feeling forced into a defensive position.

There may be occasions when you feel that you need to talk to staff about something specific and that a note, or waiting for the next open evening, will not serve the purpose: for example, if your child is being subjected to continuous bullying or if a school report has been much worse than you had expected. In such cases either ring up, or send a note, asking for an appointment with the relevant member of staff: a subject teacher or a pastoral teacher like the head of year (see pages 203–4).

The note does not need to go into details but it should briefly state the subject: 'about Susan's report, especially about her grades in . . .' or 'Tom is becoming worried about school and sometimes asks if he can stay at home.'

Talking to staff about problems

If you go to school to talk to a member of staff about a problem concerning your adolescent it is quite possible that you will find you are involved emotionally as well as at a practical level. Feelings do not always help people to communicate easily with others, especially if there is some conflict involved (see pages 187–95 for guidelines).

Be aware of your feelings and try not to let them stand in the way of what you want to say, so that the teacher understands and feels ready to co-operate. This means explaining yourself without making the teacher feel threatened.

■ Explain the problem factually:
'Sarah is very nervous of Miss Jones and afraid to ask questions in maths.'

■ Do not imply any blame for the school or staff:
There is no need to say what you think about Miss Jones's character or about her teaching ability.

■ Say how you or your adolescent are affected, putting the problem from your point of view:
'The problem is that she thinks she is falling behind and she can be anxious about going to school in the morning.'

■ Invite the teacher to help try to find ways round the problem:
'I wonder if there is anything that you can do at school, or we can do at home, to help get over the problem?'

More formal approaches

If you can get no help from a teacher, you may wish to take a problem further. Or it could be that the problem at issue is of general concern to parents and that several of you want to do something about it.

There are a number of possible courses of action:

■ Writing a letter to the board of governors explaining the problem briefly and factually, as above, and requesting a meeting with a governor.

■ With other parents, putting forward a resolution at the annual general meeting asking the governors to consider an issue.

- Making an approach to the local authority.
- Contacting a local councillor or MP.
- Writing a letter to the Secretary of State for Education.

Obviously you would want to get a complaint sorted out without going to extreme lengths and how far you decided to take it would depend on its nature and severity.

Advice and information

Your local education office can give you information on your rights about education, including:

- your choice of school;
- appeals to obtain a Statement that an adolescent is in need of special education, and appeals against a Statement;
- your rights if your son or daughter is suspended from school.

There are also addresses on page 297 of organisations which can give you more detailed advice about how to proceed with appeals or complaints.

As a general rule, if you have entered into a serious formal complaint you should keep a written record of your conversations with teachers, governors and officials and copies of all letters sent and received. You should also ask for a written statement of any action which has been agreed.

You should be careful about the sort of information you put in writing; details are not always necessary and can be counter-productive. You may need to take advice before committing anything to paper.

CHAPTER EIGHT

INDEPENDENCE IN ADOLESCENCE

THROUGHOUT THEIR TEENS adolescents become increasingly inde pendent. They no longer need the constant supervision of parents a they did when they were younger, they are more capable of lookin after themselves because, both socially and intellectually, they ar more adept than in childhood. They have increasing control over hov they spend their time and where they go. Young people reach differen levels of independence at different ages, partly because parents hav different ideas about how much independence adolescents should b given, and partly because adolescents themselves are all individuals with different temperaments and different wishes. For som adolescents, achieving independence is more complicated than fo others. Some twins, for example, may feel the need to becom independent of each other, as well as of their parents, at an earlie stage than their peers,[1] and adolescents with disabilities – and thei parents – have to find their own particular ways forward.

Much of this book is about achieving a healthy balance between th independence of adolescents and their continuing, if ever-decreasing reliance on parents. It suggests how parents can provide informatio encouragement and support of various kinds, to help youngsters grov up safely, so that eventually they can take on adult roles, unhampere by the consequences either of being given independence too early or of being encouraged to rely too heavily on their parents. So far we have looked at questions of health and of sexuality as well as at the responsibilities adolescents have to face at school. This chapter considers further areas of independence, both at home and in the community, and the questions that arise, within the family, concerning the changing relationship between parents and adolescents; adolescents' need for privacy; learning to manage and earn money; responsibilities for taking some part in housework; and about adolescents and the school holidays. The latter part of the chapter focuses on adolescents away from home, out and about in cities and towns, using public and private transport; and on parents and teenagers arriving at mutually acceptable rules about where they go and at what time they should come home. There is also a section about teenagers who leave home and the problems involved, and information about juvenile crime and the legal system.

The chapter ends by considering some of the influences which come from outside the home, such as the influence of friends and of the mass media.

Growing up and the law[2]

The law recognises that adolescents become more capable throughout their teens and gives young people increasing rights, and decreasing protection, as they progress towards legal adulthood at the age of eighteen. At the same time, the rights and obligations of parents towards their children diminish.

Young people can:

- be convicted of a criminal offence at the age of ten;
- buy a pet at twelve;
- get a part-time job at thirteen;
- go into a public house bar when they are fourteen;
- see a Category 15 film at fifteen;
- open a post office Girobank account at fifteen;
- give legal consent to sexual intercourse at sixteen, in the case of girls;
- marry with parental consent at sixteen (in Scotland they can marry with or without parental consent at the same age);
- give or refuse consent to medical treatment at sixteen; they can do so before then if the doctor thinks they understand the implications of their decision. This also applies to contraceptive advice and treatment. In Scotland girls over twelve and boys over fourteen can seek contraceptive advice without parental consent;
- leave school and get full-time work at sixteen;

- have a licence to drive an invalid carriage at sixteen;
- buy tobacco at sixteen;
- buy fireworks at sixteen;
- have alcoholic drinks with a meal in a restaurant (including a publi house dining room) at sixteen;
- hold a licence to drive most vehicles except heavy goods vehicle at seventeen;
- enter legal contracts, including mortgages and hire purchase, a eighteen;
- vote at eighteen;
- buy and drink alcohol in a public house bar at eighteen;
- enter a betting shop and place a bet at eighteen;
- marry without parental consent at eighteen;
- see their birth certificate, if they are adopted, at eighteen;
- hold a licence for any type of vehicle at twenty-one;
- become a Member of Parliament, or a local councillor, at twenty one.
- Young men can consent to private homosexual acts at twenty one.

Privacy

An important aspect of growing up and gaining independence i being given the opportunity to have some privacy at home. Fo adolescents this is more than the freedom to lock the bathroom doo without arousing comment (see page 58); it also means being allowe time and space to be alone, to think their own thoughts and to hav their own experiences.

Self-consciousness is a feature of this stage of life for many youn people. Adolescents sometimes feel that they are constantly observe by others and being able to escape from this, if they wish, is a relie If it is possible for adolescents to have a room of their own, or partitioned space within a room, it can be a refuge away from th rest of the world. As they grow up they should have the feeling tha their privacy is treated with the same respect that would be show to an adult. This includes knocking on their bedroom door befor going in and only opening their cupboards and drawers wit permission. It also means that letters are not automatically for sharin and that phone calls may sometimes be made behind closed door and without comment.

A wish for privacy is not the same thing as being secretive. I would be worrying if an eleven-year-old often seemed to be actin furtively. But adolescents who have reached their mid-teens do no want to share all their private feelings and experiences: they nee their own 'space'. As parents we have to know when to back off, when not to intrude, while at the same time being ready to listen and support when needed.

Doing things together

It is inevitable that during their teens most young people spend progressively less time with their parents. They make their own friends and have their own interests, at home and outside. Also they no longer need parents to transport them and accompany them on their various leisure pursuits. It is not that teenagers no longer need parents or enjoy being with them, or that parents do not enjoy their teenagers' company, just that over the years the pattern of activities together changes.

These changes are normal in our society but, nevertheless, parents can feel rejected if they assume that some family activity will take place as usual, only to find that adolescents no longer wish to join in. They may feel a pang of recognition that their child is growing up and sooner or later will cease to be a member of the household in its day-to-day activities. This realisation needs to be accepted: your task as parents, providing, protecting and guiding, will, eventually, be complete and the relationship with your sons and daughters will be on a different footing. When young people reach full independence, parents also take on a new freedom. The responsibilities you undertook with the birth of your first child are over and you can enter a fresh phase in your own lives with new opportunities for developing or deepening personal or professional interests.

From the adolescent's point of view there may be many different reasons for wanting to follow their own pursuits. These include new, and to them more interesting, ways of passing their time. Some adolescents seem to feel extra self-conscious at being seen with their parents in public; perhaps it causes them to feel closer to the child part of their identity and further away from the young adult they aspire to be. There is also the fact that their parents are outside their control and may unexpectedly do, or say, something really embarrassing, at least in the eyes of the young person concerned. Fortunately, with greater maturity and a surer sense of who they are, this phase passes.

But although as the years pass parents and teenagers spend less time together, there are still many activities they take part in together and enjoy one another's company. Birthdays and festivals are obvious examples when the generations get together; parties and barbecues, with other parents and teenagers, can also be fun and involving other families may be an answer when teenagers become reluctant to go on a family holiday. While family outings may become less frequer over the years, relationships carry on. Parents and teenagers watc television together, work about the house and, above all, talk.

Sharing tasks around the house

Everyone who lives in the household should play at least some pa in contributing to its smooth running. Housework, cooking, shoppin and laundry are all ways of keeping the family in good health an usually most of the load falls on mothers, even those who go out t work.[3] Although there are many pressures on young people's tim they should be encouraged to give a hand with housework. Paren need help and, equally important, young people need to gain exper ence in looking after themselves so that eventually they will be ab to function independently. Preparing adolescents for independence s far as their own health is concerned not only includes teaching ther how to make appointments to see the doctor, but also giving ther experience of caring for their own physical health by the everyda tasks of buying and preparing food and looking after family hygien by washing up, cleaning and helping with the laundry. Young peop cannot learn how to do household work unless they are given som responsibility for it.

Boys need this experience just as much as girls, yet research show that they do less to help in the house than girls and are, therefor less independent in this respect.[4] If you are a father, you can encourag a boy to do housework by taking the lead and asking him to join i It is generally easier to get adolescents to work alongside you rath than expecting them to complete tasks on their own.

If you feel that your own son or daughter is not doing a fair sha of housework, then it is best to talk to them about this before yo start to feel resentful (see page 184). Discuss with them how muc can be reasonably expected, taking into account the demands c schoolwork. It may be best to set a fairly low attainable goal, rath than aiming too high, but to be consistent in expecting that what yo have agreed between you is carried out. What you should not do take over the task yourself if it has been left undone.

The lowest acceptable amount of help to be expected is th adolescents should:

- keep their own rooms as clean and tidy as they want them to be
- see that their dirty clothes are ready for the wash;
- not leave family rooms untidy or dirty: for example, they shoul clean the bath after use, clear up their belongings rather than leav them lying around, and help with the washing-up.

Independence and Money

Parents are well aware that the cost of bringing up an adolescent is much higher than for a young child. Not only are clothes and food bills greater but life presents many different opportunities for young people to spend money on leisure pursuits. Much advertising, whether it is for take-away food, alcohol, music, clothing or cosmetics is aimed, directly or otherwise, at young people. But young people have to obtain money in order to buy these commodities and often they do so from their parents. Parents are differently placed as to how much money is available for teenagers, whether for basic necessities or for extras, depending on how many incomes (if any) there are in the family and the size of those incomes. But for all adolescents it is important that they should have the opportunity to learn how to handle money sensibly before they leave home, whether to be a student or to set up a home of their own. It is impossible for anyone to be independent in adult life unless he or she has enough money to meet material and other needs and is able to manage it responsibly. For adolescents who are still at school, the only money over which they have any control is pocket money and, for some, whatever can be earned from jobs out of school hours. Later, when full-time education is over, the majority of young people take paid work or enter paid training schemes.

Realistic information about money

Young people need to understand a little about the family income, where it comes from and how it is spent, so that they can develop a rational approach towards money. In an age when money seems to appear, almost by magic, from outlets in the wall, and when much family spending is accomplished by credit cards, concrete information can give a greater sense of reality.

You may or may not want to be specific about everything (money is another subject surrounded by powerful taboos) but at least let your son or daughter have some idea about how, in general, your income is allocated: how some proportion of it goes to meet the requirements of the family as a whole, such as housing, poll tax, heating, water, light, insurances, and food; how further sums are spent on family leisure, such as television, holidays, birthdays and other family celebrations; roughly how much is needed by individual family members for essentials like transport and clothes, and what can be afforded for pocket money. There are opportunities for much of this information to emerge naturally in conversation, for example, at the time when bills need to be paid. A young person may be less receptive if information is only provided as an answer to requests for money for some desirable purpose, which parents cannot afford. Young people also need to be informed about any major change in circumstances to do with the family income, for example, if a parent loses a job, and how this will affect the family as well as the youngster concerned.

Managing their own money

No doubt there are temperamental differences between people when it comes to dealing with money. It is quite likely that if someone is cautious in other areas of life they will also be careful with money, while impetuous people are likely to spend money on the spur of the moment. But this is not an argument against giving young people, impetuous or otherwise, the chance to manage money for themselves. Having to make decisions, supported to some extent by parents, is an experience from which they can learn to be responsible about money in comparative safety, whatever their particular temperament. Obviously this sort of experience is less possible for youngsters whose families live in poverty and where parents' finances are controlled by necessity rather than choice.

Here are some suggestions:

- Discuss with your son or daughter how much pocket money is reasonable and what it should be expected to cover.
- Give pocket money regularly, and a regular sum, so that the adolescent can rely on it and has an opportunity to manage it; this is less easy when money comes haphazardly and in varying amounts.
- When your teenager seems to be sensible enough, instead of giving money for school meals and, perhaps, fares on a daily basis, give it to them in a lump sum to cover the week. When a teenager has succeeded in managing this for some time without running into difficulties, extend the period that the money has to cover.
- Consider the possibility, in later adolescence, of a clothing allowance. This means sitting down with your son or daughter and working out what is needed each year and then dividing it into, for example, termly amounts. Handling an allowance sensibly needs some maturity, being able to put off the pleasure of making small purchases in order to save for a major expense like a jacket. Some adolescents may find this level of responsibility burdensome, while for others it is another welcome step towards adulthood.
- If a teenager has any money of their own, whether from presents, work, savings or a clothing allowance, discuss ways for them to look

after it. They can open different sorts of savings accounts and, from the age of fifteen, a post office Girobank account if you are willing to act as guarantor. Only in very exceptional circumstances will a bank give a banker's card to anyone under eighteen, even if there is an account in their name. This means that they cannot make purchases and can only save and withdraw money at the branch where their account is kept. The reason for this is because, until the age of eighteen, parents are accountable for their children's debts.

Using the phone

With growing independence, young people develop deeper relationships outside the family and friends start to fulfil some of the needs which parents have previously met. In order to keep in touch with friends, even those they have seen for many hours during the day, the phone comes into its own. Problems about teenagers and the family telephone are notorious. In the first place an enthusiastic and sociable youngster can quickly run up a large bill but there is also the problem of the telephone being in constant use so that parents' own friends find that the line is always engaged and give up trying to get through.

The best solution is to discuss the problem with your son or daughter and see if, between you, you can decide how many calls are reasonable for them to make each week, how long each call should take and whether there are certain times of the day when it is less convenient for the phone to be used than others. A clock or an egg-timer by the phone can serve as a reminder to be brief and a money-box can be left for contributions towards lengthy phone calls or for calls which exceed an agreed maximum number each week.

Earning money

Adolescents can earn money at home for doing jobs about the house but they can also get paid employment outside the home.

Paid housework

In some families pocket money is earned by work about the house, and not seen as a gift, but other parents find this practice unacceptable. There are those who maintain that pocket money must be a gift, always and reliably given with love, no matter how helpful or otherwise an adolescent has been and certainly not as payment for work. There are other parents who are against paying for housework on the grounds that taking some part in household chores is to be expected of everyone who lives within the family, not something to be paid for (see page 252). On the other hand, in a single-parent family a mother with a demanding job might choose to pay her teenager the going rate for doing regular work in the house in preference to employing outside help. Another option is for young sters to be able to earn urgently needed money by taking on task that are beyond the scope of what is usually expected of them. I these circumstances, they would not be paid for washing up but woul be remunerated for work like stripping wallpaper or painting th bathroom.

Paid employment

Many young people take on paid part-time work, either before c after school, in the holidays or at the weekends.[5] The law surroundin young people and work is complex, to some extent a matter for centra government but also in the hands of local authorities. Unfortunately i seems that the law is often broken by unscrupulous employers, an parents and teenagers need to be aware of this. The local town ha can give details about local regulations and the legal requirements c any particular job (including work in a family business). It is part c the responsibility of the educational welfare officer (see page 236) t see that laws about employment and schoolchildren are observe Educational welfare officers have power to question employers an to bring a prosecution if necessary; they can also require your adc lescent to give up a job if it seems to be interfering with schoolwor or potentially damaging in some other way.

The main *legal* considerations are[6]:

- *The age of the child* With some exceptions (for example, child actor who need a local authority licence) children below the age of thirtee cannot be taken on for part-time work. There are different regulation for young people under sixteen and for those aged between sixtee and eighteen.
- *Health and safety* There are requirements, among others, abou lifting, about dangerous machinery and about chemicals.
- *Types of work* Young people may not, for example, work in pub off-licences and betting shops during opening hours.
- *The number of hours worked* Young people may not work mor than two hours on a school day; under-sixteens may not work befor seven o'clock in the morning or after seven in the evening.

These requirements may not be strictly enforced locally, so parent and young people themselves have to be alert to possible danger for example, unguarded machinery in a workplace, lack of trainin for dangerous work, or working long hours during term-time. recent survey of children and adolescents who worked found th nearly a third reported an accident or injury at work.[7] Adolescent are also frequently underpaid for what they do. These points all nee to be covered in any discussion with your son or daughter about taking on paid work. In spite of the pitfalls, getting a part-time job can also be a positive way of using leisure-time; some youngsters enjoy their jobs and, as well as money, gain independence and experience from them and a better perspective of an adult working world.

Full-time work

From the age of sixteen, young men and women can leave full-time education and get a job, although they are entitled to full-time education until they are nineteen (see page 231). Another possibility is for them to take part in a government training or employment scheme for which an allowance is paid. They should first find out what training schemes offer in the way of actual training (some may be more interested in gaining cheap labour than giving training) and if there is likely to be a job at the end, either with the current employer or in the neighbourhood (see page 232).

The law still offers some protection to under-eighteens as to working conditions although, since 1989, less so than formerly. The type of work available for this age-group is often poorly paid and the Wages Act 1989 removed its right to a minimum wage. There is the further disadvantage that, without education or training after the age of sixteen, workers are in a much less favoured position than those who postponed work until they had obtained more qualifications. If, however, after discussion a young person very much wants to leave school at sixteen and to get a job, there are still educational options open to them in the future. Having tried work, if he or she wishes to return to full-time education, for example at a local college of further education, they are entitled to do so, free of charge, until they reach the age of nineteen. Colleges will give advice about courses which can be combined with full- or part-time work so that youngsters can obtain better qualifications for work or in order to go on to higher education.

The local education authority will also have details about 'Access' courses which are geared to young people who need to brush up on basic educational skills in order to prepare themselves to enter vocational and other courses.

Applying for work

When, eventually, a young person decides to apply for work, they need to create a good impression on potential employers. They must present themselves as potentially successful candidates when they fill in application forms, write letters and go for interviews. This includes finding out what the employer wants and recognising what aspects of their own experience, character and qualifications fit the employer's needs.

Applications

■ Before filling in an application form, or applying by letter, a would-be employee should find out what they can about the position they are applying for. They can get information from friends who have experience of working in a similar position, from the careers office at college or at school and, if not already supplied, from the personnel office concerned.

They should:

■ Note the date by which applications must be received.

■ Make a photocopy of the application form and fill in the photocopy, before starting on the real thing. Doing so makes it easier to produce a neat, well-spaced application.

■ Answer all questions and carry out any instructions such as writing in capital letters. Unless there is an instruction to the contrary, the application may be typed.

■ Ask someone to check the draft for spelling and accuracy before copying it on to the actual form.

■ If space is left for applicants to say why they are suited for the job, or if they are encouraged to do so in an accompanying letter, they need to consider what they have to offer that is relevant to that particular appointment. They should think first of all about the job and what it entails. Then check through the following list, trying to identify their own particular strengths and how they relate to the job in question.

Knowledge What special understanding do they have to bring to the work? What do they know about? Any certificates they have acquired at school or college may already have been listed on the application form. Those that are particularly relevant for the job can now be given prominence, including, if appropriate, details about any special options or projects. For example, 'I did a project on children with special needs, based on observations and reading, which received a grade A.'

Experience Although teenagers have had less work experience than older people the following are applicable:

■ *Paid work* If they have had a holiday job in the same line of work as the one they are applying for, this should be mentioned. They could also say if they have held a weekend or after-school job consistently for a reasonable length of time, for a year, say. On the other hand, if they have had a variety of part-time jobs this is also worth including: 'Since I was ... (age) I have had a variety of jobs after school and in the holidays including ...'

- *Leisure pursuits* They should think about what they enjoy doing and if in any way this relates to the job they are applying for. For example, does it give them experience of working with a group of people, of concentrating on detail, of being good with their hands? They should say something about what they have done: 'I am in the local drama club and I have helped to paint scenery for the pantomime.'
- *Extra-curricular experience* At school they may have had experiences outside the academic curriculum, which would be useful in the work for which they are now applying. For example, they may have been in a school team, had duties with younger children or done voluntary work.

Skills What can they do that is relevant to the job? What are their achievements? Here they might mention passing a driving test or having keyboard skills, acquired at home, but for which they have no formal qualification.

Attitudes What attitudes do they have which would be useful in this particular job? Do they enjoy working with people or do they like meeting a challenge? Do they like working in a well-organised way? Is the work setting one which appeals to them generally – for example, in retailing, production or social services?

To sum up, any covering letter, or additional information, should say what they have to offer and why they are enthusiastic about getting the job. It should be neat and easy to read and, if possible, no longer than a page. It will look more businesslike if it is written on unlined, white A4 paper, rather than on personal notepaper. Lined paper can be used underneath plain paper for a guide. They should ask someone to check for spelling and other mistakes.

References

The names and addresses of a senior teacher at school, a holiday employer or a family friend can be given as referees. The young person should first ask permission to give someone's name as a referee so that they know in advance and are ready for any enquiry which an employer may make, by telephone as well as in writing.

Preparing for an interview

Interviews are for the employer and the would-be employee to find out more about each other.

It is quite possible that the school has given leavers opportunities to practise interview techniques. But parents can help teenagers to prepare for an interview by explaining what usually happens and by giving practical advice.

They should:

- Be sure that they are informed about the job they are applying for and what it entails, so that they are ready to answer questions sensibly.
- Be familiar with what they have written in their application, and why they chose to highlight certain aspects of their experience. They should be ready to put across whatever strengths they have in relation to the job they want.
- They should choose clothes in which they feel reasonably comfortable and not self-conscious; at the same time they should dress quite formally rather than over-casually, or in any extreme way; the main guide is to think in terms of the job they are applying for and what sort of dress would be acceptable.
- They should be in good time for the appointment: not so early as to have to sit waiting nervously for half an hour, but allowing enough time to cover any unforeseen traffic delays and to avoid the anxiety of arriving in a last-minute rush.

The interview

A teenager being interviewed for a job should aim to be friendly in manner, without being familiar. They should greet the interviewer when they come in with 'Good morning' or 'Good afternoon' and say 'Thank you' and 'Goodbye' at the end of the interview. They should not be afraid to smile and should sit in a comfortable way, not slouched over or over-tense.

It is not possible to predict what will happen in an interview because much depends on the personality and experience of the interviewer. To put applicants at ease some start by asking fairly trivial questions, perhaps about where applicants live or which school they attended. They may then ask questions about what the applicant has written in their application.

They may check examination options and grades and give the candidate a chance to say something about them. For example, 'I see you got a grade C in English.' The applicant needs to use these prompts as an opportunity to say something positive about themselves. A plain 'yes' or 'no' to every question does not help the interviewer to get to know an applicant. An appropriate answer would be something like, 'Yes, my grades in English have improved this year,' or 'Yes, I enjoy writing essays best.' If the interviewer comments on something negative, such as 'You say in your application that you got a grade

F for maths,' the applicant should find something positive (and true) to say in response like, 'Yes, I was disappointed about that. There are some parts of maths – like geometry – that I enjoy and do quite well,' or give a reason, without seeming to be on the defensive: 'I missed a lot of work in the fourth year, when I broke my leg at football. I caught up in most subjects but unfortunately not maths.'

If the interviewer asks about leisure activities mentioned in the application, the young person should take any opportunity to talk about experience relevant to the job. But even if this is not possible they should be ready to talk with some enthusiasm about their interests and to give details, not just to answer with one word.

At some stage the interviewer will describe what the work involves and something about the conditions of employment. He or she will then give the applicant an opportunity to ask questions. At this point anything that has not been made clear can be sorted out, such as information about training opportunities, pay or holidays.

If the interviewer does not make a decision on the spot, he or she should let the applicant know when they will be informed.

Out of work

Whether school-leavers manage to find employment, or a place on a suitable training scheme, depends to a large extent on which part of the country they live in. This is something which should be taken into account in discussing the benefits or otherwise of continuing with education. Unemployment is depressing. Without money and work, real independence seems a long way off; another important aspect of work concerns the sense of personal identity that comes from being able to say what you do for a living. In addition, for youngsters who do not go out to work or to college, their days are unstructured and it needs considerable maturity to cope with life without a timetable. For some teenagers, after a month without work, there is the fear that unemployment will continue for ever. It is discouraging to apply for jobs only to find that they are already taken, or to be turned down after interview.

It requires patience to be the parent of an unemployed teenager, and the realisation that unemployment is, for many young people, an unavoidable state of affairs. They especially need parents' support at this time when their self-esteem may be at a low ebb. Be ready to listen to them and to try to understand their experience.

Should they think that no work will be forthcoming, discuss other options as well as work. These include returning to education. There is growing demand for people with technical skills and the atmosphere at a college of further education may be more to their liking than memories of school would suggest. Would they consider voluntary work? This has the disadvantage of being unpaid (although expenses may be covered) but it is a way of gaining experience, and getting references which can be offered to employers. The local authority social services department, to be found through the town hall, or a volunteers' bureau can give advice.

If your son or daughter feel they have been discriminated against at a job interview on account of sex or race, and that for these reasons they have been turned down for the job, get advice from a local legal centre or from the Equal Opportunities Commission or the Commission for Racial Equality (addresses on page 297).

Adolescents Out and About in the Community

Wherever you live, in the town or the country, it is normal for teenagers, as they become more independent, to spend more time away from home, go further afield and try out new activities. Cities and towns are rich environments, full of interesting possibilities, from football matches, shops and clubs to corner cafés for meeting friends. Parents must ask themselves at what age it is safe for their sons and daughters to exercise new levels of independence in the local community. Although young people can look suddenly and amazingly grown up, are they as mature as their appearance suggests? What about the dangers that are to be met away from home and parents' protection? This section considers what is reasonable independence for a young person; possible methods of transport; and some of the dangers that exist outside the home, including accidents and delinquency.

Deciding about independence levels

Deciding about what a youngster is allowed to do, where they may go on their own or with friends, what time they must come home and other questions linked to independence do not start with adolescence. Pre-adolescent children are often allowed to play out on the pavement near to home. Many go to school by themselves, and some use public transport. They may be allowed to go to local shops to spend pocket money, and to visit friends and relatives in the vicinity of their homes.

By the time your child reaches adolescence you should have a common understanding of what level of independence is allowed, because it has been arrived at gradually over the years, probably without any discussion between you. This gradual growth in independence may continue during the teenage years. Independence only becomes an issue of conflict when your adolescent wants to push the boundaries noticeably further than was allowed previously and perhaps to a degree which you feel is unsafe. It is only reasonable that parents should set boundaries because they have responsibility for the safety and welfare of adolescents.

How do you decide if your son or daughter is sensible enough to be allowed to stay out late for a special party, to go to a football match without an adult, to go to a distant, but attractive, shopping centre with friends, for example? Obviously age plays a part in what level of independence is feasible, but some youngsters are very sensible and others of the same age are careless. In making up your mind, the following factors are all worth taking into account:

■ Do they usually keep to your agreements or rules, for instance, about home-coming, so that you have not had to worry about them in the past?
■ Does the proposed activity present many or few unfamiliar aspects? In the case of going to the football match, is this something they want to do alone for the first time, although they have been with friends previously? With the shopping centre, are they already familiar with the journey, even if they have only been there with you or another adult? Have they used public transport alone before?
■ How well do you think they would behave in an emergency? Do they know how to get in touch with you by making a reverse-charge phone call?
■ How normal is this particular activity for other youngsters of the same age?

The answers to these questions may help you to decide if you feel happy about an adolescent taking new steps towards independence. If you consider there are real problems, then you need to discuss these with your son or daughter and let them know your reasons for suggesting a compromise: for example, you may prefer them to have the experience of making shorter, less complicated journeys, before they try longer, more complex routes. Involve them in finding a solution which will be acceptable to both of you; a possible example may be that they can go somewhere alone but that you will meet them and bring them home. Tell them that if anything unexpected occurs which presents difficulties, you want them to ring you. They should always let you know if they are going to be home later than expected for any reason.

Although adolescents may seem to shrug off your worries, you are showing that you care about their welfare and this is a source of security for them. At the same time, by discussing their demands, giving your reasons for concern, listening, looking for ways round the difficulties, you show that you respect them.

Road safety

Road accidents are a major cause of death and serious injury among adolescents and young adults. Many more of them, proportionately, have serious accidents than people in other age-groups.[8] This higher accident rate unfortunately holds true for pedestrians (although the accident rate declines throughout the teens) as well as for cyclists, moped and scooter riders, motor-cyclists and young people who drive cars.

Even though the roads are dangerous it is essential for adolescents to be able to get about their neighbourhood without adult supervision, whether on foot or using some form of transport. The good news is that there has been *some* fall in casualty rates among children and young people in recent years. Various groups and individuals can help to promote road safety. Local authorities offer training and advice, sometimes through schools, and local traffic and housing planning has a part to play. Parents can also help adolescents to be more safety-conscious.

Pedestrians[9]

Young adolescents are still careless about the dangers of traffic and those between the ages of ten and fourteen are most at risk. But there are things you can do to help them be more aware of potential danger.

When they start at a new school, help them to choose the safest route. For example, show them the pedestrian crossings. They should cross on the zebra crossing itself and not on the zigzag lines on either side. Drivers concentrate on the crossing itself and may be less aware of someone walking close by. Point out hazards, such as the danger of crossing directly behind a bus and so being hidden from on-coming traffic; point out people who are endangering themselves or others on the roads by careless behaviour.

- Stress that when they are crossing the road with friends they should check if it is safe to cross for themselves and not just follow on heedlessly.
- They should always stop and look before they cross the road.
- They should not play or walk on the kerb at the edge of the pavement where they may slip in front of traffic.
- On dark mornings and evenings, fluorescent and reflective bands attached to clothes, or school bags, can make them more visible to drivers.

Two wheels

Having the use of their own transport, whether a bicycle or a moped, or a motor-bike when they are old enough to have a licence, certainly increases adolescents' independence. If they have their own 'wheels' they are not tied to public transport with its delays and expense so they can get quickly from one place to another, quite apart from the pleasure to be had from riding. It is tragic that cycling in its various forms can be such a dangerous activity and especially for young people. Adolescents are not particularly safety-conscious and as the volume of traffic on the roads increases, conditions become ever more dangerous.

What can be done to reduce risks?

Bicycles[10]

Safety begins with choosing a bicycle

For children who have not yet started the adolescent growth spurt (see pages 9 and 14), it may be tempting to buy a bicycle that is too big in the knowledge that the child will grow into it. Trying to control an over-sized bicycle is difficult and can lead to accidents. Until a child is big enough to handle an adult bicycle they should have a children's model which is the right size. When they are tall enough for an adult bicycle, you will be able to adjust the height of the handlebars and seat to fit.

Maintaining a safe bicycle

Keep the bicycle in good working order. Frequently check the brakes to see that they grip well so that the young cyclist can be sure of stopping when necessary. For the same reason, look to see that brake cables are sound and have them renewed if necessary. Tyres should have a good tread to grip the road and prevent slipping; those which show signs of wear should be replaced. Check if front and rear lamps are working.

Learning to ride safely

Your adolescent's school may arrange cycling proficiency lessons and tests. At some schools, students are not allowed to come to school on a bicycle until they have passed their test. These sessions give a basic understanding of safe cycling, what to do and what to avoid. Wearing a comfortable, lightweight safety helmet prevents serious head injury, but it is not a substitute for careful riding.

Dangerous behaviour

Cyclists should:

- ride single file on busy roads;
- not ride on the pavement;
- keep games and stunts off the road;
- not take a passenger.

Visibility for cyclists

The roads are dangerous for cyclists – and for people riding mopeds and motor-cycles – because motorists and lorry drivers do not always see them. Youngsters who cycle should make themselves as visible as possible. At night they must, by law, use a front lamp and a red rear lamp as well as having a reflector on the back of the bicycle. These make the cyclist visible to other road users in the dark. Lamps should also be used in the rain in order to make the rider more conspicuous. It is especially important that the rear light is not hidden by overhanging clothing or luggage. Spare batteries and bulbs should be carried in case a light fails at night.

Visibility can also be increased by:

- wearing bright clothing in daylight – white shows up best at night;
- wearing reflective bands on arms and legs.

Dangerous conditions

Your adolescent should avoid:

- cycling in the rain when visibility is poor, roads are slippery and brakes are less efficient;
- cycling in snow or on ice: road surfaces are treacherously slippery under these conditions;
- cycling in the dark: motorists often do not notice cyclists during the day, much less so at night;
- using main roads: heavy traffic presents more hazards. If you are lucky your local authority will have a policy for providing safe cycle paths.

Mopeds, scooters and motor-bikes

At sixteen, young people may ride mopeds, at seventeen, a scooter or motor-bike up to 125cc. The accident rates for these forms of transport are very high for teenagers. Getting a machine is a serious decision and one which needs discussion and preparation before it is undertaken, if at all.

Teenagers must learn to ride *defensively*. This does not mean riding a vehicle which looks like a small armour-plated tank, but knowing how to protect themselves from other road users by every possible means. This includes having a safe, road-worthy machine, being highly visible by using lights, reflective bands and bright clothing, and wearing protective clothing including, of course, a helmet.

There are various training schemes available to learner motorcyclists and the local safety officer, who can be contacted via your town hall, can give details of these and about road tests (see page 297 for other addresses).

It is of great importance that no person should ride a moped, a scooter or a motor-bike after drinking alcohol or while under the influence of other drugs. Impress on your teenager, also, never to accept a lift from someone who has been drinking or taking drugs (see page 155).

Cars At the age of seventeen a young person may apply for a licence to drive a car and take a driving test. Again, young drivers have a high accident rate and again, alcohol is often implicated in these accidents. The insurance rate for this group is very high and the high cost reflects the higher risks. Whether your own son or daughter has a car, or is allowed to drive the family car, depends to some extent on family and other circumstances. Can the family, or the young person concerned, afford a car, including the high insurance? Is going by car the only possible way of getting to work or college? All of these things are a matter for discussion between parents and adolescents.

It is necessary to repeat constantly the warning about drinking and driving and drugs and driving. Young people should not drink and drive, nor drive under the influence of other drugs, nor should they accept a lift from anyone who has been drinking or taking drugs (see page 155).

School Holidays

In families where parents go out to work, school holidays can present a problem, especially for the parents of younger adolescents. School holidays and working holidays do not match and while youngsters have about three months' holiday a year, parents may have twenty days' leave, or less.

It is believed that substantial numbers of children look after themselves during school holidays if both parents work.[11] A recent survey found that 39 per cent of eleven-year-olds in one area of London looked after themselves for an average of ten days during the summer holidays.[12] Contrary to popular belief, there is no statutory law which says at what age children may be left unattended at home. But if there were to be an accident in which a child or adolescent was harmed, a fire for example, the parents would be held responsible if they had not seemed to act with 'reasonable' care.

Some adolescents can be trusted to look after themselves while their parents work, for some of the time at least. Much depends on their age, temperament and individual capability, and parents must make their own decisions according to what they know about their own child. But even when teenagers are perfectly capable of taking care of themselves, holidays can be long and boring at home alone. Parents can help the situation by:

- making suggestions about how they can occupy themselves constructively;
- making arrangements with other local parents to take turns to provide a home base, for meals and companionship;
- letting an adolescent go to stay with relatives;
- finding a residential activity holiday, of the sort which offers sport and art opportunities for teenagers up to the age of eighteen;
- finding out if there is a local authority sports coaching school, which an adolescent might enjoy for one or two weeks of the holiday.
- finding a place in a playscheme or day camp.

Sometimes parents get together to provide holiday activities for groups of teenagers (see page 298 for addresses). If there is no scheme in your area, you could enquire at your PTA if other parents are interested in joining forces to organise interesting events and outings for their adolescents to take part in.

Playschemes

Playschemes are only suitable for the youngest adolescents and are rarely attended by secondary school children. Your town hall will have details of any which they organise themselves, although such schemes are not available everywhere. Ask questions at your teenager's school about any local playscheme, to find out what sort of reputation it has. Take your teenager to visit it to see if he or she would feel happy there. Ask to be shown round and look at what the children and staff are doing. Do both staff and children seem to be enjoying themselves and getting on well together? Is there enough space for a variety of activities: quiet, comfortable places where youngsters can get away from noisy activities; well-equipped craft areas; safe outdoor play space; a large indoor playroom for rainy weather? What is a typical weekly programme? Does it include trips off-site?

As well as municipal playschemes there are also commercial day camps. These are not necessarily regulated or inspected by any public body so it is up to you to find out whatever you can, before sending your adolescent to one. The proprietors of a good private scheme should not hesitate to show you round and answer any questions you may have about, for example, how many staff there are for how many children, and what past experience they have.

In addition to private and public playschemes, some employers (including some government departments) have been persuaded to set up holiday schemes for the children of employees. If you work for a large employer this may be a possibility.

Residential holidays

Again these are not necessarily registered or controlled in any way and so it is up to you to check the quality of what is on offer.

Running Away from Home

The time comes when young people leave their parents' home. For some this comes sooner than for others, when they go to college or university, returning only for holidays. Others wait until they can afford their own accommodation and this may take several years. Some leave home to marry or to settle down with a partner. By the time this stage arrives, they are capable of looking after their own needs and of taking on responsibilities for other people and of leading an independent life.

Even young people below the age of eighteen, for whom parents are responsible in law, may leave home if they have parental consent. At what age they are allowed to leave *without* your consent is not clearly stated in law, although it is commonly believed to be sixteen. At sixteen they are allowed to leave school and get a job and are eligible, in certain, limited, circumstances for supplementary benefit, so, in theory, they could also begin to lead an independent life away from home. In practice, because private housing is expensive and council housing very scarce, few sixteen-year-olds can afford to keep themselves on the wages which are typical for their age-group.

Some youngsters, however, leave home without their parents'

consent at the age of sixteen and younger. Police records for London for 1988 showed that 495 boys and 425 girls under the age of fourteen, and 980 boys and 1,172 girls aged between fourteen and seventeen, were reported missing. The vast majority did eventually get in touch with their parents or returned home but some were still missing at the end of the year.[13]

For an adolescent to run away from home is a nightmare for parents. It can also prove a very distressing experience for the teenager. Even if he or she is old enough to take a full-time job this will be difficult to find without a permanent place to live, which may itself prove impossible. An adolescent may find temporary, emergency accommodation but they may find that they have to sleep rough, subjecting themselves to physical and other dangers, and that without a permanent address it is very difficult, if not impossible, to obtain any social security benefit.

If someone under the age of sixteen runs away from home, the police are the first people for parents to contact. If the police find the adolescent in question, they will use their powers to return him or her to their parents.

With sixteen- and seventeen-year-olds the situation is, in practice, different. The police do not use their powers to return older teenagers to their parents, unless they are in moral or criminal danger.

Whether they are over or under sixteen, another possibility for parents of missing youngsters is to get in touch with the agencies which supply accommodation or advice for homeless young people. These are to be found in the large cities which are the target of many youngsters. However, there is no legal obligation for the staff of such services to let parents know who uses them. They will, however, be prepared to take a message to pass on, in case an adolescent should contact them. Most would not put parents in touch with sons or daughters without the young person's consent, although they might do what they could to encourage the youngster to give their consent or to make the contact themselves. Such agencies have to maintain this confidentiality because otherwise they would not be acceptable to the young people they set out to help. In addition, some of their clients have good reason for not wishing to return to parents who may, for example, be violent.

Names and addresses of organisations who may be in touch with runaway adolescents are given on page 298.

Gambling

Most gambling is illegal for under-eighteens and, although it is possible that some of them do occasionally break the law by placing a bet on a horse or by playing cards, this has never been seen as a problem which affects many young people. The exception to the legal prohibition on gambling under age is that young people are permitted to gamble on amusement machines that pay out less than £4 in prize money.

Fruit and video machines

Fruit machines, their lights flashing, promise showers of cash for the lucky and skilful; sophisticated video machines invite passers-by to test their co-ordination in exciting games and to compete against their own and their friends' best scores. Amusement machines are a regular feature in places frequented by adolescents such as neighbourhood fish and chip shops, take-aways and cafés. There is, however, legal regulation of these machines. They come under the control of the local authority which gives, or withholds, planning permission for amusement arcades and permits for individual machines in other places.

Under-sixteens are mostly prohibited from amusement arcades. This is not the result of legislation but of the proprietors' voluntary code of practice. This voluntary code does not hold, however, in seaside towns where children and adolescents are allowed to enter arcades and play machines unaccompanied by an adult.

Many young people enjoy playing fruit and video machines, and it is a much debated issue whether there are large-scale problems associated with this mild form of gambling. The danger arises if playing machines becomes a compulsive pastime for adolescents and leads to other forms of gambling. A survey of thirteen- to sixteen-year-olds, undertaken by the National Housing and Town Planning Council in 1988, found that 69 per cent of boys and 45 per cent of girls played machines at least once a month. Those who played every week, or more frequently, were in the minority. Ten per cent of boys and six per cent of girls spent more than £3 each time they played. The National Housing and Town Planning Council's report for 1988 claimed that regular gambling is associated with heavy spending (including of lunch money), truancy and stealing, and advocated the banning of fruit machines for young people.[14]

A more recent survey – of ten- to sixteen-year-olds, commissioned by the Home Office in 1989 – came up with lower percentages of young people using machines; it was found that 45 per cent of boys had played machines during a sample month.[15] This survey concluded that playing machines is mostly a sociable activity between friends who exercise control over one another's playing and spending, and in its subsequent report the Home Office saw no need for any further restrictions over adolescents using gambling machines.

The message for parents from both surveys is that using amusement machines is an activity which many young people take part in from time to time and which for the majority of youngsters presents no problems. It only becomes a matter for concern if an adolescent seems to be more interested in gambling on machines than in other leisure activities, or if parents suspect that he (or less likely she) is taking time out of school and possibly stealing in order to do so.

If parents are worried, they should discuss the situation with their adolescent and explain their concern. Those needing outside help should contact Gam-Anon (see page 298 for address), an organisation which provides support and encouragement for relatives of people who gamble, and which runs youth groups for young people who have a gambling problem and who want to do something about it.

Juvenile Delinquency

Juvenile crime has increased sharply since the late 1950s in the UK and in other industrialised societies and, although many social changes have been found to be linked to the rise in delinquency,[16] saying that something is *linked* to a rise in the crime rate is not the same as saying that it *causes* it. And there is considerable doubt about which, if any, of the social changes that have taken place in the last half of the twentieth century are responsible. There are certainly more opportunities for crime today than there were fifty years ago and this in itself plays some part. The following can all have had an effect:

- The self-service facilities in local shops, supermarkets and department stores which make theft from shelves easier.
- The fact that more women nowadays go out to work, leaving homes empty, and providing increased opportunities for break-ins.
- The huge increase in the numbers of cars and, consequently, of on-street parking; both add to the temptation of breaking into cars and taking them for joy-rides.

How many young offenders are there?

Official crime rate

There are two different answers to this question.

This is based on the number of children and young people aged ten or over who are either formally cautioned by the police (see page 276) or brought to court and found guilty. The percentage of young people who figure in the official crime rate is higher in the middle and later teens than it is earlier on.

In 1987, for example, among ten-year-olds, 861 out of every 100,000 were either cautioned or found guilty; for girls the number was 175. By the age of fifteen, 7,897 boys per 100,000 – almost one in every twelve – were cautioned or found guilty. The proportion of girls was much less – 1,783 per 100,000, which is fewer than one in fifty. Youngsters in their mid- to late teens have the highest crime rate of any group in the community.[17]

Teenagers admitting to crime

The number of young people who admit that they have committed offences is much higher than the official crime rate suggests. In a survey undertaken by the Home Office, fourteen- and fifteen-year-olds were questioned about any delinquent behaviour during the past year. (It is around this age that official crime figures peak.) This method, called self-reporting, is well-established and always produces higher figures than the official crime rate. The survey found that 49 per cent of boys and 39 per cent of girls admitted to some form of delinquency. These were mostly offences involving theft or dishonesty: shoplifting, stealing from the family, fare evasion, or acts of vandalism like smashing milk bottles in the street or damaging school property.[18]

Given that this survey only covered one year, and did not include drug offences, it seems likely that many more adolescents commit criminal acts which could get them into trouble with the police than any other section of the community. This is also evident from a number of other self-report surveys, although for the most part it would seem that the offences young people admit to are relatively minor and isolated.[19]

Young people who commit offences

Young people who commit offences are a very mixed group but, speaking generally, there are differences between delinquent and non-delinquent youngsters. The most striking of these is that, both in this country and internationally, more boys than girls are delinquent. Girls are much less likely to commit crimes involving damage to property or injury to other people. When girls come before the court it is frequently for reasons to do with their own protection, because they are thought to be 'in moral danger' or 'beyond parental control'.

It is also the case that those who are repeated offenders are much more likely to have important social, emotional and behavioural problems than other young people. Those who commit fairly minor offences or whose crime is a 'one-off', on the other hand, do not have significant problems and many are little different from other adolescents.

The part played by schools in delinquency

Adolescents spend many waking hours in school and their experience there can indirectly influence their behaviour outside school, and whether or not they come to the attention of the police. The way schools are organised, the relationship between students and teachers, how they treat less academically able youngsters, are all important factors here. Schools that are able to motivate youngsters and to give them a sense of self-value and achievement, irrespective of academic ability, seem better able to protect their students against delinquency than schools where there is an authoritarian regime and where less able young people are made to feel failures. Failing at school is known to be associated with delinquency and truancy and disruptive behaviour are also implicated.[20]

In choosing a school (see page 207) parents should look at the way in which discipline is maintained; whether, alongside clear statements about what is and what is not acceptable behaviour, there is also a readiness to show consideration for a boy or girl as an individual and to take into account different backgrounds and different levels of ability.

Parents and delinquency

Most delinquency takes place when adolescents are away from home and not under direct parental control. Nevertheless, parents still exercise a form of supervision by the rules they have made about what teenagers are allowed to do, where they may go and when they must return home. The Home Office survey of teenagers and their own reports of delinquent behaviour (see page 273) also examined whether the quality of indirect parental supervision was linked to delinquency.[21] Most parents in the survey admitted that they expected to be kept informed about their teenagers' activities and whereabouts and had agreed times for their coming home, but more parents were found to be concerned about girls than about boys.

Despite this, however, the survey showed that delinquent girls were much more likely to have parents who were uninformed about their activities than other girls and much less likely to tell their parents what they did when they were with their friends. For delinquent boys, on the other hand, it did not seem to matter whether their parents were highly supervisory or not. Why this should be so is a matter for speculation. It could be that girls, who are generally given less freedom than boys,[22] may experience lack of supervision as neglect, or because some parents who do not supervise their daughters are uncaring in other ways, which also have an effect on their behaviour.

Quite apart from the risks of delinquency, there are other good reasons why parents should know about their adolescents' activities when they are away from home. These concern their personal safety at a time when they are still, to some extent, in need of protection.

Delinquent friends

In the Home Office survey, as in many others, boys and girls who were delinquent were found to be more likely to have friends who were also delinquent. Friends can be a great source of support for adolescents but going round with friends who break the law is risky. It should be remembered, however, that friends choose one another's company and it does not seem realistic to apportion blame to the rest of a group without asking why any particular adolescent has chosen to be a member of that group.

What can parents do to protect adolescents from delinquency?

If you are worried about your adolescent, because of the people he or she mixes with, express your worries (see pages 283–4). As always, it is necessary to talk and to listen. Explain what can happen to young people who break the law and that you do not want them to get into trouble. But be careful not to condemn a youngster's friends, even if you say that you are worried about what they do. You may be mistaken and, whether you are or not, you face your adolescent with divided loyalties if you attack them. Listen to what an adolescent has to say, take an interest in their friends and welcome them to the house. Welcoming them gives the family an opportunity to get to know them while, at the same time, it helps teenagers to see where their friends' values differ from those of their parents. Young people can be very sensitive to such differences and can easily start to distance themselves from friends who do not fit in at home.[23]

If you have reason to think that your adolescent is breaking the law, discuss your suspicions with them. Explain why delinquent behaviour worries you, because of its effects on other people (for example, in the case of vandalism), because of the physical danger to the adolescent concerned (for example, with some forms of drug abuse [see pages 164–7]), and because of the legal consequences.

Do not, however, turn the situation into a drama, whether your suspicions are justified or not; many young people who commit offences do not go on to a life of crime. Even those who have often been delinquent, and have gone through the legal processes more than once in their youth, mostly give up crime by the time they reach their twenties.[24] Talk things over and find out if there is anything wrong, at school, or with their relationships, and take whatever action is appropriate.

If they are detected in a crime, whether by you or by someone else, assure them of your concern and support. Although young people may at first make light of minor offences, they will feel differently when they realise that what they have done is taken seriously by the adult community and that their behaviour can have serious consequences. Let them know that you will stand by them whatever happens, that you love them and that you will do all you can for them, even if an offence comes to the notice of the police. Whether this happens or not, parents can feel upset and ashamed if they know that their son or daughter has committed an offence, and wonder where they have gone wrong. Although these feelings are natural, it is important for parents to remember that delinquency is very common, that its 'causes' are complex and that they include many different social and personal factors. At this point self-doubt and guilt should not stand in the way of parents' maintaining communication with their adolescent and helping him or her to rescue whatever can be salvaged from the situation.

Police action

If the police have reason to believe that an adolescent has committed an offence – whether a minor theft, breaking and entering or vandalising property – they may take formal or informal action. Whatever they choose to do is at their discretion, however, and even trivial offences may be dealt with formally. Informal action could include reprimanding the youngster on the spot. It could also include coming to talk to parents and explaining what has happened. Most police forces have juvenile bureaux whose members (themselves police officers) decide whether young people should go to court. In order to do this, they talk to parents, to the adolescent concerned, to the local social services department and to the school, and in the light of these enquiries they may decide to take no formal action.

Cautioning

The police may, however, decide that an offender should be cautioned, and this is a formal legal action. There are four conditions to be met for cautioning to take place: there must be sufficient evidence for the police to be able to take the case to court, should they decide to do so; offenders must admit to the offence and that they knew it to be wrong; parents must agree to the cautioning; and the victim of the crime must be willing to leave the matter in the hands of the police and not want to go to court over the case.

The cautioning is usually carried out in a formal manner, by the police, and the seriousness of the situation is impressed on the young offender.

Going to court

In some cases the police decide to take young people to court rather than to caution them. The decision to do so is influenced by the offender's age, the seriousness of the offence and whether the defendant has any previous record. There is also evidence that the young person's attitude, their social class and their racial background can influence the decision. People who are polite, white and middle class are more likely to be cautioned and less likely to be taken to court than others.[25]

Juvenile courts deal with cases where a young person under the age of seventeen is said to have broken the law. At least one parent or guardian should accompany a young defendant to court, otherwise the magistrate may refuse to hear the case. It is highly advisable for there to be a solicitor to speak for the young person, and the Citizens Advice Bureau will advise parents about obtaining legal aid to pay for this.

Sentencing

The court can take various steps with young offenders:

- Give them an *absolute* or *conditional discharge.* Both of these mean that the offender now has a criminal record, but that the court judges the offence a minor one and gives no formal punishment. But, in the case of a conditional discharge, if there is a subsequent offence that breaks the conditions of the discharge, the first offence may also be punished.
- *Bind them over,* that is, require a signed promise that a youngster will be of good behaviour for a certain length of time. Parents can also be asked to sign on their adolescent's behalf. Breaking the promise results in paying a specified amount of money.
- Require them to pay a *fine.*
- Require them to pay *compensation.*
- Require them to pay *costs.*
- Put them on *probation.*

■ Require them to attend a *centre, an activity scheme* or *do community service* in the evenings or at weekends.

■ *Place them in care.* This means that responsibility for a child or adolescent passes from parents to the social service department of the local authority. It may or may not mean that they are taken away from home.

■ Send them to a *detention centre* or into *youth custody*.

■ At the time of writing, parents have no legal responsibility for their adolescents' crimes. Legislation that may alter this is currently under discussion.

Criminal record

A criminal record, however small the offence, can stand in the way of a young person's career. It must be declared when he or she is applying for certain jobs and in applications for travel visas.

Sexual Attacks on Adolescents

One of the risks against which children and adolescents need protection is the risk of sexual attack.

Many young people, both boys and girls, experience sexual attacks, some more serious than others but all of them unwelcome. They range from what amounts to bullying remarks at school about their physical development (although the perpetrators may describe it as teasing), meeting someone exposing himself in the street, being subjected to obscene remarks and phone calls, being touched and rubbed against on public transport, being coerced into sexual contact by another young person or by an adult and, most seriously, rape.

From early childhood your son or daughter will no doubt have been warned about the dangers of talking to 'strangers', and accepting lifts from them although there are also risks from people who are known to the child.[26] In adolescence, with their own growing sexual maturity and their greater independence, the risks remain. As a parent you need to reinforce earlier lessons which should also be covered at school. Tell them that no one has the right to make them feel embarrassed about their physical development, whether by staring or calling out or making personal remarks. If such incidents happen in the street, or if an adolescent sees a 'flasher', they should ignore them, but they should tell you so that you can inform the police, for the sake of other youngsters. They should also tell you if unpleasant incidents occur at school, and either you or they should report the matter to a member of the school pastoral staff (see page 203).

Tell your son or daughter that no one has the right to touch them in a way which they do not want; that even with a boyfriend or girlfriend, there is no need to accept any sort of kiss or touch, on the grounds that everyone else does it, or that they are too embarrassed to say 'no', or that they have been going out together for some time, or for any other reason; that if the other person tries to persuade them against their will, whether by cajoling or blaming, they do not have to comply. They should say 'no' firmly and in such a way that the other person realises that they mean what they say (see page 156).

Explain, too, that no one, adult or teenager, now or in the future, has any right to sexual intercourse with them without their consent, and consent is based on choice, not on pressure.

If an attack happens

Safety from sexual attack will be one of the considerations behind the arrangements you make with your teenager for letting you know where they are going and who they are with, how late they may return home, and whether you need to pick them up. In spite of parents' care, however, some boys and girls *are* sexually attacked and some are raped. Sometimes this is by a member of the family, sometimes by an acquaintance and sometimes by a stranger.

Rape

In the case of rape or attempted rape, you can get in touch with a Rape Crisis Centre (see page 298 for address) for advice if needed. With older teenagers it is for them to decide if the police should be informed, but they should be encouraged to do this for the safety of other young people. They should not wash or change their clothes, no matter how much they would like to, or take alcohol or medicines, until they have been seen by a doctor for an internal or external examination. They can ask to see a woman police doctor or their own GP if they wish. Take warm clothes for them to change into after the examination. Tell them that you will stay with them and give them all the support you can. Do not add to their distress or any misplaced feelings of guilt by blaming them in any way for what has happened.

Rape is a shocking experience and one which takes time to get over. A teenager who is raped can react in many different ways and may or may not be prepared to talk about her feelings immediately. She may feel angry, depressed, shocked, unclean and guilty; and her parents may also share some of these feelings. She may also feel nervous about going out alone. Over the months following the rape parents should be sensitive towards her feelings and ready to listen, to reassure and to provide support from outside the family, if necessary.

A local Rape Crisis Centre can be of great help in adding their resources to those of parents. They can give information about pregnancy prevention, VD and AIDS, police and legal procedures and financial compensation. They can also give on-going support.

Sexual abuse in the family

Sexual abuse within the family is a serious and painful subject. If your adolescent tells you that he or she has been sexually abused by another member of the family, they need your support and protection. Tell them that you believe them and that you are glad that they have told you; reassure them that they are in no way to blame for what has happened and that you will protect them. Confront the person concerned and say that you are not prepared to allow the situation to continue. You can telephone the local social services department, a health visitor, the NSPCC child protection team or the police (see page 298 for addresses) for help in protecting your child.

Sexual abuse is a criminal matter and the offender is sometimes, but not always, taken to court where the victim may be required to give evidence. In 1986 court proceedings were considered in a minority of cases. It is also possible in cases where sexual abuse is suspected that an abused youngster might be taken into the care of the local authority and removed from home. Again this is not automatic and happens in a minority of cases only.[27] A care order cannot be made on someone who has reached the age of seventeen.

Influences Outside the Family

As they grow towards independence young people are influenced, consciously or otherwise, by people and institutions outside the family: by friends, youth organisations, television, magazines, the music industry, and advertising, while for some politics or religion are important. All of these can help to shape adolescents' attitudes and behaviour. A major influence is, of course, the school they attend and this has a chapter to itself (see pages 196–247).

Parents will want to ask themselves whether these influences help adolescents to develop into competent adults, able to look after themselves and take a responsible role in society, or whether they stand in the way. Are these outside influences in competition with parents and with parents' values or are family influences stronger?

Friends

Parents need only look back to their own adolescence to remember how important friendship is at this stage: the hours spent discussing fashion, music, sport; the mutual support about difficulties at school and at home; the confidences exchanged; the adventure of setting out on grown-up excursions together for the first time; the quarrels and, sometimes, the feeling of being without friends.

How adolescents understand friendship at different ages

Adolescence is a lengthy business and the nature of adolescents' friendships, and their understanding of friendship, changes as they move through their teens. During adolescence they become more capable of sophisticated thinking (see page 21) and this applies also to their understanding of what it is to be a friend.

There are five different 'levels' in understanding what makes up a relationship, which children and adolescents pass through as they grow up. They come to grips with more advanced social understanding through their experience of what happens in their own relationships. At the lowest level, very young children do not understand that other people have feelings and thoughts which are different from their own, and so they do not make allowances for this in the way they relate to others. At this stage 'friends' are seen as children who play together, rather than anything deeper. Children at this age tend to deal with any problems that arise between friends by using physical means, such as taking away a toy from someone who has just purloined it, or running away from a 'trouble maker'.[28]

During childhood a more realistic idea of other people, and of the basis of friendship, develops. By adolescence youngsters understand that different people have different needs and experiences, and expect these to be taken into account by both parties in a relationship. In other words, they expect friendships to be reciprocal. They also come to an understanding that conflict between friends can be dealt with: problems can be discussed, not walked away from, and a mutually agreeable solution found.

At a more sophisticated level still, in late adolescence or early adult life, young people realise that other people are influenced by how they have been brought up, by their experience of life and the society in which they live. They are able to make allowances for these influences in their relationships and to accept the other person as they are, without wanting to change them.

Group friendships

Early adolescence is a time when many young people like to go about in a clique of like-minded people of the same sex. It is at this age that their peer group has the greatest influence on young people, affecting their leisure activities, their choice of clothing, of hairstyles and other customs.[29]

Later in adolescence cliques may combine into larger groups, of both boys and girls, who 'hang around' together. They may meet at clubs or converge on certain coffee bars or other places of entertainment. Youngsters can find these 'crowds' a safe way of meeting members of the opposite sex, surrounded as they are by their own clique of protective friends. Eventually some of the crowd may start 'going out together'.[30]

How friends help one another towards independence

Adolescents know that they are on the road to adult life, even though at times it may seem impossibly far away. Their friendship groups are a means of getting there, together with other youngsters who are sharing the same sorts of experience. Together they create a territory that is their own, for which adults are not allowed to hold a passport. To be accepted by the group a teenager must want to join in the same activities, whether these consist of playing pool or talking about ponies, they must have similar tastes in fashion and in music and use the same sort of slang. These are the kind of things that parents are told they just do not understand and which can change from one month to the next. Having their own tastes and customs, which are different from those of their parents, is one way in which adolescents experience their own separateness and dawning independence. Group membership contributes to young people's sense of identity at a time when the changes of early adolescence can make their feelings somewhat ambiguous; it tells them that they are individuals who are different not only from their parents but also from youngsters in other groups.

It is in their early teens that youngsters are most likely to conform closely to the customs and styles of the rest of the group. Obeying its unwritten rules removes uncertainties about how to behave, and at the same time gives a teenager a feeling of independence. Looking to the group for decisions about what sort of clothes to wear is more 'grown up' than letting parents decide, or than going to them for advice. This is one way in which being a member of a group allows adolescents to loosen their ties with parents and to take a further step towards becoming adults in their own right.

In the group, also, they learn about getting on with one another, what is acceptable social behaviour, how to deal with conflict and how to make their own contribution in discussions, and they learn these skills among equals, with no adult smoothing their path. These lessons prepare adolescents for the relationships involved in adult life, for life partnerships, for working with other people and for citizenship. The group also pools information, not necessarily accurate, about things which interest or puzzle them, from news about football clubs to details about sex. As well as sharing information, within their friendship groups youngsters also offer one another valuable advice and support about problems they may be facing.

The need to conform to a group does not remain strong throughout adolescence. By their mid-to-late teens young people are more confident about being an individual and no longer have the same need to be part of a crowd.[31]

Individual friendships

Although many youngsters belong to a group of friends, they also have close individual friends with whom, increasingly throughout adolescence and into young adult life, they can share their feelings, their hopes and their worries. Their friends may include people of the same sex and those of the opposite sex. These close relationships are another way of loosening (not breaking) their emotional ties with their parents and of preparing for the mature partnerships of adult life.

Worries about friends

Teenage friends can have a great influence over each other and sometimes parents find this worrying. Will their children's friends encourage them not only to adopt weird hairstyles but to commit crimes, to smoke, to take drugs?

Earlier we looked at the influence of friends on young people who commit criminal offences (see page 275). To repeat what was said there, parents should get to know their son's or daughter's friends and welcome them into the home. Young people can be polite, considerate and fun, so meeting them, and getting to know them, can be enjoyable and reassuring for parents.

Helping your teenager's friends to feel at home means accepting them with all their differences. If you feel uneasy about some aspect of their behaviour you need to decide if you are going to talk to your son or daughter about it or keep it to yourself. It is not a good idea to criticise the appearance of their friends or any other superficial characteristic that does not present any threat to other people. If you nag about unimportant details your adolescent may be less willing to co-operate over important matters.

If, on the other hand, you have a serious concern about something

which could lead to real problems, then it is necessary to express thi
to your adolescent (see page 187). Explain why you are worried an
be ready to listen, in turn, to what your son or daughter has to say
Try to arrive at a clear understanding between you of what i
acceptable behaviour. Just a few words may be enough for you t
realise that you are in agreement. On other occasions, when it seem
that a youngster does not want to listen, you may still be having
positive effect by reinforcing something he or she already realises. I
is very likely that your adolescent shares your own deepest values
after all you have spent many years in a close relationship. And whil
he or she shares the tastes of friends in music and clothes, yo
probably have the greatest influence in important matters.[32]

Above all, it is important to keep communicating freely wit
adolescents, listening to them and expressing your own concerns.

Youth Services

Youth services are facilities for young people provided by the loca
authorities, by churches, political groups and voluntary organisations
They include youth clubs and traditional uniformed organisations lik
the Boy Scouts and Girl Guides, the Girls' Brigade and the Boys
Brigade. There are also, in some neighbourhoods, youth workers wh
work with youngsters out in the community, without being attache
to a club.

Different types of youth services have different aims, according t
who provides them and who works in them. Traditionally youth wor
has aimed to keep youngsters off the streets, away from danger. I
has done this by providing leisure facilities which are within thei
means, compared with more expensive commercial enterprises. Yout
clubs are places where youngsters can meet and enjoy some of thei
leisure-time together. They may be based in a church hall or in
specially built youth centre. Sometimes they set out to do no mor
than provide a free-and-easy atmosphere with coffee, soft drinks
games, music and dancing so that youngsters can enjoy themselves
A few deliberately set out to imitate the sort of decor, bar and seating
arrangements to be found in a public house, and do not resemble th
traditional youth club at all (see page 158). This is in order to provid
an enjoyable, non-alcoholic alternative to the public house whic
young people might otherwise frequent.

In other clubs and centres there are more organised activities suc as games, crafts and drama, perhaps in addition to a relaxed club-room. Here, too, there are possibilities for young people to enjoy themselves and to make friends.

An important emphasis in much youth work is to provide social and informal education, away from school. In part this is the role of the youth worker, who encourages young people to participate in the programme of activities, without putting them under pressure. Youth workers also try to help youngsters to get on with one another, individually and as a group. They aim to set standards partly by their own example and partly by the sort of interactions they encourage among members, so that individuals are listened to and their points of view taken into account. Part of the informal education offered by a youth club is the opportunity for young people to take responsibility in planning and organising the programme. Many youth workers also see their work as supporting individual young people; they try to make themselves available for listening, without passing judgement, when a young person has problems.

The uniformed organisations, such as Scouts and Guides, have their own special aims and, in particular, have stressed character-building and the acquisition of practical skills and service to other people.

Youth work aimed especially at girls is available in some places, or at certain times in a club's programme. This is so that girls can take advantage of all the activities on offer without competition from boys, who sometimes take over games and equipment.

Religious and political youth services share many of the activities and educational aims of local authority youth work but they have in addition their own particular aims, broadly speaking to promote their own attitudes and values.

Just as integration of students with special needs is now considered desirable in schools – although it is not always achieved – so many youth clubs and organisations have a policy to integrate young people with disabilities into their programmes. This does not mean that adolescents with disabilities pay occasional visits to clubs but that they take a regular part in the activities and mix in with other members. The local authority youth officer at the town hall can give advice about which clubs and organisations have an integration policy in the neighbourhood. Parents may also approach individual youth workers and youth leaders to enquire, for example, if there is adequate access to a building, to fire escapes and to lavatories for adolescents who have physical disabilities. Parents should also find out if youth leaders have practical ideas about integrating a person with a disability into their activities and what preparation, if any, is needed. Because parents are themselves experts in their adolescent's condition, they are in a position to give advice about practicalities to youth workers and to management committees and to recommend books and other sources of information.

Information about the different youth services in your area may be obtained from the youth officer via the town hall. See page 297 for address of the National Youth Bureau.

Religion and Politics

We live in a society in which people have different values and beliefs, including their beliefs about politics and religion. For some parents these are important dimensions of life while for others they are less so, and frequently adolescents follow their parents in these matters.

But in late adolescence and early adult life some young people make their own choices about politics and religion. At this stage many are beginning to think about moral and political issues in a sophisticated way and they may test out previously held beliefs and values (see page 29) and develop their own ideals. In addition, they are at a point when they are achieving a separate adult identity which may also lead them to adopt political and religious ideals which are different from those of parents. Being independent from parents is the essence of adult life and parents can do little other than try to understand their grown-up sons' and daughters' decisions and to respect them. None the less, while realising that they cannot control what their teenagers believe, parents may still feel saddened, angry and guilty if children turn away from the values and practices of their family background.

Cults and sects

There are some religious movements to which young people may turn in their late teens and which make parents feel particularly anxious. These are the so-called 'cults' or sects. They include, among others, the Unification Church of Sun Myung Moon (the moonies), Hare Krishna, and the Church of Scientology. Some of these organisations are openly religious, others are much less so, but they all offer members a promise of experience which will lead to 'eternal salvation' or will, eventually, put the young person in touch with his or her 'true self'. Whether parents have their own religious beliefs or not the new religious movements can seem very threatening to their adolescent's welfare.

In part this anxiety arises because parents know little about these movements, except for news stories about young people who have been completely estranged from family and friends when they have joined a cult.

If an adolescent is attracted towards a cult it is important for parents to learn all they can about it. They can then discuss it with understanding, rather than through hearsay, and put into context what their son or daughter tells them.[33] Parents should realise that the different movements are rooted in different backgrounds, different beliefs and different practices, and that not all cults 'brain-wash' their adherents. Nevertheless, difficulties can arise for young people who become involved in them. They can be estranged from family and friends, they may decide to interrupt their studies in order to take a more active part, and in some cases may spend more money on them than they, or their parents, would have believed possible.

Some groups are more authoritarian than others and put pressure on young people to abandon their homes, families and education in order to join them. In such cases researcher Eileen Barker advises against parents arranging for their children to be forcibly removed and deprogrammed, explaining that some may nevertheless return to the group while others may suffer an identity crisis, feeling unsure of their ability to make decisions about their own lives.

Whatever happens parents should keep in touch with their sons and daughters who join cults or sects, and keep communications open. While many young people have some contact with such groups, for most this proves to be a passing episode and some will need parental support when their involvement ceases, in order to take up their ordinary lives again.

The Media and Adolescents

The subject of the mass media, especially television and video, and their possible effects on adolescents, can raise strong feelings. Violence, frank portrayals of sex, pornography, sexist stereotypes, bad language, advertisements which promote greed and anxiety – not to mention tobacco and alcohol – are all topics which add fuel to the debate in different political quarters. The questions raised include to what extent media output should be censored and how parents should react towards their adolescent's use of the media.

Television programmes, videos, newspapers and magazines are as

much a part of an adolescent's world as they are of their parents'. W
all enjoy watching television, flicking through magazines and readin
the newspaper, which we find relaxing, amusing and informative. Bu
some of the material presented can be at variance with individu
parents' standards and those they want for their children. Some parent
may be offended by the under-representation of women in seriou
political discussion programmes on television; others may object t
the portrayal of gratuitous violence. There is also the question c
whether magazines and television get in the way of homework an
other 'worthwhile' activities.

Advantages

It would be unrealistic to dwell only on those aspects of televisior
magazines and videos which parents may consider unsuitable fo
young people. The following should also be remembered:

- The mass media provide youngsters with an opportunity to unwin which, given the stresses of school and adolescent life, is useful.
- Television presents a huge amount of information about the worlc political, natural and social.
- Television portrays situations which youngsters do not all mee at first hand. The 'soaps', the most popular of programmes, presen life-and-death experiences which parents and adolescents watch, an can talk over, together. Different characters often have contrastin opinions about the same event: whether an abortion, a loveles marriage, infidelity or drug abuse. This can make discussion at hom all the richer; part of intellectual, social and moral development is t realise that different people have different points of view.
- Charitable appeals and the various marathons shown on televisio engage young people's altruism.
- Teenage magazines may present rather rigid role models for gir but they can also contain useful information about health and se presented in a readable fashion. The problem page, also, can make positive contribution to understanding teenage relationships.

When the standards and behaviour portrayed in television pro grammes and magazines are at complete variance with your own, thi gives you an opportunity to point the fact out and provide a vehicl for discussion. Listen carefully to what your son or daughter has t say. Discussions of this sort can reinforce your influence and you ar very likely to find that in broad terms they share your point c view, not about fashion or music, perhaps, but about deeper feeling concerning the way people should behave towards each other. Youn people are not sponges who soak up media values uncritically. *You standards and your influence are the most important factor in shaping their opinions.* Have confidence in your adolescent and in the way you have brought him or her up. Television and the other media have some impact on attitudes and behaviour but it is small compared to the part played by parents.[34]

Points of conflict

'They do nothing but watch television,' is a frequent complaint of parents. In fact this is less likely to be the case for adolescents than for younger children.[35] Teenagers find other things to do with their time including homework, talking and going out with friends. Nor does it seem that watching television is a replacement for reading. A survey of adolescents carried out by Exeter University found that young people who watched most television were also those who read most[36]; perhaps these were youngsters who preferred quiet indoor occupations.

If you are worried that your son or daughter is watching too much television, decide why you are worried. Does it seem to stand in the way of friendships and social activities? Or are you worried because television and homework are in competition? Whatever the reason talk to your adolescent about it, say why you are worried, listen to what he or she has to say and tackle whatever problems (if any) emerge between you (see pages 187–90).

Video nasties

Young people have ready access to pornographic videos and magazines[37] and it can shock parents to discover that their teenagers have been watching them. In part this may be because it is an indication that a son or daughter is sexually mature, but there may also be religious or moral reasons for their disapproval. In our society, people do not all share the same standards about what is acceptable sexual behaviour, let alone what should be depicted and what adolescents should be allowed to see. What some parents consider to be acceptable portrayal, others will condemn as pornographic.

You may decide that what an adolescent reads or watches is his or her own business, especially in late adolescence. But if you find that your son or daughter has been reading magazines or watching videos that you disapprove of, and you decide to confront them about it, explain *why* you disapprove: whether because it involves treating women as sex objects, because it is violent, or because it offends other moral or religious values. Do not use emotive words like 'disgusting' about it or about watching it. In fact, do not blame your son or daughter, who may feel embarrassed at being found out and neither want to talk nor to listen. Just explain your point of view.

Conclusion

This guide may have appeared to dwell almost entirely on the problems that can arise for adolescents and, therefore, for parents. But being the parent of adolescents has its own delights. There is a specia pleasure in seeing young people taking assured steps forward, using new skills and competencies, whether in making their first trips to the local town with friends, surviving examinations, using thei developing strength and stamina to good effect on the sports field o assisting in the community. And much that happens in these sometimes eventful years can put parents in touch with some of the excitements of their own adolescence.

Over the years, as youngsters develop intellectually and become better informed about the world – better than parents on some subjects – it is possible to enjoy conversations and to share interest at a much more adult level. Just by living with them, talking and listening, parents can come to appreciate that their sons and daughter have their own standards and ideals, probably close to theirs but with their own particular emphases and individuality.

The teenage years are not uniformly joyful, as this guide make clear, and this should be openly acknowledged. While for most young people adolescence seems to be, relatively speaking, untroubled, othe teenagers, even in the same family, do not make a smooth transitio into adult life. For some, social conditions and political and commercia influences outside the home make the going harder, whether thes have an effect on health, on schooling, or on employment. These ar issues which parents can do little about alone, although it is possibl to join with others, locally and nationally, either through pressur groups or as voters, to try to alleviate the problems that are experienced in parenting adolescents.

Within the home parents have their own strengths and resource on which they can draw to support their adolescents through th crises which sometimes occur and there is a particular satisfaction t be found in seeing young people leave potential disasters behind them and achieving greater maturity as a result. Where parents think that it is necessary to seek outside help, it is hoped that this book provides useful information about getting it.

The transition between childhood and adulthood can be a bitter-sweet time for parents who glimpse the approach of the end of their task. Inevitably, throughout their teens, the relationship of adolescents with their parents will change as they become less dependent on them. For parents this requires finding a balance between progressively letting their children go, both emotionally and materially, while at the same time ensuring that they know they are loved, and that their parents are available when needed. Sons and daughters will, in time, no longer need parental support although in young adult life they may sometimes turn to their parents for help.

For some parents, watching their sons and daughters leave home, find work, and enter adult partnerships, is a matter of pride and satisfaction. This may well be mixed with relief; bringing up children is, after all, demanding work. Others experience the 'empty nest', and the loss of their role as parents, with sadness. This may depend on many circumstances, for example, if parents have interesting work, close friends, a satisfying relationship with a partner, or whether they have the opportunity for creative interests in arts, crafts and sports, or working in the community.

The end of adolescence is not, of course, the end of the relationship. As adults, sons and daughters bring new people and new interests into parents' lives. For many, there is the special relationship of grandparent and grandchild to look forward to. In the end, when we have 'let go' of our grown-up children and, by doing so, have allowed them to 'let go' of us, we can enjoy the new experience of beginning to relate to them as independent human beings.

Useful Addresses

CHAPTER 2 Sex Education and the Adolescent

Sources of information about many health- and sex-related subjects:
Health Education Authority
Hamilton House
Mabledon Place
London WC1H 9X
01 631 0930

Women's Health Information Centre
52–54 Featherstone Street
London EC1Y 8RT
01 251 6332

Family Planning Information Services
27–35 Mortimer Street
London W1N 7RJ
01 636 7866

DHSS Leaflets Unit
PO Box 21
Stanmore
Middlesex HA7 1AY

CHAPTER 3 Gender and Sexuality in Adolescence

Homosexual information and advice:
Gay Youth Movement
BM Gym
London WC1N 3XX
01 317 9690

The Joint Council for Gay Teenagers
BM JGGT
London WC1N 3XX

Lesbian Line
BM Box 1514
London WC1N 3XX
01 251 6911

For the parents of homosexuals:
Parents Enquiry
16 Henley Road
London SE26 2HE
01 698 1815

CHAPTER 4 Contraception, Pregnancy and Sexually Transmitted Diseases in Adolescence

Advice about abortion and pregnancy:
British Pregnancy Advisory Service
Austy Manor
Wootton Wawen
Solihull
West Midlands B95 6BX
05642 3225

Life [advice for those who wish to continue with pregnancy]
118–120 Warwick Street
Leamington Spa
Warwickshire CV32 4QY
0926 21587

Brook Advisory Centres [advice about relationships and contraception for teenagers]
153a East Street
London SE17 2SD
01 708 1234

Family Planning Association
27–35 Mortimer Street
London W1N 7RJ
01 636 0366

National Advisory Service on Aids
0800 567 123

CHAPTER 5 Adolescent Health Care

Information about food and diet:
The Vegan Society
33–35 George Street
Oxford OX1 2AY
0865 722166

The Vegetarian Society
53 Marloes Road
London W8 6LA
01 937 7739

London Food Commission
88 Old Street
London EC1V 9AR
01 253 9513

British Heart Foundation
102 Gloucester Place
London W1H 4OH

The Coronary Prevention Group
60 Great Ormond Street
London WC1N 3HR
01 833 3687

Overeaters Anonymous
PO Box 539
London W11 2EL
01 584 3157

Eating Disorders Association
The Priory Centre
11 Priory Road
High Wycombe
Buckinghamshire
0494 21431

Anorexic Family Aid (AFA)
Sackville Place
44 Magdalene Street
Norwich NR3 1JE
0603 621414

Information about sports and the following associations may also be obtained from the Sports Council, 16 Upper Woburn Place, London WC1 01 388 1277

Archery:
The Grand National Archery Company
7th Street
National Agricultural Centre
Stoneleigh
Kenilworth
Warwickshire CVS 2LG

Athletics:
Amateur Athletics' Association (AAA)
Francis House
Francis Street
London SW1P 1DE

Badminton:
Badminton Association
National Badminton Centre
Bradwell Road
Loughton Lodge
Milton Keynes MK8 9LA

Baseball:
British Baseball Federation
197 Newbridge Road
Hull HU9 2LR

Basketball:
English Basketball Association (EBBA)
Calomax House
Lupton Avenue
Leeds L59 0EE

Canoeing:
The British Canoe Union
Flexel House
45–47 High Street
Addlestone
Weybridge
Surrey KT15 1JV

Cycling:
British Cycling Federation
16 Upper Woburn Place
London WC1H 0QP

Fencing:
Amateur Fencing Association
83 Perham Road
West Kensington
London W14 9SP

Golf:
(men) Royal and Ancient Golf Club
St Andrews
Fife KY16 9JD;
(women) Ladies' Golf Union
The Scores
Fife KY16 9AT

Gymnastics:
British Amateur Gymnastics Association
Ford Hall
Lilleshall National Sports Centre
near Newport
Shropshire TF10 9NB

Handball:
The British Handball Association
60 Church Street
Radcliffe
Manchester

Horse-riding:
British Equestrian Centre
Stoneleigh
Kenilworth
Warwickshire CVS 2LG

Ice-hockey:
UK Ice Hockey Association
48 Barmouth Road
Shirley
Croydon CR0 5EQ

Lawn tennis:
Lawn Tennis Association
Queen's Club
West Kensington
London W14 9EG

Netball:
All-England Netball Association Ltd
Francis House
Francis Street
London SW1P 1DE

Rowing:
Amateur Rowing Association
6 Lower Mall
Hammersmith
London W6 9DJ

Sailing:
Royal Yachting Association
Victoria Way
Woking
Surrey GU21 1EQ

Skiing:
The British Ski Federation
118 Eaton Square
London SW1W 9AF

Sports for the Disabled:
British Equestrian Centre
Stoneleigh
Warwickshire CVS 2LG; *or*
British Sports Association for the Disabled
Hayward House
Barnard Crescent
Aylesbury
Buckinghamshire HP21 9PP

Squash:
(men) Squash Rackets Association
Francis House
Francis Street
London SW1P 1DE;
(women) Women's Squash Rackets Association
345 Upper Richmond Road
West Sheen
London SW14 8QN

Swimming:
Amateur Swimming Association
Harold Fern House
Derby Square
Loughborough
Leicestershire LE11 0AL

Table tennis:
English Table Tennis Association
21 Claremont
Hastings
E. Sussex TN34 1HF

For information about foot care:
Society of Registered Chiropodists
53 Welbeck Street
London W1M 7HE

For information about dental care:
British Dental Health Foundation
88 Gurnards Avenue
Fishermead
Milton Keynes MK6 2BC
0908 667063

The Phobia Society
4 Cheltenham Road
Chorlton-cum-Hardy
Manchester M21 1QN

The British Society of British and Dental Hypnosis
42 Links Road
Ashstead
Surrey K221 2HT

For advice about hospitals:
National Association for the Welfare of Children in Hospital
Argyle House
29–31 Euston Road
London NW1 2SD
01 833 2041

For advice about alcohol and tobacco:
Action on Alcohol Abuse
Livingstone House
11 Carteret Street
London SW1H 9DL
01 222 3454

Alcoholics Anonymous (AA)
61 Great Dover Street
London SE1 4YF
01 403 0888

Alcohol Concern
305 Gray's Inn Road
London WC1X 8QF
01 833 3471

Teachers' Advisory Council on Alcohol and Drug Education (TACADE)
Third Floor
Furness House
Trafford Road
Salford
Manchester M5 2XJ
061 848 0351

Action on Smoking and Health (ASH)
5–11 Mortimer Street
London W1N 7RH
01 637 9843

ASH Scotland
c/o The Royal College of Physicians
8 Frederick Street
Edinburgh EH2 2HB
031 225 4725

For advice about drugs:
Narcotics Anonymous
PO Box 246
London SW10 0RS
01 351 6794/6066

RELEASE [for legal advice]
1 Elgin Avenue
London W9 3PR
01 289 1123

Solvent Abuse: Re-solve
St Mary's Chambers
19 Station Road
Stone
Staffordshire ST15 8JP

Standing Conference on Drug Abuse (SCODA)
1–4 Hatton Place
London EC1N 8ND

CHAPTER 6 Communication and Crises in Adolescence

The following associations can give advice about local sources of help for stress and crisis:
MIND
22 Harley Street
London W1N 2ED
01 637 0741

National Association of Young People's Counselling and Advisory Services (NAYPCAS)
17–23 Albion Street
Leicester LE1 6GD
0533 558763

CRUSE (Bereavement Care)
Cruse House
126 Sheen Road
Richmond
Surrey TW9 1UR
01 940 4818

Family Welfare Association
501–505 Kingsland Road
Dalston
London E8 4AU
01 254 6251, and local numbers

For advice about divorce, stepfamilies and one-parent families:
Relate
Local offices are in the telephone book

The National Stepfamily Association
162 Tenison Road
Cambridge CB1 2DP
0223 460312

National Council for One-Parent Families
255 Kentish Town Road
London NW5 2LX
01 267 1361

Gingerbread (England and Wales) [for lone parents]
35 Wellington Street
London WC2E 7BN
01 240 0953

Department of Education and Science
Elizabeth House
York Road
London SE1 7PH
01 943 9000

Campaign for the Advancement of State Education
The Grove
110 High Street
Sawton
Cambridge CB2 4HJ

National Confederation of Parent-Teacher Associations
2 Ebbsfleet Industrial Estate
Stonebridge Road
Gravesend
Kent DA11 9DZ
0474 560618

Equal Opportunities Commission
Overseas House
Quay Street
Manchester M3 3HN
061 833 9244

Education Otherwise [for parents wishing to educate children at home]
25 Common Lane
Hemingford Abbotts
Cambridgeshire PE18 9AH

Schools' Council Information Centre
45 Notting Hill Gate
London W11 3JB
01 299 1234

Girls into Science and Technology
Manchester Polytechnic
9a Didsbury Park
Manchester M20 0LH
061 434 2817

CHAPTER 7 Adolescents at School

For general advice:
Advisory Centre for Education (ACE)
18 Victoria Park Square
London E2 9PB
01 980 4596

For information about independent schools:
Independent Schools Information Service
56 Buckingham Gate
London SW1E 6AG
01 630 8793

For advice about reading problems:
British Dyslexia Association
98 London Road
Reading
Berkshire RG1 5AU

For information about changes in education:
Department of Education and Science
Elizabeth House
York Road
London SE1 7PH
01 943 9000

Welsh Office Education Department
Crown Buildings
Cathays Park
Cardiff CF1 3NQ
0222 82511

Scottish Education Department
New St Andrew's House
Edinburgh H1 3SY
031 556 8400

Department of Education for Northern Ireland
Rathgael House
Balloo Road
Bangor BT19 2PR
0247 270077

For advice about racism:
Commission for Racial Equality (CRE)
Elliot House
10–12 Allington Street
London SW1E 5EH
01 828 7022

For advice about special needs:
Independent Panel of Special Educational Experts
c/o John Wright
12 Marsh Road
Tillingham
Essex CM0 7SZ
0621 87781

Centre for Studies on Integration in Education
4th Floor
415 Edgware Road
London NW2 6NB
01 452 8642

For advice about careers:
The Careers and Occupational Information Commission (COIC)
W1108 Department of Employment
Moordfoot
Sheffield S1 4PQ
0742 704563/4/9

COIC Scotland
5 Kirkloan
Corstophine
Edinburgh EH12 7HD
031 334 9821

For advice about how to proceed with appeals or complaints against schools:
The Children's Legal Centre
20 Compton Terrace
London N1 2UN
01 359 6251

Advisory Centre for Education
18 Victoria Park Square
London E2 9PB

CHAPTER 8 Independence in Adolescence

For information about youth services:
National Youth Bureau
17–23 Albion Street
Leicester
0533 471200
and your local education authority

Road safety:
Royal Society for the Prevention of Accidents
Cannon House
The Priory
Queensway
Birmingham B4 6BS
021 200 2461
and the local authority safety officer

Possible sources of advice about missing teenagers:
Runaways
The Piccadilly Advice Centre
100 Shaftesbury Avenue
London W1V 7DH
01 434 3773

Alone in London
Advice Centre
188 Kings Cross Road
London WC1X 9DE
01 278 4224

Young Runaways Project
10 Rutford Road
Streatham
London SW16 2DH
01 677 8407

Sexual abuse:
National Society for the Prevention of Cruelty to Children (NSPCC)
67 Saffron Hill
London EC1N 8RS
01 242 1626

Royal Scottish Society for the Prevention of Cruelty to Children (RSSPCC)
Melvill House
41 Polworth Terrace
Edinburgh EH11 1NU
031 337 8539

The Rape Crisis Centre
PO Box 69
London WC1X 9NJ
01 837 1600

For general information about the law:
The Children's Legal Centre
20 Compton Terrace
London N1 2UN
01 359 6251

Advice for relatives of gamblers:
Gam-Anon
17–23 Blantyre Street
Cheyne Walk
London SW10 0DT
01 352 3060

For childcare and play-schemes information:
Daycare Trust
4 Wild Court
London WC2B 5AU
01 405 5617

Working Mothers' Association
77 Holloway Road
London N7 8JZ
01 700 5771

National Out of School Alliance (NOOSA)
Oxford House
Derbyshire Street
London E2 6HG
01 739 4787

Further Reading

CHAPTERS 1–4

Baldwin, D. *For Growing Boys.* Family Circle, 1985. For ten- to thirteen-year-olds on how their body develops.

Baldwin, D. *For Growing Girls.* Family Circle, 1985. For ten- to thirteen-year-olds on how their body develops.

Docherty, Dr James. *Growing Up: A Guide for Children and Parents.* Modus Books for The Royal Society of Medicine, 1986. The changing responsibilities of adolescence, for ten-year-olds upwards.

Meredith, S. *Growing Up: Adolescence, Body Changes and Sex.* Usborne, 1985. For ten-year-olds upwards.

Tucker, J. (ed.). *The Advice Book.* Virgin Books, 1987.

Parker, S. *Your Body.* Kingfisher, 1985. A pocket-size book that includes areas like: growing up, smoking and dentistry for nine- to thirteen-year-olds.

Vevers, H. G. *Your Body.* Bodley Head, 1986. A cartoon-style book for eight- to twelve-year-olds.

Loulan, J. G. *Period.* Volcano Press, 1985. A frank look at menstruation. For nine- to thirteen-year-olds.

Hayman, Suzie. *It's More Than Sex!: A Survival Guide to the Teenage Years.* Wildwood House, 1986. For the mid-teens.

MacFarlane, Aidan and McPherson, Ann. *The Diary of A Teenage Health Freak.* Oxford Paperbacks, 1987. Aimed at teenagers.

Thomson, R. *Have You Started Yet?* Pan Books, 1987. A book for growing girls on how to cope with menstruation.

McCormack, A. E. and McCall Smith, E. *All About Sex.* Chambers, 1987. A teenage guide dealing with the emotional and physical aspects of growing up.

Gee, R. *Babies: Understanding Conception, Birth and the First Years.* Usborne, 1985. For ten-year-olds upwards.

Wellings, K. *First Love, First Sex.* Thorsons, 1986. Explores, with practical advice, early sexual relationships.

Saunders, D. *Let's Discuss Sex.* Wayland, 1987.

McCarthy, W. and Fegan, L. *Sex Education and the Intellectually Handicapped: A Guide for Parents and Care Givers.* ADIS Press, 1984.

Davies, M. *Sex Education for Young People with a Physical Disability.* SPOD, 1985.

Cousins-Mills, Jane. *Make it Happy – Make it Safe.* Penguin Books, 1988.

Craft, Ann. *Mental Handicap and Sexuality: Issues and Perspectives.* Costello, 1987.

Grabrucker, Marianne. *There's a Good Girl: Gender Stereotyping in the First Three Years of Life – a Diary.* The Women's Press, 1988.

Hart, John. *So You Think You're Attracted to the Same Sex?* Penguin Books, 1984.

Trenchard, Lorraine (ed.). *Talking About Young Lesbians*. London Gay Young Teenage Group, 1984.
Sharpe, S. *Falling For Love: Teenage Mothers Talk*. Virago, 1987.
Schofield, C. B. S. *Sexually Transmitted Diseases*. Churchill Livingstone, 1979.
Watcher, O. *Sex, Drugs and AIDS*. Penguin Books, 1987.
Wilkinson, G. *Let's Discuss AIDS*. Wayland Publishers, 1987. Aims to help young people understand the threat of AIDS.
Belfield, T. and Martins, H. *Introduction to Family Planning*. Family Planning Information Service, 1984.
The Children's Legal Centre, *Briefing on Gillick*. Undated.
Pipes, M. *Understanding Abortion*. The Women's Press, 1985.

CHAPTER 5

Crisp, A. H. *Anorexia Nervosa: Let Me Be*. Academic Press, 1980.
Institute for the Study of Drug Dependence. *Drugs: What Every Parent Should Know* ISDD, 1985.
Institute for the Study of Drug Dependence. *Drug Abuse Briefing: A Guide to the Effects of Drugs and to the Social and Legal Facts about their Non-Medical Use in Britain*. ISDD, 1988.
Jaffe, Jerome, et al. *Addictions, Issues and Answers*. Harper & Row, 1980.
Pownall, Mark. *Inhalants (Understanding Drugs)*. Gloucester Press, 1987.
Cannon, Geoffrey. *The Politics of Food*. Century Hutchinson, 1988.
Palmer, R. L. *Anorexia Nervosa*. Penguin Books, 1986. A guide for both families and sufferers.
Jacobson, B. *Beating the Lady-Killers: Women and Smoking*. Pluto Press, 1986.
Armstrong, S. *Smoking: What's in it for You?* Chambers, 1986. For eleven-year-olds upwards.
Baldwin, D. *Health and Exercise*. Wayland, 1987. For ten-year-olds upwards.
Fraser, K. and Tatchell, J. *You and Your Fitness and Health*. Usborne, 1986. For nine- to thirteen-year-olds.

CHAPTER 6

Jewett, Claudia. *Helping Children Cope with Separation and Loss*. Batsford, 1986.
Coleman, Dr John. *Teenagers under Stress* and *Teenagers in the Family*. Trust for the Study of Adolescence, 1988. Tapes and booklets for parents.
Skynner, R. and Cleese, J. *Families and How to Survive Them*. Methuen, 1984.
Krementz, J. *How it Feels when Parents Divorce*. Gollancz, 1985.
Mitchell, A. K. *When Parents Split Up: Divorce Explained to Young People*. Chambers, 1986.
The Children's Legal Centre. *When Parents Separate*. Undated.
Hodder, Elizabeth. *Preparation for Step-Parenthood*. The National Stepfamily Association, 1988.
De'ath, Erica. *Step-Parenting*. Family Doctor Publications, 1988.
Atkinson, Christine. *Step-Parenting – Understanding the Emotional Problems and Stress*. Thorsons, 1986.

CHAPTER 7

Arnot, Madeleine and Weiner, Gaby. *Gender and the Politics of Schooling*. Hutchinson Education, 1987.
Wragg, Ted. *Education: An Action Guide for Parents*. BBC Publications, 1986.
Advisory Centre for Education. *Education Reform Act 1988. Governors' Handbook*.

Newell, Peter. *ACE Special Edition Handbook: The Law on Children with Special Needs.* Advisory Centre for Education, 1988.

Department of Education and Science. *Education Reform: The Government's Proposals for Schools.* Central Office of Information, 1987.

Department of Education and Science. *Our Changing Schools.* Central Office of Information.

The Children's Legal Centre. *Education Rights Handbook – An Adviser's Guide to the Legal Rights of School Students.* 1987.

CHAPTER 8

Stones, Rosemary. *Too Close Encounters and What to Do about Them: A Guide for Teenagers.* Methuen, 1987. Sexual abuse and harassment.

Department of Transport, Scottish Development Department, Welsh Office, Department of the Environment (Northern Ireland), Central Office of Information. *Lesson for Life – The Best Way to Teach Road Safety for Parents of 1–14-year-olds.* HMSO, 1988.

Stone, Chas. *Safer Cycling.* Department of Transport, 1986.

The Children's Legal Centre: *Running Away; Child Sexual Abuse; Young People in Work.* All undated.

The Children's Legal Centre. *You and the Police – Fact Card for Young People.* 1986.

Notes

INTRODUCTION

1 J. Demos and V. Demos. 'Adolescence in Historical perspective'. *Journal of Marriage and the Family*, 31, 1979.

2 Bruno Bettelheim. *A Good Enough Parent*. London: Pan Books, 1987.

CHAPTER 1 The Developing Adolescent

1 Gupta et al., *Journal of Clinical Endocrinology and Metabolism*, 1975 (pp. 636–43).

2 Richard West. *The Family Guide to Children's Ailments*. London: Hamlyn, 1983.

3 W. A. Schonfeld. 'The Body and the Body Image', G. Caplan and S. Lebovici (eds). *Adolescence: Psychosocial Perspectives*. New York: Basic Books, 1969.

4 S. M. Garn. 'Continuities and Change in Maturational Timing', O. G. Brim Jr and J. Kagan (eds). *Constancy and Change in Human Development*. Cambridge, Mass: Harvard Press, 1980.

5 J. M. Tanner. 'Physical Growth', P. H. Carmichael (ed.). *Manual of Child Psychology*. New York: Wiley, 1970.

6 Schonfeld, 1969, *op cit*.

7 J. Brooks-Gunn and D. N. Ruble. 'The Experience of Menarche from a Developmental Perspective', J. Brooks-Gunn and A. C. Petersen (eds). *Girls at Puberty: Biological, Psychological and Social Perspectives*. New York: Plenum, 1985.

8 J. R. Klein and I. F. Litt. 'National Health Examination Survey', Brooks-Gunn and Petersen (eds), 1985, *op cit*.

9 A. C. Kinsey et al. *Sexual Behaviour in the Human Male*. Philadelphia: Saunders, 1948.

10 R. M. Lerner and S. A. Karabenick. 'Physical Attractiveness, Body Attitudes and Self Concept in Late Adolescence'. *Journal of Youth and Adolescence*, 3, 1974.

11 Lerner and Karabenick, 1974, *op cit*.

12 B. Inhelder and J. Piaget. *The Growth of Logical Thinking from Childhood through Adolescence*. New York: Basic Books, 1958.

13 L. Kohlberg, 'The Cognitive-Developmental Approach to Moral Education', P. Scharf (ed.). *Readings in Moral Education*. Minneapolis: Winston Press, 1978.

14 Jean Piaget. *The Moral Judgement of the Child*. New York: Free Press, 1948.

15 Cited by Kohlberg, 1978, *op cit*.

16 Cited by Kohlberg, 1978, *op cit*.

CHAPTER 2 Sex Education and the Adolescent

1 Isobel Allen. *Education in Sex and Personal Relationships*. London: Policy Studies Institute, 1987.

2 Judith Bury. *Teenage Pregnancy in Britain*. London: The Birth Control Trust, 1984.

3 Christine Farrell and Leonie Kellaher. *My Mother Said ...: The Way Young People Learned about Sex and Birth Control*. London: Routledge and Kegan Paul, 1978.

4 Stewart Meikle et al. *Teenage Sexuality*. London: Taylor and Francis Ltd, 1985.

5 Allen, 1987, *op cit*.; Gallup. *Gallup Youth Survey, Contemporary. Denver Post*, 10 June 1979.

6 Allen, 1987, *op cit*.

7 Allen, 1987, *op cit*.; Meikle et al., 1985, *op cit*.

8 Allen, 1987, *op cit*.

9 Shirley Prendergast and Alan Prout. *Knowing and Learning about Parenthood: A Study of Parenthood Education in Secondary Schools*. Cambridge: Health Education Authority, Research Report 17, 1987.

10 Ann Craft. *Mental Handicap and Sexuality: Issues and Perspectives*. Tunbridge Wells: Costello, 1987.

11 Hilary Brown. 'Working with Parents', Ann Craft (ed.), 1987, *op cit*.

CHAPTER 3 *Gender and Sexuality in Adolescence*

1 R. J. Francoeur. *Becoming a Sexual Person*. Chichester: John Wiley & Sons, 1982 (p. 97).

2 Z. Rubin et al. 'The Eye of the Beholder: Parents' View on the Sex of Newborns'. *American Journal of Orthopsychiatry*, 44, 1974.

3 C. Seavey et al. 'Baby X: The Effects of Gender Labels on Adult Responses to Infants'. *Sex Roles*, 1 (2), 1975.

4 Margaret Mead. *Sex and Temperament in Three Primitive Societies*. New York: American Library, 1935.

5 J. T. Spence and R. L. Helmreich. *Masculinity and Femininity: Their Psychological Dimensions, Correlates and Antecedents*. University of Texas, Austin, Texas, 1978.

6 A. C. Kinsey et al. *Sexual Behaviour in the Human Female*. Philadelphia: Saunders, 1953. W. Simon. 'The Development of Sexuality in Adolescence', J. Adelson (ed.). *Handbook of Adolescent Psychology*. New York: Wiley, 1980.

7 W. Masters and V. Johnson. *Human Sexual Response*. Boston: Little Brown, 1966.

8 Allen, 1987, *op cit*.

9 Allen, 1987, *op cit*.

10 Gallup. *Gallup Youth Survey, Contemporary. Denver Post*, 10 June 1979, cited in J. Conger and A. Petersen. *Adolescence and Youth: Psychological Development in a Changing World*. New York: Harper and Row, 1984.

11 Conger and Petersen, 1984, *op cit*. (p. 356).

12 Driscoll, 1978.

13 Susan Ross. *The Youth Values Project*. New York: State Communities Aid Association, 1979.

14 Conger and Petersen, 1984, *op cit*.; Allen, 1987, *op cit*.; Bury, 1984, *op cit*.

15 Farrell and Kellaher, 1978, *op cit*.

16 Conger and Petersen, 1984, *op cit*.

17 Sorensen, 1973, *op cit*.

18 Conger and Petersen, 1984, *op cit*; Allen, 1987, *op cit*.; Bury, 1984, *op cit*.

19 Farrell and Kellaher, 1978, *op cit*.

20 Ann Phoenix. Thomas Coram Research Unit, University of London, personal communication.

21 Ross, 1979, *op cit*.

22 *Sex and the Law*. FPA Education Unit, 1987.

23 Kinsey, 1948, *op cit*.; Kinsey, 1953, *op cit*.; Sorensen, 1973, *op cit*.

24 Kinsey, 1948, *op cit*.

25 Petersen, 1985, *op cit*.

26 Celia Kitzinger. *The Social Construction of Lesbianism*. London: Sage Publications, 1987.

27 Conger and Petersen, 1984, *op cit*. (pp. 310–13).

CHAPTER 4 *Contraception, Pregnancy and Sexually Transmitted Diseases in Adolescence*

1 Bury, 1984, *op cit*. (p. 36).

2 FPA Education Unit, 1987, *op cit*.

3 Bury, 1984, *op cit*.

4 A. B. Elster and M. E. Lamb. 'Adolescent Fathers: The Understudied Side of Adolescent Pregnancy' (ed.). Jane Lancaster and B. Hamburg (eds) *School-age Pregnancy and Parenthood: Biological Dimensions*. New York: Aldine de Gruyter. And Ann Phoenix. *Young Mothers?* Cambridge: Polity Press, in press.

5 A. B. Elster and S. Panzanine. 'Unwed Teenage Fathers: Emotional and Health Educational Needs'. *Journal of Adolescent Care*, 1, 1980.

6 S. M. Smith et al. 'Parents of Battered Babies – A Controlled Study.' *British Medical Journal*, 4, 1973. G. R. McAnamey and H. A. Thiede. 'Childbearing – What We Have Learned in a Decade and What Remains to be Learned'. *Seminars in Perinatology*, 5 (1), 1981.

7 Bury, 1984, *op cit*.

8 Bury, 1984, *op cit*.

9 R. W. Blum and J. Goldhagen. 'Teenage Pregnancy in Perspective'. *Clinical Paediatrics*, 20 (5), 1981.

10 Blum and Goldhagen, 1981, *ibid*.

11 *Population Crisis Report*. Prop of Abortions, internationally, 1981.

12 Based on FPA, HEA and BPAS material and conversations.

13 FPA Education Unit, 1987, *op cit*.

14 The Children's Legal Centre Briefing. Undated.

15 *Et seq.* Sources include various HEA and DES educational material; O. Watcher. *Sex, Drugs and Aids.* London: Penguin Books, 1987; C. B. S. Schofield. *Sexually Transmitted Diseases.* Edinburgh: Churchill Livingstone, 1979.

CHAPTER 5 Adolescent Health Care

1 *The Diets of British Schoolchildren.* London: DHSS, 1986.
2 NACNE Report. *Proposals for Nutritional Guidelines for Health Education in Britain.* London: HEA, 1983; COMA Report. *Diet and Cardiovascular Disease (Report on Health and Social Subjects 28).* London: DHSS, 1984.
3 The Coronary Prevention Group. *Children at Risk: Should Prevention of Coronary Heart Disease Begin in Childhood?* London: A Policy Statement from the Scientific and Medical Advisory Committee, 1988.
4 Tim Lobstein. *Fastfood.* London Food Commission, 1988.
5 NACNE, 1983, *op cit.*
6 NACNE, 1983, *op cit.*; COMA, 1984, *op cit.*
7 Royal College of Physicians' Report on Medical Aspects of Dietary Fibre, 1980.
8 DHSS, 1986, *op cit.*
9 CPG. *Heart*, 8, 1988.
10 Peter H. Fentem. 'Exercise and Coronary Heart Disease', Tom Heller et al (ed). *Coronary Heart Disease: Reducing the Risk.* The Open University in association with the Health Education Council. Chichester: John Wiley & Sons, 1987.
11 Sports Council, *Sport in Society*, undated; see also Professor Barry Lewis et al. *Children at Risk: Should Prevention of Coronary Heart Disease Begin in Childhood?* London: CPG, 1988. Recommendations include: 'Measures should be Devised to Encourage Teenagers to Continue Sport and Exercise after Leaving School'.
12 Anita White and Jay Coakley. *Making Decisions: The Response of Young People in the Medway Towns to the 'Everthought of Sport' Campaign.* Sports Council, undated, *op cit.*
13 Sports Council, undated, *op cit.*
14 Ronald Marks. *Acne: Advice on clearing your skin.* London: Dunitz, 1986.
15 R.S. Levine. *The Scientific Basis of Dental Health Education.* HEC, 1986; Blinkhorn et al. *Notes on dental health education.* Scottish Health Education Group in association with HEC, undated.
16 R.S. Levine, 1986, *op cit.*
17 Blinkhorn et al., undated, *op cit.*
18 The sources are: HEA educational leaflets and David Atherton. *Immunisation in Children with Atopic Eczema. Exchange*, 49, 1988.
19 John Balding. *Young People in 1987.* HEA Schools Health Education Unit, 1988.
20 DoH Press Release. *New Arrangements for NHS Sight Tests.* 10 March 1989.
NHS Vouchers for Glasses. London: HMSO, 1988.
NHS Prescriptions. London: HMSO, 1988.
Help with NHS costs. HMSO, 1988.
21 NAWCH Policy Paper 3.
22 Institute for the Study of Drug Dependence. *Drug Abuse Briefing.* ISDD, 1988.
23 Young People and Alcohol. *British Medical Journal*, 1986.
24 Brewers' Society. *UK Statistical Handbook.* Brewers' Publications Ltd, 1985.
25 Alan Marsh et al. *Adolescent Drinking.* A survey carried out on behalf of the Department of Health and Social Security and the Scottish Home and Health Department. London: HMSO, 1986.
26 Alan Marsh et al., 1986, *op cit.*
27 Alan Marsh et al., 1986, *op cit.*
28 Anne Hawker. *Adolescents and Alcohol.* London: Bedsall and Co., 1987.
29 TACADE/HEC. *Alcohol Education Syllabus.* 1984.
30 R. Doll and R. Peto. *The Causes of Cancer.* Oxford: OUP, 1981.
31 Fowler. *CDH Reducing the Risk.* (ed.) Heller et al. Chichester: John Wiley & Sons, 1987.
32 Eileen Goddard and Clare Ikin. *Smoking among Secondary Schoolchildren in 1986, OPCS.* London: HMSO, 1987.
33 Bachman et al. 1986.
34 Fowler, 1987, *op cit.*
35 *Women and Smoking, Report to the Surgeon-General.* Washington DC: Health, Education and Welfare, 1980.
36 A. Macfarlene et al. 'Teenagers and their Health'. *Archives of Disease in Childhood*, 62, 1987.
37 Gillian Penny and James Robinson. *Stressful Life Events, Psychological Resources and Coping Behaviour in Relation to Adolescent Cigarette Use.* London: HEC, 1986.
38 Anne Charlton. 'Children's Advertisement Awareness Related to Their Views on Smoking.' *Health Education Journal, Health Education and the Media*, 45(2), 1986; D.S. Leather et al. (ed.). Oxford: Pergamon Press, 1981 (p. 425).

9 Anne Charlton. 'Children Who Smoke'. *Health at School*, 1, 1986.

0 H. Swadi. *British Journal of Addiction*, 1988.

1 M. Plant et al. *Alcohol, Drugs and School-leavers.* London: Tavistock, 1985.

2 C. Brown and J. Lawton. *Illicit Drug Use in Portsmouth and Havant.* London: Policy Studies Institute, 1988.

3 MacFarlane, 1987, *op cit.*; Brown and Lawton, *op cit.*, 1988.

4 *Drugs: What You Can Do as a Parent.* DHSS and Welsh Office, 1986; *Drug Use and the Young.* DHSS and Welsh Office, 1985.

5 Swadi, 1988, *op cit.*

6 Institute for the Study of Drug Dependence. *Drugs: What Every Parent Should Know.* London: ISDD 1985.

CHAPTER 6 Communication and Crises in Adolescence

1 Michael Rutter. *Helping Troubled Children.* London: Penguin Books, 1975.

2 Claudia Jewett. *Helping Children Cope with Separation and Loss.* London: Batsford, 1984.

3 Jewett, 1984, *op cit.*

4 K. Paddock and S. Thorman. 'Attitudes of Young Adolescents towards Marriage, Divorce and Children of Divorce.' *Journal of Early Adolescence*, 3, 1981.

5 Ann Mitchell. *Children in the Middle.* London: Tavistock Press, 1985.

6 Anne Hooper. *Divorce and Your Children.* London: Unwin, 1984.

7 Ann Mitchell, 1985, *op cit.*

8 Anne Hooper, 1984, *op cit.*

9 Christine Atkinson. *Step-Parenting.* Wellingborough: Thorsons, 1986.

10 Conger and Petersen, 1984, *op cit.* (pp. 235–44).

11 V. Cicirelli. 'Family structure and interaction: Sibling effects on socialisation', M. McMillen and M. Segio (eds). *Child Psychiatry, Treatment and Research.* New York: Bruner Mazel, 1977; V. Cicirelli. 'Sibling influence throughout the lifespan', M. Lamb and B. Smith (eds). *Sibling Relationships.* Hillsdale, New Jersey: Eribaum, 1982.

12 G.M.G. McClure. 'Recent changes in suicide among adolescents in England and Wales'. *Journal of Adolescence*, 9 (2), 1986.

CHAPTER 7 Adolescents at School

1 *Education Reform.* DES, 1987.

2 *Education Reform in Northern Ireland, The Way Forward.* The Department of Education for Northern Ireland, 1988.

3 *Sex Education At School.* DES, 1988.

4 Felicity Taylor. 'Governors and the Curriculum', *Governor's Handbook.* ACE, 1988.

5 Alison Kelly. 'The Construction of Masculine Science', Madeleine Arnot and Gaby Weiner (eds). *Gender and the Politics of Schooling.* London: Hutchinson, 1988.

6 Morton Jenkins. *Human Biology GCSE.* Letts Study Aids, 1987.

7 Julian Ford-Robertson. *Revise Biology GCSE.* Letts Study Aids, 1987.

8 *Subject Options at School.* Equal Opportunities Commission, undated.

9 Nigel Blagg. *School Phobia and its Treatment.* Croom Helm, 1987.

10 Blagg, 1987, 2, *ibid.*

11 Blagg, 1987, 2, *ibid.*

12 Blagg, 1987, 2, *ibid.*

13 Blagg and Yule, 1984.

14 Louis Cohen and Lawrence Manion. *Perspectives on Classrooms and Schools.* Holt, Rivenhart and Winston, 1981.

15 Delwyn Tatum and David Lane (eds). *Bullying in Schools.* Trentham Books, 1988.

16 Sue Lee. 'The Structure of Sexual Relations in Schools', Madeleine Arnot and Gaby Weiner (eds). *Gender and the Politics of Schooling.* Hutchinson Education, 1987.

CHAPTER 8 Independence in Adolescence

1 Mary Rosambeau. *How Twins Grow Up.* London: The Bodley Head, 1987.

2 A more detailed account is given in *At What Age can I?* The Children's Legal Centre, undated.

3 *Social Trends*, 19. London: HMSO, 1989.

4 Pat Petrie and Penny Logan. *Out-of-School Study.* Report to Economic and Social Research Council, 1983.

5 Emma MacLennan et al. *Working Children.* Low Pay Unit, 1983.

6 See also *Young People in Work.* The Children's Legal Centre, undated.

7 Low Pay Unit, 1983, *op cit.*

8 Department of Transport. *Road Accidents Great Britain – The Casualty Report 1987.* London: HMSO, 1988.

9 Based on *Lesson for Life*. Department of Transport, 1988 and DoT Casualty Report, 1988, *op cit*.
10 Based on Peter Dobson. *The Corgi Book of Bicycles and Bicycling*. Corgi Books, 1985; Department of Transport. *Be Safe Be Seen*. 1985; and Department of Transport. *Safer Cycling*. 1986.
11 Robin Simpson. *Day Care for School Age Children*. Equal Opportunities Commission, 1978.
12 Pat Petrie and Penny Logan. *After School and in the Holidays*. Thomas Coram Research Unit Working and Occasional Papers, University of London, Institute of Education, 1986.
13 *Running Away*. The Children's Legal Centre, undated.
14 *Gambling Machines and Young People: Detailed Findings of a National Survey*. National Housing and Town Planning Council, 1988.
15 *Amusement Machines: Dependency and Delinquency*. Home Office Research Study 110, 1989.
16 Michael Rutter and Henri Giller. *Juvenile Delinquency: Trends and Perspectives*. Penguin Books, 1983.
17 Home Office. *Criminal Statistics, England and Wales, 1987*. London: HMSO, 1988.
18 David Riley and Margaret Shaw. *Parental Supervision and Juvenile Delinquency*. Home Office Research Study 83. London: HMSO, 1985.
19 Rutter and Giller, 1983, *op cit*.
20 John Graham. *Schools, Disruptive Behaviour and Delinquency: A Review of Research*. Home Office Research Study. London: 96 HMSO, 1988.
21 Riley and Shaw, 1985, *op cit*.
22 Petrie and Logan, 1983, *op cit*.
23 John Coleman. *Teenagers in the Family*. Brighton: Trust for the Study of Adolescence, 1988.
24 S. G. Osborne and D. J. West. 'Do Young Delinquents Really Reform?' *Journal of Adolescence*, 1, 1980.
25 Rutter and Giller, 1983, *op cit*.
26 A. W. Baker and S. P. Duncan. 'Child Sex Abuse: A Study of Prevalence in Great Britain'. *Child Abuse and Neglect*, 9 (4), 1985.
27 NSPCC. *Protect your Child*. Undated. A guide about child abuse for parents.
28 Robert L. Selman. *The Growth of Interpersonal Understanding*. New York: Academic Press, 1980.
29 T. J. Berndt. 'Developmental Changes in Conformity to Peers and Parents'. *Developmental Psychology*, 15, 1979.
30 Dunphy. 'The Social Structure of Urban Adolescent Peer Groups'. *Sociometry*, 26, 1963.
31 J. C. Coleman. *Relationships in Adolescence*. London: Routledge and Kegan Paul, 1974.
32 J. C. Coleman. 'Friendships and the Peer Group in Adolescence', J. Adelson (ed.). *Handbook of Adolescent Psychology*. New York: Wiley, 1980.
33 Eileen Barker. *New Religious Movements: A Practical Introduction*. Norwich: HMSO, 1989.
34 Rutter and Giller, 1983, *op cit*.
35 BBC Broadcasting Department. *Daily Life in the 1980s*. London: 1984.
36 T. Hincks and J. W. Balding. 'On the Relationship between Television Viewing Time and Book Reading for Pleasure: the Self-reported Behaviour of Eleven- to Sixteen-Year-Olds.' *Reading*, 22, 1, 1988.
37 Allen, 1987, *op cit*.

Index